Triumph
over
Silence

Recent Titles in Contributions to the Study of Religion
Series Editor: Henry W. Bowden

A Cultural History of Religion in America
James G. Moseley

Religious Mythology and the Art of War: Comparative Religious
Symbolisms of Military Violence
James A. Aho

Saints, Slaves, and Blacks: The Changing Place of Black People
Within Mormonism
Newell G. Bringhurst

Southern Anglicanism: The Church of England in Colonial South
Carolina
S. Charles Bolton

The Cult Experience
Andrew J. Pavlos

Southern Enterprize: The Work of National Evangelical Societies,
in the Antebellum South
John W. Kuykendall

Facing the Enlightenment and Pietism: Archibald Alexander and
the Founding of Princeton Theological Seminary
Lefferts A. Loetscher

Presbyterian Women in America: Two Centuries of a Quest for
Status
Lois A. Boyd and R. Douglas Brackenridge

Marchin' the Pilgrims Home: Leadership and Decision-Making
in an Afro-Caribbean Faith
Stephen D. Glazier

Exorcising the Trouble Makers: Magic, Science, and Culture
Francis L. K. Hsu

The Cross, the Flag, and the Bomb: American Catholics Debate
War and Peace, 1960–1983
William A. Au

Religious Conflict in Social Context: The Resurgence of Orthodox
Judaism in Frankfurt Am Main, 1838–1877
Robert Liberles

Triumph over Silence

WOMEN IN PROTESTANT HISTORY

EDITED BY
Richard L. Greaves

Contributions to the Study of Religion,
Number 15

GREENWOOD PRESS
WESTPORT, CONNECTICUT
LONDON, ENGLAND

Library of Congress Cataloging in Publication Data
Main entry under title:

Triumph over silence.

(Contributions to the study of religion ; no. 15,
ISSN: 0196-7053)
  Bibliography: p.
  Includes index.
  1. Women in church work—Protestant churches—History.
  2. Protestant churches—History. I. Greaves, Richard L.
  II. Series.
  BX4817.T7 1985   280'.4'088042   85-961
  ISBN 0-313-24799-4 (lib. bdg.)

Library of Congress Catalog Card Number: 85-961
ISBN: 0-313-24799-4
ISSN: 0196-7053

First published in 1985

Greenwood Press
A division of Congressional Information Service, Inc.
88 Post Road West
Westport, Connecticut 06881

Printed in the United States of America

The paper used in this book complies with the
Permanent Paper Standard issued by the National
Information Standards Organizations (Z39.48-1984)

10 9 8 7 6 5 4 3 2 1

To the families of the authors
and to the
women whose contributions were indispensable
to the
advance of Protestantism

Let a woman learn in silence with all submissiveness. I permit no woman to teach or to have authority over men; she is to keep silent.

1 Timothy 2:11-12

Help these women, for they have labored side by side with me in the gospel.

Philippians 4:3

There is neither male nor female; for you are all one in Christ Jesus.

Galatians 3:28

Contents

SERIES FOREWORD   ix

PREFACE   xi

INTRODUCTION
Richard L. Greaves   3

1   The Matrix of Reform: Women in the Lutheran and Calvinist Movements
Charmarie Jenkins Blaisdell   13

2   God's Powerful Army of the Weak: Anabaptist Women of the Radical Reformation
Keith L. Sprunger   45

3   Foundation Builders: The Role of Women in Early English Nonconformity
Richard L. Greaves   75

4   Shaking Patriarchy's Foundations: Sectarian Women in England, 1641–1700
Dorothy P. Ludlow   93

5   "The Hidden Ones": Women and Religion in Puritan New England
Gerald F. Moran   125

6 Expanding Horizons: Women in the Methodist
   Movement
   Frederick A. Norwood   151
7 To Make the World Better: Protestant Women in
   the Abolitionist Movement
   Blanche Glassman Hersh   173
8 Questions of Power and Status: American
   Presbyterian Women, 1870–1980
   *Lois A. Boyd and
   R. Douglas Brackenridge*   203
9 Participation of Women in the Public Life of the
   Anglican Communion
   V. Nelle Bellamy   229
   SUGGESTIONS FOR FURTHER READING   261
   INDEX   275

Series Foreword

One of the truisms worth remembering about scholarship is that each generation writes its own history. Revisions occur when contemporary circumstances change enough to foster new perspectives in the minds of those who ask questions about the past. New awareness creates a fresh sensitivity to what can be learned from previous experience. Asking new questions often leads to discovering neglected materials, documents that existed all along but were never used through lack of interest. Students in succeeding generations ask questions that earlier students never thought of; they use freshly available materials, and as a result they see the past more clearly. This collection of essays is a good example of how historical revision benefits our general understanding of things. Here we have before us the latest and most incisive analyses of women's roles in European and American Christianity during the past five centuries.

The traditional notion about women in religion has been that they were silent and subjugated, acquiescent in passive roles while males took command of this important area of human affairs. This interpretation stemmed from a viewpoint that valued pulpit activity to the exclusion of virtually everything else.

Since women were denied the pulpit, most observers concluded that they did not participate in religious activities. Modern awareness of religion has questioned the adequacy of defining Christian life through sermons, and, as a result of this challenge, contemporary students are able to see that women have made many important contributions to religion in a number of different capacities. This volume helps us see as never before that women were neither silent nor subjugated; over several centuries they have moved from junior partnerships to increased parity with male counterparts.

The essayists in this volume bring together a significant number of specializations under a topical focus. Each contributes an expertise in distinct chronological periods. They pool a shared awareness that larger social contexts contribute to understanding religious action in various epochs. Moreover, the authors add familiarity with differing confessional and denominational groups. The resulting anthology derives cumulative merit from precise focal points that dovetail with each other to yield an informative complementarity on the chosen subject.

Women have constituted more than half of Protestant Christianity throughout its 500-year history. Because their roles are only now being appreciated, the fundamental building blocks of church history over this time period are being reshaped. It is necessary to rethink the very basis of religious history, what it has encompassed and who contributed materially to it. While this important volume does not claim to meet that ultimate need, it nevertheless supplies valuable information for that purpose. Essays herein provide essential data for reassessing the roles of women since Protestantism first appeared in sixteenth-century Europe. They represent successful efforts to expand the horizons of both a new comprehensive religious history and a more complete social history. They cover mainline church traditions and left-wing movements, private and social roles, spiritual and cultural issues, quietist perfectionism and public ordination. As the eclectic field of women's studies extends its scope and sophistication, this book's pioneering investigations will be recognized as a considerable stimulus to further investigation into religious thought and action.

Henry W. Bowden

Preface

The history of the Protestant churches has normally been written with minimal attention to the role of women, in part because historians in general were typically insensitive to the contributions of women and in part because church historians have given excessive importance to the role of the clergy in the development of Protestantism. In the last two decades, however, there has been a growing interest both in the way organized religion has treated women and in the contributions women have made to their churches. Most of the existing studies have been oriented toward specific historical periods, such as the Reformation or Colonial America, with almost no attention to the evolution of women's role over the full expanse of Protestant history. The essays in this book provide the opportunity for reflection on a broader scale, though spatial limitations prohibited anything like a comprehensive survey. There is a crying need for a full-length study of women in Protestant history, and we hope the studies in this book will aid in the ultimate achievement of that goal.

The task of an editor is both challenging and rewarding. Working with the contributors to this volume has been a special pleasure. Their scholarship, enthusiasm, and dedication were of the highest order. It is a delight to acknowledge their labors and their patience in seeing this project to its completion. As editor, I have also benefitted from the advice and support of Dr. Henry Bowden, president of the American Society of Church History and Series Editor of Contributions to the Study of Religion. Among the many others who offered suggestions and encouragement I must thank Dr. Miriam Chrisman, professor of history, University of Massachusetts; Dr. Joanna Bowen Gillespie, president of the Episcopal Women's History Project; Dr. Brian Heeney, vice-president and professor of history, Trent University; Dr. Michael McGiffert, editor of the *William and Mary Quarterly*; Dr. Albert C. Outler, professor of church history, Perkins School of Theology, Southern Methodist University; Dr. Nancy Lyman Roelker, professor of history, Boston University; Dr. John Woolverton, Editor of the *Historical Magazine of the Protestant Episcopal Church*; and Dr. Robert Zaller, professor of history, University of Miami. Preparing this work for the press was greatly facilitated by the professional skill and good-humored patience of our typists, Mrs. Polly S. Edmiston and Mrs. Dianne B. Weinstein.

Richard L. Greaves

Triumph over Silence

Introduction

Richard L. Greaves

The Protestant conviction that Scripture alone is the sole authority in matters of religion reinforced traditional biases against the participation of women in most positions of leadership in the church. The Pauline insistence on women keeping silent in church is but the most famous example of a general biblical tendency to teach a concept of female subordination. Wives were counselled by Paul to be subject to their husbands, whose lordship was compared to that of Christ over his church. Women were clearly depicted as the weaker sex and admonished not only to learn in silence but to do so in a submissive manner. The author of the first epistle to Timothy explained that he permitted "no woman to teach or to have authority over men," a position he justified by citing the Edenic story of Eve succumbing first to the wily temptations of the serpent and then persuading her husband to transgress the divine commandment (1 Tim. 2:11–14). Just as man reflects the glory of God, according to Paul, so woman manifests the glory of man (1 Cor. 11:7).

Simultaneously, however, the New Testament contains the outline of a view of women which laid the foundation for their ultimate involvement as equal partners in the work of the church.

In his letter to the Galatians, Paul espoused a doctrine of the mutual identity of male and female in Christ: "There is neither Jew nor Greek, there is neither slave nor free, there is neither male nor female; for you are all one in Christ Jesus" (Gal. 3:28). In keeping with this notion of oneness or mutual identity, Paul also taught the interdependence of male and female, both of whom had their origins in God (1 Cor. 11:11–12). Eve originally appears in the creation account because God is convinced that Adam must have a helper, a partner, and from this act the Hebrews derived the belief that husband and wife became one flesh in marriage. Thus biblical teaching juxtaposes on the one hand the idea of female subjugation and silence in the church and on the other the vision of men and women achieving a mutual identity in Christ and a partnership in marriage.

No less important as a pattern for the behavior of female Protestants were the actual practices of women in the pages of the Bible, particularly the New Testament. The belief in a miraculous virgin birth exalted the status of motherhood and added a crucial element of femininity to religious consciousness that was less apparent in traditional Judaism. Moreover, when Jesus was crucified, those who gathered at the foot of his cross were mostly women, all but one of his male disciples having fled. The first of Jesus' followers to risk a visit to his tomb was Mary of Magdala, who therefore became the first person to proclaim the resurrection. Far from being silent in the apostolic church, women not only prayed but prophesied (1 Cor. 11:5; Acts 2:42, 21:9). Women travelled with the apostles as they spread the Christian message, a practice stoutly defended by Paul himself (1 Cor. 9:5). There is no more eloquent expression of the ideal of a partnership between men and women for the propagation of the gospel than Paul's appeal to the church at Philippi to "help these women, for they have labored side by side with me in the gospel together with Clement and the rest of my fellow workers" (Phil. 4:3). Other women served as deaconesses, providing relief to the needy, or as widows who enjoyed the church's support in return for undertaking a special ministry of prayer.

The earliest Protestants demonstrated a willingness to embrace the idea that women could be partners with men in the work of spreading the gospel. Neither Lutherans nor Calvinists were willing to admit women to the formal work of the ministry in the sixteenth century, though Luther was willing to allow women to preach if men were unavailable. Various women nevertheless made substantial contributions to the spread of the Reformation. Wives of Lutheran ministers, such as Katherine Luther and Katherine Zell, provided crucial support to their husbands but were generally confined to working in the context of the parsonage. Unlike Calvin's followers, Lutheran midwives were allowed to continue the traditional Catholic practice of baptizing infants in danger of imminent death. The same practice was allowed in the Church of England, though it was opposed by the Puritans. In general, however, Calvinist women were active in a broader range of religious activities than their Lutheran counterparts. This is particularly true of those ladies of aristocratic status, who used their wealth, prestige, and influence to provide patronage and political backing for Calvinist clergy. The different level of female participation between the Lutherans and Calvinists is in keeping with the more pronounced tendency among Calvinists toward social and political activism as well as a greater willingness to break with tradition. Yet not even Calvin was willing to repudiate the notion of a wife's subordinate status to her husband as head, so that women remained junior partners in marriage. By rejecting the idea of celibacy as a superior state, however, the Protestants enhanced the overall position of marriage in the Christian commonwealth. Coupled with this, the Protestant attack on the monastic life was a strong inducement to marriage as a means both of personal fulfillment and of divine vocation. In accepting this calling, Protestant women took on themselves not only the usual duties of a wife and mother but the responsibility to nurture their children and sometimes their servants in the principles of Christianity.

The most stringent criticisms of the old church and traditional society were made by adherents of the "radical" reformation, particularly the Anabaptists. Their espousal of freedom of conscience and the necessity of believers' baptism postulated a freedom of choice that implied an equality between the sexes, at least in religion. But the Anabaptists did not open the pulpit to women, nor did they significantly alter the traditional concept of a wife's subordination to her husband. In a movement as diverse as Anabaptism there were, of course, exceptions. On one extreme the millenarian zealots who followed Jan van Leiden in the infamous experiment at Munster in 1534–35 degraded women by imposing polygamy and denying single women the right to decline an offer of marriage. On the other extreme were women who not only tried to assume positions of leadership but fell into delusions (like others, male and female, in other centuries) of divinity. Magdalena Muller of St. Gall claimed to be Christ, as did her friend Frena Bumenin, who once sat naked before her followers waiting to give birth to the Antichrist. In sharp contrast, most Anabaptist women were piously respectable, contributing to the cause of the gospel by such varied activities as writing hymns, undertaking works of charity (especially those who held the office of deaconess), founding new churches, and providing financial support. Like the Quakers of seventeenth-century England and the women of the apostolic church, Anabaptist women sometimes accompanied men on preaching itineraries. No less than the men, Anabaptist women demonstrated the depth of their convictions by undergoing cruel persecution.

The English experience suggests that religious persecution led to greater participation by women in the life of the church. In the most dramatic period of religious persecution in English history, the burning of Protestants by the government of Queen Mary I in the 1550s, more than fifty of the nearly 300 martyrs were women, mostly poor widows. When Protestantism was restored in 1559 by Elizabeth I and her Parliament, women were still excluded from the pulpit. As the Puritan movement developed, however, women became involved in the quest to accomplish further reforms in the established church—to remove what they regarded as the "dregs of popery." The concept of a partnership between the sexes for the propagation of the gospel received concrete expression as Puritan women actively catechized children and servants, using their patronage to provide benefices to Puritan ministers, intervened on their behalf at the royal court, encouraged the publication of godly literature, and even demonstrated in public on behalf of their cause. A handful even made their own translations of the writings of Protestant reformers.

Among the Separatists, who considered the Church of England incapable of reform and therefore defied the law by worshipping in private congregations, the role of women was even more extensive. In the face of persecution that typically took the form of fines or imprisonment, they opened their homes to their ministers, sometimes for the purpose of holding worship services. Others helped establish new churches and in some instances even preached themselves. Unfortunately, almost nothing is known of these early Separatist women who preached in England. Not until the revolutionary era of the 1640s is there much evidence about their activity, but they were there, following in the footsteps of Lollard women who had defied the authorities of Catholic England by their preaching in the century or so that preceded the Reformation. Puritan and Separatist women alike helped publish works espousing their cause, and like their Puritan sisters the Separatist women were not afraid to demonstrate for their faith, even in the face of repression.

As traditional authority eroded and censorship collapsed in the 1640s and 1650s, revolutionary England became a crucible where all sorts of religious ideas and practices were instigated. Building on the foundation of the pre–1640 period, women began to preach in the sects more and more openly, until finally the Society of Friends (Quakers) accorded them virtually full access to the ministry, contingent on their divine calling and possession of the requisite gifts. Quaker women travelled throughout the British Isles and to points as far afield as the American Colonies and Turkey preaching their message. Some indication as to precisely how revolutionary this was is illustrated by the fact that historians of both the Congregationalists (Independents) and Baptists (both Particular, or Calvinist, and General, or Arminian) have traditionally written the stories of their movements in this period with scarcely a mention of women, whereas no historian of the Society of Friends could do so. Women were, of course, very active among the Congregationalists and Baptists, but their *public* role was regularly overshadowed by the men, who dominated the preaching function and the church offices. The Baptists allowed women to serve as deaconesses and to share in the responsibility of visiting, counselling, and reproving wayward members. Yet the Congregationalists in

England did not ordain their first female minister until 1917, and a woman did not chair the Congregational Union until 1956. As recently as 1984, the Southern Baptist Convention in the United States passed a resolution encouraging "the service of women in all aspects of church life and work other than pastoral functions and roles entailing ordination."

Apart from the Quakers, the women in the seventeenth century who attracted attention because of their religious roles were adherents of the more radical sects. One such was the Fifth Monarchist Mary Cary, a millenarian zealot who demanded the right of women to preach, wrote a number of religious tracts, and urged major social reform. Less extreme was the Congregationalist Katherine Chidley, author and evangelist. As with the Continental Anabaptists, the breaking of traditional religious bonds in England paved the way for the appearance of a small number of fanatics, both male and female. Among them was the Ranter Mary Gadbury, who called herself "the Bride of the Lamb."

As Protestantism spread to the new world, a crucial role was played by women, particularly among the Quaker missionaries who defied persecution to spread their message. Among more traditional Protestant churches in New England, women regularly outnumbered men, but they were nevertheless not accorded an equal role in the churches' work. Their piety was recognized and warmly appreciated, but on the whole they were expected to exercise their faith within the confines of the home. In fact, New England religious leaders even thought that women had an advantage over men in their opportunity for spiritual growth because they were shielded from a good deal of earthly concerns and temptations. Ministers were quick to recognize the value of this reservoir of spiritual strength within their congregations and looked to female congregants to help convert the men and to nurture the young children in the Christian faith. New England women were also active in the voluntary meetings of the laity to promote spiritual growth, meetings that look forward to the important voluntary societies that developed in the nineteenth century for such activities as the encouragement of missionary work. Women were also very active in the Great Awakening in the eighteenth century.

The eighteenth century was important too because of the founding of the Methodist movement, which began within the conservative Church of England and consequently initially manifested the same position toward women as did the larger Anglican Communion. Before long, however, John Wesley somewhat reluctantly recognized that women as well as men could receive the extraordinary call which enabled lay persons to teach and preach. The decision was made for pragmatic as well as theological reasons, for the expansion of the Methodist movement created a need for preachers that could not be met by men alone. Thus almost from the beginning the Methodists, like the Quakers, included women in the preaching ministry of the church as well as in the more traditional roles of patrons, teachers, and ministerial wives. In the nineteenth century Methodist women in America took a major step forward by founding the Woman's Foreign Missionary Society, publishing their own magazines, and supporting their own missionaries. Nevertheless men still enjoyed superior status in the various Methodist churches. It was not until the year 1900 that the Methodist Episcopal Church in the United States granted women the right to sit as equal lay representatives in its General Conferences, and full-fledged ordination was only recognized in 1889. The latter right lapsed in 1946 and had to be restored a decade later, making full equality for Methodist women a relatively recent achievement.

In addition to Methodism, the eighteenth century also gave rise to the anti-slavery movement, which had a particularly divisive effect on churches in the United States in the following century. In general, the newer denominations tended to be the most outspoken in their hostility to slavery. The Quakers, for example, were the first major Protestant group to attack slavery, doing so as early as 1671. English Quakers provided the backbone of the Abolition Society, founded in 1787. Although women were already active in philanthropy and missionary work in the United States, the decision to work for abolition was controversial, and began only with their own spiritual struggle to reconcile scriptural principles, the conviction of the necessity for social reform, and traditional biases concerning the proper place of women. In the end, those who became active abolitionists did so out of a pronounced sense of moral duty and spiritual vocation. In some cases, the conservatism of their churches was so strong that they either repudiated them or lapsed into denominational inactivity. Some of the leading female abolitionists came from the more liberal churches, such as the Unitarians, the Universalists, or the Quakers. Among the Quaker ministers who fought in the abolitionist crusade were Lucretia Mott and Elizabeth Comstock. As the abolitionist women began in the 1830s to demand an equal role in the movement with the men, they asserted the principles of feminism. Out of the antebellum feminist-abolitionist movement came the drive to attain female suffrage.

In the nineteenth century then, women dramatically demonstrated their involvement as major partners in the work of the church through such activities as foreign missionary societies and the abolitionist movement. Their expanding role was in keeping with a growing awareness in the West for women's rights. One of the earliest statements of this theme came in 1792 from the English reformer Mary Wollstonecraft, author of *Vindication of the Rights of Women*. In 1819 Emma Hart Willard called in New York for major reforms in the education of females, but it was not until the 1830s that women had the opportunity to pursue college-level education in the United States. As women began to graduate from colleges and seminaries for women, there was no longer any excuse to bar them from leadership positions in the church on educational grounds. At the Seneca Falls Women's Rights Convention in 1848, a resolution was unanimously approved calling for an end to the monopoly of the pulpit by men. In fact, some of the greatest leaders of the movement for women's rights were female preachers, particularly the Quaker Lucretia Mott and the Methodist Dr. Anna Howard Shaw. The Universalist Mary Livermore and the Unitarian Julia Ward Howe also preached from time to time. It should be noted that the groups which ordained these women were not the older, more traditional Protestant churches. Even Dr. Shaw could not be ordained by the main body of Methodists, the Methodist Episcopal Church, but had to seek ordination from the Methodist Protestant Church, a smaller, reform-minded group. By 1882 there were enough female ministers in the United States to enable the formation of the Women's Ministerial Conference. As some of the older Protestant churches began to drop the barriers to female clergy, the Rev. Madeline Southard, a Methodist, founded the American Assocation of Women Ministers in 1919. In 1970 this group became the International Association of Women Ministers.

The history of the Presbyterian Church, U.S.A. provides an instructive example of the struggle of women for a more substantive place in the governance and preaching ministry of the church. Like the Methodists they too established their own missionary organizations, including regional boards for foreign missions and the Women's Executive Committee for Home Missions, founded in 1878. Presbyterian women also exemplified their role as partners in the work of the church through expanding activities in such areas as philanthropy, education, and social reform. Despite their invaluable contributions, women had to continue to fight against traditional biases against their equality in the church. In 1929, at a conference convened to address the question of women's status and service in the church, a call was issued to terminate sexual discrimination. Although women could be ordained to serve as elders, it was not until 1956 that the ministry was opened to women in the Presbyterian Church, U.S.A., thereby going a long way to fulfill the call of equality enunciated nearly three decades earlier. By 1984, however, American Presbyterians had not yet elected a woman to serve as Stated Clerk (chief administrator) of their church. For that matter, no woman has ever headed a major Christian church, despite the gains which women have made in moving toward full equality in the Christian community. The Presbyterians would have been the first had they accepted the recommendation of a special nominating committee that the new Stated Clerk be the Rev. Patricia McClurg.

Of the major Protestant churches, none has been more reluctant to ordain women as ministers than the Anglican Communion. Yet in certain respects they have moved ahead more rapidly than their sister denominations, as in the case of deaconesses. Although the Baptists and Congregationalists in England did not introduce formal deaconess organizations until the early twentieth century, the Church of England revived the ancient order of deaconesses as early as 1862. Ordaining women to the priesthood, however, was another matter, and here the lead was taken by younger Anglican churches. An Anglican woman was first ordained in 1944 in order to administer the sacraments in the Macao area because no men were available. Presumably this met the criterion espoused for women to minister as early as the sixteenth century by John Whitgift, archbishop of Canterbury. Nevertheless the ordination was so controversial that the woman involved, Florence Lee Tim Oi, resigned. Anglican churches in Hong Kong, Canada, the United States, and New Zealand eventually ordained women to the priesthood; but the mother church in England has remained adamant in its opposition.

The essays in this volume suggest a pattern concerning the emerging role of women in the Protestant churches. From the beginning women have exercised an important function as partners with men in the propagation of the gospel. To be sure, the partnership was at first no more than a junior one, and it involved less for Lutheran women than for those of Calvinist persuasion. As the work of reform pressed ahead in late sixteenth- and seventeenth-century England, the role of women began to expand, until the Quakers made them almost equal partners and even allowed them to preach, something that not even the radical Anabaptists of the previous century had done. As the churches slowly evolved toward the acceptance of women as equal partners, there was a growing willingness to let them speak in the churches, and this in turn has finally led in recent decades to the gradual acceptance of women as ordained ministers. The "right" of women to preach and to be ordained was thus a direct outgrowth of the Pauline concept of the apostolic partnership of the sexes in the work of the church. In a broader context, the full blooming of the partnership was facilitated by concomitant movements granting women equal opportunities in education and suffrage. While those battles have been won, the long struggle for equality in the churches remains unfinished.

1

The Matrix of Reform: Women in the Lutheran and Calvinist Movements

Charmarie Jenkins Blaisdell

A study of the role of women in the Lutheran and Calvinist movements in the sixteenth century involves several different approaches: the theological concepts of the reformers and how they related to women; the religious and social impact of the ideas of the movements on women; and the appeal of these movements to women. The latter approach has already been successful for French noble and middle-class women. Another alternative is a biographical approach, a path which is already well trodden. Each of these methods has advantages but also serious limitations because women, like men, were not isolated individuals but operated within a matrix of social, religious, intellectual, political, and economic forces. Here we will examine the role of women in the Lutheran and Calvinist movements from all of these points of view in order to achieve a broad picture of women and the Magisterial Reformation on the Continent. This would not be possible without important work done on this subject in the last fifteen years.[1]

We will begin with what Luther and Calvin each had to say about women's sexuality, spiritual equality, and marriage starting with Eve and the Creation. We will examine the impact of these ideas on women's functions within the family, church, and society. We will discuss important Lutheran and Calvinist women for the insight their lives may give on changes which the movement brought about in women's lives and women's roles in general. Underlying this investigation is the question of the appeal of the Magisterial Reformation to women and what they gained from it.

Luther and Calvin considered themselves theologians above all else. Yet, secular matters were also important to both of them. Since individuals put their faith into practice and work out their salvation in this world, Luther and Calvin believed that it was their primary task as theologians to instruct Christians in the proper conduct of their lives and the exercise of the Christian faith. Both reformers, Luther particularly, were specialists in scriptural exegesis and the works of the Church Fathers. According to Luther and Calvin, God's work is definitive, and Scripture is meant to be applied to human life. Both men were, however, influenced by the ideas of the late medieval church and their own society. Both, therefore, interpreted Scripture and wrote from social, economic, political, and religious assumptions and prejudices of their times. Their scholarly exegesis influenced and formed the treatises, sermons, and letters which both men used to convey their ideas to their followers. Those ideas were based on very traditional attitudes; and we will find little that is new in their thinking on women, sexuality, the relationship between the sexes, and marriage.

Medieval discussions about marriage were of two kinds: one favored virginity and celibacy and advocated the conventual life as the ideal Christian vocation; the other praised marriage but stressed the need for women to be submissive to their husbands. The reformers rejected celibacy for all but the impotent, physically deformed, or monkish types and promoted marriage as the more natural state. Having made that choice, Luther and Calvin were notably conservative in their attitudes toward women's roles in married life or society. Thus we may be forced to conclude that the Reformation changed women's lives very little.

Luther's ideas about women and relationships between the sexes can be found in a number of different places in his writings. In 1519 he wrote a "Sermon on the Estate of Marriage;" and in

1522, three years before his own marriage, he enlarged his ideas on the subject with an essay entitled "The Estate of Marriage." A section of his famous treatise on "The Babylonian Captivity of the Church" is on marriage. He wrote several lectures, on the first three chapters of Genesis, in which he dealt with the issue of woman and sin. There he went beyond the traditional interpretation of the Eve story and emphasized woman's unique role as a companion to man and co-creator of the family. A collection of his conversations with students and friends ("Table Talk") and several of his letters also contain references to women, sexuality, and the family.[2] Since his thought evolved during his career as a scholar and pastor, his ideas are not necessarily consistent.

Scholars generally agree that Luther was traditional in his views on women.[3] He viewed women as creatures inferior to men, subject to impulse, governed by emotion, incapable of profound thought, vain, gossipy, and unsuited for responsibility beyond the home. His attitudes toward women were influenced by his own marriage and family life and later, after he became a public figure, by his acquaintance with women from a wide variety of backgrounds. While he treated women with respect, he never overcame his conviction that women had limited abilities and should be subject to man. Because of Eve's sin men and women are not totally equal.

Yet Luther acknowledged women's spiritual equality with men—an equality which the Roman Church never denied but, on the other hand, never emphasized because of Eve. This equality was a logical outcome of justification by faith and what came to be referred to as "the priesthood of all believers." This latter idea was not so much a belief in the individual's ability to intercede directly with God as it was acceptance of the importance of members of the church community teaching and supporting each other in the ways of the Christian life.[4] Women were included in this task; although following St. Paul, Luther believed they were not to teach or preach in church.[5]

Luther, the scholar and exegete, drew heavily on Scripture for his views on women. God originally created Adam and Eve equal in all respects, according to a definite plan. If Eve had not been deceived by the serpent and had not sinned, women would have remained equal to men in all respects. But God imposed Eve's subjugation to Adam as punishment after he discovered her sin. In addition all women must bear children in pain and carry the burden of raising children and running the household. But, according to Luther, Eve is not to be despised. She was neither abandoned by God nor separated from companionship with Adam for his sin. While she might have to bear children in pain, she recognized that the glory of motherhood belonged to her and regarded the pain as a joyful punishment.[6] Woman's purpose in life is procreation, companionship to man, management of the household, and, because of her sin in the Garden, to be an antidote to lust.

Luther emphasized accepting sexuality as a God-given gift, for even though it was damaged by sin, faith in God's grace could make it good and positive. Human sexuality as a God-given component of human existence is a fundamental idea that underlies all of Luther's observations on relations between the sexes and his views on marriage.[7]

Luther was both traditional and innovative in his views on marriage, declaring it was a better state than monasticism and a natural and honorable calling for all but a few human beings.[8] According to his interpretation of Genesis 2:18–24, God singled out man and woman and placed them above the animals when he created marriage for them alone before the Fall. Marriage would have been a lovely state if it had remained uncorrupted by sin; but since the Fall, it had become a means for restraining powerful human sexual appetites in addition to its originally intended purposes of companionship and procreation. Since the Fall, marriage had become a means of channeling and containing sexual passion.[9]

In 1519 Luther still considered marriage a sacrament but he gradually denied this, emphasizing both its worldly and spiritual significance.[10] Marriage had a worldly significance in that it provided a means of containing lust which, because of the Fall, might otherwise run rampant in society.[11] Luther spoke openly of conjugal duty in this respect, and the Augsburg Confession in 1530 contained the statement that marriage was commanded by God to avoid fornication.[12] But although marriage may help to contain sexual lust, it does not exist for sexual gratification alone but for establishing a household and bringing up children.[13] While Luther believed that sex in marriage should not be limited to procreation, he believed raising children was the primary purpose of marriage. Marriage was a "school for character" where men, women, and children learned to live by faith through struggling with everyday problems.[14] Thus, beginning with Luther, there was a shift in thought about marriage away from the traditional emphasis on sexual intercourse solely for procreation and on marriage as a mere remedy for sexual incontinence.[15]

Luther rejected monasticism on two grounds: it did not aid in salvation, and men were unable to control their carnal appetites and remain celibate. Since most men must marry to avoid sin, women thus became an instrument of men's moral improvement, an idea which seems to have begun with Luther and dominated western ideas about women at least as late as the Victorian period.[16]

As far as the spiritual side of marriage was concerned, Luther believed that marriage was a natural and honorable calling for all but a few human beings.[17] He especially recognized the importance of emotional contentment in marriage. He was concerned about the freedom of men and women to choose to marry, yet he recognized the need for individuals to select their marriage partners. These were important ideas in a period when young men and women, of the upper classes especially, were often forced to accede to parental wishes to marry for the family's social or material aggrandizement. Luther emphasized the need for love and companionship between husband and wife. He once wrote: "What is more desirable . . . than a happy and tranquil marriage where there is mutual love and the most delightful union of souls?"[18] Marital love, companionship, and mutual support of husband and wife became an important Protestant ideal, especially among Puritans.[19]

In 1525 Luther married Katherine von Bora, a former nun, and together they created the first parsonage, which established an example of the Protestant concept of Christian family life.[20] An inveterate letter writer, Luther never hesitated to tell his friends directly or indirectly of his contentment in his marriage to Katherine.[21] Luther's ideas of marriage enshrined the family at the center of the church and society, with the result that the role of wife and mother gained new prestige and importance.

Not only did Luther emphasize the importance of companionship and compatibility in marriage, but he also had a concept of something approaching partnership in marriage. Cooperation and mutual respect were important between the couple. The raising of children was a partnership, with the father and mother working together for the benefit of the child. His ideas sometimes have a modern ring as, for example, when he suggested that husbands should help their wives and ease the burden with such mundane tasks as feeding and diapering the small children. By advocating partnership, Luther raised the status of women's work. Yet he also believed that women performed child-rearing tasks better than men.[22]

Although Luther recognized the important contribution women made to the family and society, he still believed they should be subject to their husbands and justified this with Scripture.[23] Exactly how the married couple were to have a partnership at the same time that the wife was to be subject to her husband Luther never made clear.

The recognition of the importance of a good marriage relationship led Luther to consider the issue of dissolving bad marriages. He also acknowledged that there could be conditions, other than those permitted by the Roman Church, under which men and women might need to end a bad marriage. In his treatise "On Married Life," Luther discussed the subject of divorce.[24] He acknowledged that there were instances in which divorce might be necessary, as when a husband or wife had a previously unknown physical deficiency or adultery. He based his view on adultery on the words of Jesus in Matthew 19. Although Luther recognized that adultery might be an acceptable reason for divorce, it is clear that he did not like the idea of divorce. Accordingly, he made suggestions to civil and religious authorities for divorce procedures that would discourage all but the most determined couples and prescribed stringent measures against the adulterer. The third basis for divorce that Luther recognized was the refusal of one party to fulfill conjugal duties or to live with the spouse. Luther believed that the stubborn party should be publicly rebuked in church. If the offender remained recalcitrant, divorce might follow. The civil authorities could also intervene, he suggested, and threaten the resistant spouse with the death penalty. Luther made a veiled reference to a fourth justification for divorce: incompatibility, an idea which followed naturally from his emphasis on companionship in marriage. Luther's discussion of divorce was theoretical. In practice he found the idea of divorce detestable and bigamy preferable, especially for public persons who were supposed to set an example for others.[25] That Luther even discussed divorce is, however, significant because it opened the issue of the need for an emotional relationship between married couples. It came at a time when marriages were being severely strained by economic, social, and religious changes, and in many cases religious differences. Throughout his writing on divorce Luther appears to have assumed that women had an equal status with men.

Luther liked women and acknowledged that men were extremely dependent on them in many spheres of life. Without women, he said, "the home, cities and economic life and government would virtually disappear."[26] He believed that the wife had certain rights in marriage, especially the right to bear children, so that if her husband could not provide her with children she might resort to bigamy or a secondary contract with one of his male relatives in order to achieve that end.[27] In a number of conversations recorded in "Table Talk," it is clear that Luther based his views as much on practical experience in his marriage with Katherine von Bora as on Scriptural exegesis.[28] "I would not trade my Katy for all of France and Venice," he once lovingly remarked.[29]

Luther's views of women's roles were in fact notably traditional and patriarchal. Women were not only forbidden to teach or preach in church, but they were not to participate in politics or rule at home.[30] Luther's most famous passage on women reveals the conventional trend of his thinking on the subject:

Men have broad and large chests, and small and narrow hips, and more understanding than women who have small, narrow breasts, and broad hips, to the end that they should remain at home, sit still, keep house and rear and bring up children.[31]

Luther clearly saw woman's role tied to her capacity to bear children, and he saw it as a glorious destiny rather than a curse.[32]

With Luther and most Protestant leaders the concept of family remained rooted in the principles of patriarchy. But the rationale for a family was no longer principally economic survival. It was also a setting for practicing Christian values, building Christian character, and a microcosm of the correct relationship between ruler and subjects.[33] In the sixteenth-century world view, to upset the family was to threaten the stability of the state. In spite of the acceptance of subjugation of women to their husbands, recognition of the dignity of married and family life made a positive contribution to concepts of women's roles in early modern Europe. With the family unit and motherhood given an emotional, religious, and social importance, women's roles gained new respect. We must be careful not to allow the twentieth-century feminist view on the family to prevent us from recognizing that an important shift in attitude toward the role of the mother was taking place in the sixteenth century. Bearing and rearing children, supervising the household, and teaching the catechism and Psalms to the children became a respected role and duty of the mother. These duties of Protestant mothers were probably not very different from those of Catholic mothers. But Protestant pastors, with their sermons and homilies, consciously raised the role of wife and mother to a new level of importance and respect. Vocation or Christian calling included more than the religious life of the convent. The vocation of wife and mother gained recognition as God-given with religious and social importance.[34]

Luther's ideas about women set the tone for sixteenth-century Protestant thought. Pastors of the Lutheran, Reformed, and Anglican Churches spoke about the position of women and the spiritual and emotional significance of marriage with very little deviation from Luther's ideas. They questioned the value of clerical celibacy and the ability of most people to live the chaste and cloistered life. At the same time they praised marriage as the proper state for most human beings. They accorded women spiritual equality but also advocated their subordinate position in the family and church community. They followed Luther in assuming that wives who failed to be properly submissive to their husbands deserved to be chastised. Above all, they were certain that women should not teach or preach in church.

Martin Bucer, a former German Dominican monk who supported Luther as early as 1518, was for many years the leading reformer in the city of Strasbourg and a key person in neighboring Protestant Churches in the cities of Augsburg, Ulm, and Constance. Bucer also exerted important influence on the English Reformation during the reign of Edward VI. Thus his influence on Protestant thinking was important and widespread. Bucer believed in women's spiritual equality on the Scriptural authority that "there is neither male nor female in Christ." Yet Bucer was certain that a woman should be under the control of a husband. The good husband should be the governor, the representative within the family of God the Father in heaven. The subjugation of wife to husband did not cancel the right of an honest woman to divorce a husband who hates her, abuses her, or commits adultery.[35] Bucer's view would have given unheard of divorce rights to women, including remarriage. For a brief time, this had some impact on the divorce laws in parts of Germany, the Netherlands, and Scandinavia. In general, however, the religious and civil authorities were unwilling to change. Laws concerning divorce and remarriage changed very little in spite of Bucer's persuasive arguments, even in his own city of Strasbourg.[36] Divorce remained as difficult to obtain in Protestant areas as in Catholic.

Protestant stress on the Word of God, reading Scripture in the vernacular, and teaching children the Bible and catechism at home accentuated the importance of literacy for men and women in the sixteenth century. Humanism also helped to accelerate a trend toward education which had begun in the later Middle Ages. With Protestant emphasis on spiritual equality for women, an improvement in female literacy could be expected. Yet, although women's literacy rose in the sixteenth century, men's literacy rose faster.[37]

As early as 1524, Luther called upon civil authorities to establish schools to educate children.[38] If Zwickau is an example of Lutheran territories, education of girls lagged behind that of boys. Visitation committees appointed to oversee the quality of education limited a girl's education to reading, writing, needlework, and sewing. The intellectual content and rigor of the educational program for girls was less important than the moral content which was designed to inculcate traditional standards of modesty, decency, and submissiveness.[39] In Strasbourg, which had one of the most developed educational systems found anywhere in the sixteenth century, education for girls consisted of reading and writing in order that, as mothers, they might teach their children to read Scripture at home.[40] It is important to note that with the exception of Katherine Zell, the major contribution of women to the Lutheran movement was as help-mates to their husbands and as managers of the domestic scene, which may have included keeping accounts and managing land. Lutheran women left little that would indicate a high level of learning.

The Lutheran movement did not noticeably improve the position of women except, perhaps, to accord them greater respect in their roles as wives and mothers. Yet the movement attracted a number of interesting women. They may have found something exciting in its nonconformity and some comfort in the implication of spiritual equality contained in the messages of justification by faith and the "priesthood of all believers." Luther, as the reformers who followed him, did not aim to change women's role in society; yet women found themselves involved and sometimes participating in the political and social turmoil created by the Protestant challenge.[41]

Many of the women who were important in the Lutheran movement were former nuns who became wives of reformers and shared in their husbands' concerns. They supported their husbands' work instead of being individually active in the movement, as would be the case with Calvinist and Anabaptist women later in the century. Like Luther's wife, Katherine von Bora, Lutheran women's contributions were in the domestic sphere and in the example of their middle-class lives as pastors' wives, mothers, and household managers.

Katherine von Bora was a former nun whom Luther married in 1525.[42] She was a woman of impressive inner strength and character, hard-headed and practical. She kept track of Luther's affairs and managed the family finances. She also provided a hostel for refugees and followers who came from as far away as England and Hungary for long stays in the Luther household. Had it not been for Katherine's clever management, the Luthers' limited resources would have been depleted. She nursed Luther's innumerable illnesses, bore six children, shared issues of the Reformation with him, and supported his endeavors to accomplish religious reform in Germany. She never entered the public arena herself. Yet she presided over the first Christian parsonage and created an example for German domestic life, which dominated German middle-class life until the nineteenth century. Luther was fond of saying: "Let the wife make her husband glad to come home, and let him make her sorry to see him leave."[43] This example of partnership and mutual respect, revealed in the Luther household and Luther's writings, may have had an impact on the psychological evolution of Protestant women.[44]

Like Katherine von Bora, Wibrandis Rosenblatt made her contribution to the Reformation in the domestic sphere.[45] Married three times, she created a parsonage and haven for two husbands who were leaders of the Reform, one in Basel and the other in Strasbourg. Like Katherine she was sensible and practical. She managed the family finances and created stability, first in the household of Wolfgang Capito, her second husband, and then in the household of Martin Bucer. Her achievements in balancing the budget and keeping the household going while the Bucer family was in exile in England were noted by another foreign reformer, Peter Martyr Vermigli.

Not all Lutheran women led private lives. Some, like Katherine Zell, the wife of Matthew Zell, one of the leaders in Strasbourg, worked beside her husband to further the cause.[46] At his death she delivered a public eulogy, an act unheard of for a woman. She negotiated with the City Council to visit Melchior Hoffman, one of the most troublesome of the radical sectaries, in prison. Bucer described Katherine as "imperious" and believed that Matthew, because of her influence, sometimes dragged his feet on political and theological reform in Strasbourg while others forged ahead.

Some women made important public contributions to the spread of Lutheranism by participating in public controversies and acting as independent agents of the Reform. In most cases, however, these women were of noble background and better educated than their middle-class sisters. One example was Argula von Grumbach who came from a noble Bavarian family.[47] She entered the lists of the Reform when she wrote a critical letter to the university authorities at Ingolstadt in which she protested the forced recantation of Lutheran theology by a young professor. A copy of her letter was sent to the magistrates of the city and the duke of the territory. She corresponded with Luther and also George Spalatin, the chaplain of Duke Frederick the Wise, who was a friend of Luther. She seems to have discussed Scripture authoritatively in these exchanges. At least twice she was imprisoned for inciting the populace to disobedience by circulating Lutheran books. She was accused of seducing them away from church services, conducting private services in her home, and officiating at funerals. Argula was not typical of female followers of Luther. Not only did she speak her mind to university officials and public authorities, but she also once scolded Luther because he was not yet married. After the death of her first husband she remarried and retreated to a more typical domestic life of the German female, managing her estates and raising four children. Her upper-class origins and humanist education undoubtedly gave Argula freedom of movement and intellectual confidence that many of her middle-class sisters lacked.

Both Elizabeth of Brandenburg and her daughter, Elizabeth of Braunschweig, were members of the German nobility and more influential in the politics of the Reformation than most Lutheran women. Elizabeth of Brandenburg is an example of female nobility, found not only in Germany but elsewhere in Europe, who defied their Catholic husbands, converted, and became outspoken supporters of the Reform.[48] The senior Elizabeth's actions finally forced her to abandon her marriage and go into exile. Even after her husband's death she refused to return and settle on property promised her by her sons unless they agreed to permit her to introduce Lutheran worship. Ten years later when she was permitted freedom of conscience for her household and a Lutheran minister, she did go home, but it was understood she would not proselytize. Her story reminds us of some French and Italian noblewomen who defied and divided their families in the name of the Reform.

Elizabeth's daughter, Elizabeth of Braunschweig, joined the

reform movement thirteen years after her marriage to Duke Erich Braunschweig.[49] Although her husband refused to leave the Catholic faith himself, he did not prevent Elizabeth from participating in her new-found faith. Elizabeth converted the duke's subjects both in the cities, such as Gottingen and Hanover, and the countryside. Her activities soon embroiled her in the inextricably entwined political controversies. The duke's political position was constantly being threatened by the religious activities of his wife. Like many aristocratic women, she educated her young son in the reformed faith, thoroughly grounding him in the Lutheran catechism. Her political activities and religious leadership between 1538 and her death in 1558 are amply recorded in her correspondence with political leaders such as Albert of Prussia and religious leaders such as Antonious Corvinus.

It is clear that there were many women in the Lutheran movement who stepped into public life. It is also clear that these women would have been public figures anyway because of their status in society. There was no thought given to allowing women to share ministerial responsibilities with men, for to do so would be to associate Lutheranism with the Anabaptist movement. St. Paul made it quite clear that women were to keep silent in church and have no voice in church affairs. The first generation reformers leaned heavily on St. Paul in their scholarship and ministry.

The strong patriarchal strain in Protestantism was continued by John Calvin and his followers. Calvin, like his predecessors, argued for spiritual equality for women, marriage as a God-ordained institution, removal of the double standard in divorce and adultery, and subjugation of the wife to her husband. Calvin too was definite in his opinion that women should not assume ministerial functions, such as teaching, preaching, administering baptism, or participating in congregational decision making.

Calvin's views on women were not always consistent. Like other leaders who have formulated theory and created institutions to support it over a period of time, Calvin changed his point of view or emphasis to fit particular situations. His views of women are found in the *Institutes of the Christian Religion*, the book which was the foundation of the Reformed Church, in his *Commentaries* on books of the Bible, and in his sermons and letters.[50] It is important to note that aside from his sermons,

Calvin's works appeared first in Latin, which made them inaccessible to most of his followers except indirectly.[51]

Calvin believed in qualified subordination of women and benign supremacy of men in all human relationships as was ordained and established by God at the time of creation.[52] In his commentary on Genesis 1:27, Calvin reminded his followers that Eve, like Adam, was created in the image of God and, like him, "a preeminent specimen of divine wisdom, justice and goodness." Eve was one degree removed from man: she, like Adam, had dominion over the beasts and nature but was to be forever under the dominion of man by God's ordinance. God assigned Eve as the aid and accessory to man, Calvin said, and "the order of nature implies that women will be helper to man."[53]

Calvin did not speak demeaningly about women as Luther sometimes did. Subordination did not mean degradation. He specifically repudiated what he called "the vulgar proverb"— the idea that woman was "the wellspring of the mischief that befell mankind."[54] The Fall was not the cause of woman's subordinate position to man. In contrast to Luther, Calvin argued that her subordination was rooted in her creation. God ordained woman's subordinate position because it suited him. So, following St. Paul and the account of creation in Genesis, Calvin argued that since woman was created out of man and after man and that since man was the source of the physical constitution of woman, man's leadership is implied.[55]

As far as the Fall was concerned, Calvin believed that though Eve was "the cause of all our undoing," that ultimately the responsibility lay with both Adam and Eve: both were guilty and both deserved to be deprived of authority because they went against God. But God chose not to deprive Adam of authority since if he did, there would be no remnant of order left in nature. If, through the Fall, man had lost his prerogative to rule, woman's position would have been improved in the order of things by virtue of her sin and that, said Calvin the lawyer, could not be.[56]

Before the Fall, woman's subjection to man had been a free and easy one. The Fall caused her to be placed in a kind of serfdom. Redemptive grace raised her from that level so that she is honored as an image bearer of God.[57]

For Calvin, the principle of supremacy and subordination applied to all relationships between men and women. In commenting on 1 Corinthians 11:3, Calvin said that as far as spiritual things are concerned Christ is the head of man and woman; but in political arrangements and outward behavior, man should follow Christ, and woman should follow man.[58] Commenting on verse 7, Calvin said that woman is the glory and distinguished ornament of man, for it is a great honor that God has appointed her as a partner to man for life and has made her as subject to him as the body is to the head.[59] Commenting on verses 11 and 13, Calvin went on to say: "Let the man therefore carry out his function as head ruling over her; let the woman perform her function as the body helping him. Let that be rule not only for married people, but also the unmarried."[60] The man should exercise his authority with moderation and not abuse the woman who has been given to him as a partner. Although a man's wife is subject to him, he must love her as Christ loved the church. He must exercise his authority responsibly and must not ill-treat the woman who has been given to him as a companion.[61] For a woman to refuse to accept the subject role is for her to defy God.[62]

Calvin replaced Catholic esteem for celibacy, which dominated the Roman Church since the Patristic Age, with the Hebraic esteem for conjugal love. He was cautious in his position on celibacy and sometimes appeared to support the traditional view at the same time. He deftly avoided the Catholic position that celibacy conferred a spiritual superiority. He believed that continence was a rare gift from God and not within everyone's reach. Like Luther he believed that the celibate life was an exceptional vocation, and he made it clear that he opposed the Roman requirement of clerical celibacy.[63] Calvin believed that sexual intercourse within marriage was honorable and holy in itself because it was created by God and should be enjoyed without guilt.[64]

Calvin found evidence in the Old Testament that marriage was an essential part of God's design to fulfill the human personality. While he sometimes spoke of the "yoke" of marriage, he also spoke of marriage as the most sacred of all relationships.[65] Both were attitudes similar to those expressed by Luther. Calvin, like Luther, believed that marriage had several purposes, including procreating, rearing children, and containing human sexual drive. Like Luther, he emphasized the need for companionship between husband and wife.

Calvin also spoke of companionship and the actual sharing of duties within the household. He assured husbands that marriage would take on new meaning if, in addition to working to support the family, they would also support their wives at home by helping with the burden of caring for infants. We are reminded of Luther's views on companionship and sharing in the raising of children.[66]

Calvin was never explicit about how partners in marriage were to maintain benign subjection of the wife consistent with companionship. Arguments in the commentaries and sermons on the position of women were not consistent. On the one hand, woman is equal to man in her humanness, according to the first creation story in Genesis 1. On the other, she is forever subject to man as stated in the second creation story, in Genesis 2.[67] Calvin's exegesis evolved over a number of years, and the contradictions we observe surveying the entire body of his work were probably not as apparent to his contemporaries.

The most significant way in which Calvin revealed his attitudes on marriage was to take a wife and, like Luther, to establish the tradition of the Christian family within the setting of the parsonage. In contrast to our knowledge of Luther's marriage, very little is known about Calvin's childless marriage to Idelette de Bure in 1539.[68]

For Calvin, as for Luther and other sixteenth-century reformers, the highest female vocation was marriage, serving her husband and raising children. Among French Calvinists, many mothers gave their children spiritual instruction. The *métier* of wife and mother was highly esteemed among Calvinists. When we recall the importance of "calling" or "vocation" for early followers of Calvin, the maternal vocation scrupulously followed took on special significance for women whose work was respected as an instrument of God's will, which if accomplished in a godly spirit was equal in value and dignity to man's work.[69]

Calvin, like Luther, had trouble reconciling his belief in the importance of a true companionship in marriage on the one hand with the reality of the necessity for divorce, sometimes, on the other. He reluctantly admitted that there are times when divorce is advisable, pointing out that the reason for divorce is the persistence of sin. On the issue of divorce Calvin was both traditional and innovative. He always insisted on equality for both sexes as far as the right to divorce an unfaithful spouse went.[70] Yet in his letters to noblewomen who suffered violence or persecution from their husbands because of their religion, he counselled patience and discouraged separation except as a last resort if their lives were in danger. He urged such women to try to convert their husbands rather than seek a divorce.[71] In 1561 the Geneva City Council supported Calvin's point of view on equal rights of the sexes to instigate divorce proceedings in cases of marital infidelity.[72] By the end of the century, however, the pendulum of opinion had returned to the traditional position, and the law was rescinded.[73]

Calvin, like Luther, emphasized women's spiritual equality with men. Both sexes share equally in the redemptive mission of Jesus. Calvin reminded his followers that the resurrection was first proclaimed by women who found the tomb empty.[74] But spiritual equality was not to be interpreted as the right to power or leadership within the church or state. Calvin took his arguments from Scripture, the Church Fathers, Church Councils, and even events in Roman history.

Commenting on Mary Stuart's accession to the throne of Scotland to his colleague Heinrich Bullinger in Zurich, Calvin wrote that although female rule is at variance with the legitimate order of nature, sometimes God (as he did for Deborah) elevates a woman endowed with a heroic and manly spirit to reproach men for their sluggishness.[75] Calvin dedicated the first edition of his *Commentary on the Book of Isaiah* to Elizabeth's half brother, King Edward VI. The second edition was dedicated to Elizabeth, who wrongly suspected him of co-authoring with John Knox the *First Blast of the Trumpet Against the Monstrous Regiment of Women*.[76] Calvin understood political power even when it was vested in a woman.

If Calvin did not approve of women ruling the state, he also did not approve their ruling or preaching in church. St. Paul had written that women were to remain silent in church; and even though Calvin acknowledged their spiritual equality with men, he counselled them to silence and limited their participation to congregational singing.[77] In some Reformed churches, and later in Puritan churches, the women were segregated from the men, and the men took communion first.[78] The French pastor Pierre Viret explained that while men and women were spiritually equal, the order of nature and society required that women not preach or teach in church. A woman's task was to instruct the young in the faith, and a gifted woman might be a schoolmistress to girls.[79] Some congregations tried to revive the diaconate among women for the purpose of nursing and distributing alms to the poor, but the leaders of the Reformed church in Geneva would not consent to women's participation even to that extent.[80] When, in 1562, the Calvinist pastor Jean Morély proposed that women serve as deaconesses, Calvin openly condemned his ideas.[81] Both Calvin and François de Morel, the pastor to the French noblewoman Renée de France, vehemently opposed any female participation in congregational affairs and decision making.[82] Thus, neither Calvinist nor Lutheran women gained the right to participate or lead in church affairs in the sixteenth century. In spite of the prohibitions against participation, Calvinism appealed to women.[83]

After 1536 there was some small improvement in the education of children in general and girls in particular following the Reformation in Geneva. Whereas there had been no education for girls prior to that time, after 1536 all children in Geneva were required to attend school, and the schoolmaster was paid by the City Council to ensure the education of children of poor families.[84] Boys and girls learned reading, writing, arithmetic, and the catechism.[85] The "Colloquies" of the Geneva schoolmaster, Maturin Cordier, which superseded all others as a text for teaching grammar, were clearly written to instill attitudes of piety at the same time the student learned classical Latin.[86] After 1541 girls seemed to have had their own school for primary instruction, but there were complaints that no public secondary schools existed for girls.[87] Calvinist girls, unless they were from aristocratic families, seemed to fare no better than their Lutheran sisters when it came to education. In France, at least by the sixteenth century, humanism seems to have had at least as much impact as the Reformation on the education of girls.

Many French noblewomen especially had supported the humanist movement for reform in the 1520s and 1530s. In the 1550s they supported the spread of Calvinism in France, particularly when Geneva-trained pastors were sent to establish congregations. They often used their power to protect these preachers and their congregations against attacks from local authorities and the Catholic populace. During the 1550s the Reform became institutionalized in France and conversions among the nobility increased rapidly. With conversion came persecution by a besieged and threatened crown. One of the earliest mass persecutions, the "affaire of the Rue St. Jacques," took place when a Calvinist communion service in a private house was invaded and 130 participants were arrested. Among the prosecuted were thirty-seven women, mostly members of aristocratic families. One young woman, Philippe de Luns, was tortured and put to death—an early feminine martyr for the Calvinist cause.[88]

In France in the 1560s, Catholics and Protestants formed into religious and political factions and prepared for war. Women played a vital role in the reformation of Huguenot policies and negotiations between the rival parties. The first woman to become a prominent leader was Madelein Mailly, comtesse de Roye, daughter of an early convert to the Reform and a later supporter of the Huguenot cause.[89] Madame de Roye converted her two daughters and Louis de Condé, a man who was to become one of the military leaders of the party. The comtesse became prominent in 1559 when she attempted to influence royal policies toward the Calvinist community. She arranged for a secret interview between the most distinguished of the Parisian pastors and the queen mother, Catherine de Medici. The interview gave Calvinists access to the queen mother even after the outbreak of war. Madame de Roye was persecuted and imprisoned by the Catholic party. Following her release she went to Strasbourg to negotiate with the German Protestant princes for financial and military aid for the Huguenots. In March 1563 she helped frame a peace treaty which ended the first of the bitter Wars of Religion in France.

A similar role was played a few years later by Jacqueline de Rohan, marquise de Rothelin.[90] Jacqueline was widowed at twenty-eight, and after a struggle in the name of her son for his right to inherit the city of Neuchatel, she secured his claim. She began sympathizing with the Calvinist movement in the 1550s, and she and her children eventually converted. Although the children returned to the Roman Church after a year, Jacqueline remained a Calvinist the rest of her life. In 1567 she mediated between Huguenots and Catherine de Medici, preventing the renewed outbreak of war. Both the praises of the Venetian ambassador to the French court and the fears of the pope that she would succeed are tributes to her skill as a negotiator.

Renée de France, duchess of Ferrara, is another female who participated in the Calvinist movement.[91] Renée was raised at the court of Francis I. As a pawn in the politics of the French crown, she married an Italian prince, the duke of Ferrara. Her court at Ferrara became a known refuge for Italian and French reformers, including, perhaps briefly, John Calvin. In Italy, heretics, as the reformers were called, counted on her protection and financial support. Calvin personally encouraged Renée in her reform practices and pleaded with her to declare her faith openly, which she never did. Because of her behavior her husband unleashed the forces of the Inquisition against her. Following her husband's death in 1559, she returned to France. There she became involved in the complicated court struggles which followed the death of King Henry II of France and included the formation of rival political-religious factions. She settled on her lands at Montargis, opened her court to refugees, and established a Protestant church and an academy for educating Huguenot children. From time to time she went to the royal court where she attempted to defend the Protestant cause. She was more successful as patroness and protector of the movement at her own court. When she died in 1575, she left specific instructions for a Protestant burial—"without candles, black drapes and masses."

The best known of the Calvinist women was Jeanne d'Albret, the daughter of Marguerite de Navarre, a Catholic, who had sympathized with Calvin and the Reform but never left the Roman Church.[92] She publicly espoused Calvinism at services on

Christmas day 1560. In her sovereign domains, in Béarn near the Pyrenees, Jeanne established public preaching and a Protestant academy. She was the architect of important Huguenot policy, especially foreign. She was an acknowledged Huguenot leader until her sudden death in 1572. One of her most important legacies was, of course, her son Henry IV who brought the Civil Wars in France to an end with the Edict of Nantes and established peace and toleration for the Huguenots which lasted almost a hundred years.

The question of the appeal of Calvinism to women, especially noblewomen, is a fascinating question. Why, despite the dangers involved, did these women choose Calvinism when it would have been so much simpler for them to have remained Catholic?

As we have seen, Calvin's sermons and commentaries conveyed an acceptance of women and an acknowledgement of their importance, especially in their vocations as wife and mother. Calvin's concept of the mother's responsibility for the spiritual instruction of her children gave Calvinist women an important status in the family. Calvinist attitudes and the movement itself induced women to espouse a "cause" which had the socially useful goal of "setting things right" in society, activities which are an extension of the mothering-tutoring role for which most women were bred and socialized. Calvinism obviously appealed to women who were strongly motivated intellectually and enjoyed the opportunity to read and debate Scripture. Reformed liturgy, while it did not give women a unique place, permitted everyone including women and children to participate in prayer services and gave them an active role in congregational singing and perhaps a sense of belonging.[93]

Little is known about middle- and lower-class women in the Reformed Church. Calvin pitched his appeal to politically powerful women of the nobility, but many early converts in France and the Low Countries were middle class. These women left very little in the way of records about themselves. Working women of the artisan class in Lyon participated in the riots and violence that accompanied the antagonisms between Catholics and Huguenots. They spoke up in church and argued with pastors and provided meeting places in their inns and taverns for newly formed Huguenot groups. There is evidence that, in Lyon,

Calvinism appealed to urban middle-class women because its doctrine of Christian vocation—serving God well in the world—complemented and supported their already active lives in business, artisan specialties, and the home. The Calvinist message may have appealed because it lent dignity to what they were already engaged in doing.[94]

Although Calvin devoted less attention to the movement in the Low Countries, Dutch women were also important to the movement—supporting and protecting fugitives, image breaking, and providing safe meeting places for leaders. Calvinists were effective in the Netherlands' struggles for political and economic independence from the Spanish crown. As in France, Calvinism was as much a religious faith as a political party. The so-called Eighty Years War was precipitated in 1566 by the "Compromise of the Nobility," a document presented to the Spanish regent, Margaret of Parma. This document urged the King of Spain to repeal his laws against heretics. Women were not permitted to sign the document. However, it is known that they directly influenced many of the men who did sign.[95]

Englishwomen also promoted the Calvinist or Puritan cause. Catherine Willoughby, duchess of Suffolk, and Frances Radcliffe, countess of Sussex, supported ministers and established schools for spreading the Reformed faith. Catherine attended Martin Bucer's lectures at Cambridge. He persuaded her to adopt a stance more radical than "Anglicanism." When Mary Tudor ascended the throne, Catherine fled to Poland with her family. She returned to England during Elizabeth's reign and became a dedicated supporter of the Puritan cause.[96]

One of the most outstanding middle-class English Calvinists was Anne Locke, friend and correspondent of John Knox and translator of some of Calvin's works into English. Between 1556 and 1562, Locke and Knox exchanged letters that reveal a great deal about him and the state of the Reform in England and Scotland. Through the devotion of Anne Locke, some of Knox's lesser-known works have been preserved. The Locke-Knox correspondence is interesting because of parallels with Calvin's letters to women. Like Calvin, Knox respected his friend and tried to use her exceptional talents to further the movement. He sent her copies of his tracts and the Scottish Confession of Faith for comment and distribution. When he urged her to leave her husband and go into exile for the sake of religion, she obeyed. But Locke differed from most of Calvin's female correspondents because she was a commoner lacking in influence.[97]

In summary, Calvin and Luther did not bring about any major changes in attitudes towards women or the roles permitted them in the early modern period. Women, however, contributed outside the structure of the Reformed Church in spite of traditional male instructions for passive, submissive behavior. They acted as if somehow male prescriptions for female submissiveness did not apply to them, and they seemed to find personal, spiritual, and emotional satisfaction in the movement whether or not it changed their status.

Calvin and Luther were men of their time. Equality requires particular social, political, and economic conditions. Within the context of the sixteenth century, terms such as subjugation and subordination were less emotionally charged than they are today. Most people were subjects. According to modern social theory, categories or symbols such as equality are recognized only when they become culturally significant in an explicit way.[98] Open rebellion against patriarchal attitudes does not occur until the categories, symbols, and vocabulary take on a significance for a majority. Except for the outbursts of a few exceptional men and women, this did not occur until at least the nineteenth century. Furthermore, the rejection of traditional sex roles and symbols cannot take place until new concepts exist to replace them. It is doubtful that religious ideology alone is sufficient to create change in behavior and attitudes without the political, social, and economic climate for the ideas to take root.

The sixteenth century saw the beginning of important changes in religious outlook and social structure. For example, Calvinist men and women no longer had the option of denying or rejecting the world. Instead, they were to affirm the world and this life and to follow a vocation to the greater glory of God. In a similar vein, transformation began in sex images and roles so that spiritual equality between men and women and the dignity of the female role, at least as mother, were integral in Calvinist and Lutheran thought. An articulated concern for female equality was not possible among sixteenth-century Lutherans or Calvinists. The cultural consciousness necessary to effect lasting change came later. Time was needed for religion and society to support the ideas of equality. Thus it is not surprising that Luther and Calvin straddled tradition and innovation in their attitudes toward the female role.

NOTES

1. See, for example, Roland R. Bainton, *Women of the Reformation in Germany and Italy* (Minneapolis: Augsburg Publishing House, 1971); Roland R. Bainton, *Women of the Reformation in France and England* (Minneapolis: Augsburg Publishing House, 1973); Miriam U. Chrisman, "Women and the Reformation in Strasbourg, 1490–1530," *Archiv für Reformationsgeschichte* 63 (1972): 143–68; Elizabeth Clark and Herbert Richardson, "Luther and the Protestant Reformation: From Nun to Parson's Wife," in *Women and Religion*, ed. Elizabeth Clark and Herbert Richardson (New York: Harper and Row, 1977), pp. 131–48; Natalie Z. Davis, "City Women and Religious Change," in *Society and Culture in Early Modern France* (Stanford: Stanford University Press, 1975); Jane D. Douglass, "Women and the Continental Reformation," in *Religion and Sexism: Images of Woman in the Jewish and Christian Traditions*, ed. Rosemary Radford Ruether (New York: Simon and Schuster, 1974), pp. 292–318; Susan C. Karant-Nunn, "Luther's Attitude Toward Women" (Paper presented at the American Society for Reformation Research, Washington, D.C., 1978); Susan C. Karant-Nunn, "Continuity and Change: Some Effects of the Reformation on the Women of Zwickau," *Sixteenth Century Journal* 12 (1982): 17–42; Nancy Lyman Roelker, "The Role of Noblewomen in the French Reformation," *Archiv für Reformationsgeschichte* 63 (1972): 172–93; Nancy Lyman Roelker, "The Appeal of Calvinism to French Noblewomen in the Sixteenth Century," *Journal of Interdisciplinary History* 2 (Spring 1972): 391–418; Sherrin M. Wyntjes, "Women in the Reformation Era," in *Becoming Visible: Women in European History*, ed. Renate Bridenthal and Claudia Koonz (Boston: Houghton Mifflin, 1977), pp. 165–91.

2. Martin Luther, "A Sermon on the Estate of Marriage," in *Luther's Works*, vol. 44, *The Christian in Society: I*, ed. James Atkinson (Philadelphia: Fortress Press, 1966), pp. 7–14; Luther "The Estate of Marriage," in *Luther's Works*, vol. 45, *The Christian in Society: II*, ed. Walther I. Brandt (Philadelphia: Muhlenberg Press, 1962), pp. 17–49; Luther, "The Babylonian Captivity of the Church," in *Luther's Works*, vol. 36, *Word and Sacrament: II*, ed. Abel R. Wentz (Philadelphia: Muhlenberg Press, 1959), pp. 92–106; Luther, *Luther's Works*, vol. 1, *Lectures on Gen-*

esis, ed. Jaroslav Pelikan (St. Louis: Concordia Publishing House, 1958); Luther, *Luther's Works*, vol. 54, *Table Talk*, ed. Theodore G. Tappert (Philadelphia: Fortress Press, 1967). The above are hereafter referred to as *LW*.

3. Steven Ozment, *When Fathers Ruled: Family Life in Reformation Europe* (Cambridge: Harvard University Press, 1983). The following unpublished papers have been useful: Susan C. Karant-Nunn, "Martin Luther, Advocate of Change or Continuity in the Status of Women?" (Pacific Northwest Renaissance Conference, Eugene, Oreg., March 1973); Susan C. Karant-Nunn, "Luther's Attitude Toward Women" (American Society of Church History, Washington, D.C., December 1976); Susan C. Karant-Nunn, "The Transmission of Luther's Teaching on Women and Matrimony: The Case of Zwickau" (Sixth International Congress for Luther Research, Erfurt, August 1983); Merry E. Wiesner, "From Woman to Wife" (Quincentennial Celebration of Luther's Birth, St. Louis, Mo., June 1983); Jonathan W. Zophy, "Luther's Attitudes Toward Women" (Sixteenth Century Studies Conference, Milwaukee, Wis., October 1983). I am grateful to the authors of these unpublished papers for sharing their work with me.

4. See Martin Luther, "On Christian Liberty," *LW*, vol. 31, *Career of the Reformation: I*, ed. Harold J. Grimm (Philadelphia: Muhlenberg Press, 1957), pp. 333–77, especially pp 345, 351; Luther, "The Babylonian Captivity of the Church," *LW* 36: 192–96; Luther, "To the Christian Nobility of the German Nation," *LW*, 44: 123–217; Douglass, "Women and the Continental Reformation," pp. 293, 296, makes this point very well.

5. Luther, *LW*, vol. 40, *Church and Ministry: II*, ed. Conrad Bergendorff (Philadelphia: Muhlenberg Press, 1958), pp. 388–90.

6. Luther, "Lectures on Genesis," *LW*, 1: 198–203 (Gen. 3:16).

7. Luther, "A Sermon on the Estate of Marriage," *LW*, 44: 8–10.

8. This has been well demonstrated in the works cited in note 3.

9. Luther, "A Sermon on the Estate of Marriage," *LW*, 44: 7–9; Elizabeth Boehme, "The Development of Luther's Attitude Toward the Secular in His German Writings to the Peasants' War" (Ph.D. diss., Boston College, 1976), pp. 19–24, 131–43.

10. Luther, "A Sermon on the Estate of Marriage," *LW*, 44: 7–10; Ozment, *When Fathers Ruled*, pp. 1–50.

11. Luther, "Babylonian Captivity of the Church," *LW*, 36: 2, pp. 92–96; Luther, "A Sermon on the Estate of Marriage," *LW*, 44: 10.

12. Philip Schaff, *The Creeds of Christendom*, 3 vols. (New York: Harper, 1877), 3: 52, article VI.

13. Luther, "The Estate of Marriage," *LW*, 45: 11–49.

14. Ibid.

15. For an excellent discussion of this point see Douglass, "Women and the Continental Reformation," p. 310.

16. Karant-Nunn, "The Transmission of Luther's Teachings on Women and Matrimony," makes this point very well.

17. Luther, "The Estate of Marriage," *LW*, 45: 13–15.

18. Luther, "Lectures on Genesis," *LW*, 1: 138; 2: 23–24.

19. See for example Schaff, 3: 304, chap. XXIX; 3: 655, chap. XXXIV; John Calvin, *Commentary on the Harmony of the Evangelists*, trans. W. Pringle (Grand Rapids: Wm. B. Eerdmans, 1949), 2: 384; Andre Biéler, *L'homme et la femme dans la morale calviniste* (Geneva: Labor et Fides, 1963); Gervase Duffield ed., "Calvin on Marriage," in *John Calvin: A Collection of Essays*, (Grand Rapids: Wm. B. Eerdmans, 1966); W. Fred Graham, *The Constructive Revolutionary* (Richmond: John Knox Press, 1971), pp. 151–60; Louis B. Wright, *Middle Class Culture in Elizabethan England* (Chapel Hill: University of North Carolina Press, 1955), pp. 201–97; William and Malleville Haller, "The Puritan Art of Love," *Huntington Library Quarterly* 5 (1941–42): 235–72; Roland Mushat Frye, "The Teaching of Classical Puritanism on Conjugal Love," *Studies in the Renaissance* 2 (1955): 148–59; John Yost, "The Value of Married Life for the Social Order in the English Renaissance," *Societas* 6 (1976): 25–39; Lawrence Stone, *The Crisis of the Aristocracy, 1558–1641*, abridged ed. (Oxford: Clarendon Press, 1967), pp. 269–302.

20. The following are the best studies of Katherine in English: Yvonne Davy, *Frau Luther* (Montain View, Calif.: Pacific Press, 1979); Clara Schreiber, *Katherine, Wife of Luther* (Philadelphia: Muhlenberg Press, 1954); Bainton, *Women of the Reformation in Germany and Italy*, pp. 23–45.

21. Luther, *LW*, vol. 49, *Letters: II*, ed. Gottfried G. Krodel (Philadelphia: Fortress Press, 1972), see for example, no. 157; Karant-Nunn, "The Transmission of Luther's Teachings on Women and Matrimony."

22. Luther, "The Estate of Marriage," *LW*, 45: 13–15.

23. Ibid.; Luther, "Lectures on Genesis", *LW* 1: 198–203 (Gen. 2:23 and 3:20).

24. "The Estate of Marriage," *LW*, 45: 13–15; Luther, "The Babylonian Captivity of the Church," *LW*, 36: 105.

25. Luther, "The Babylonian Captivity of the Church," *LW* 36: 105.

26. Luther, "Table Talk," *LW*, 54: 160–61, no. 1658.

27. Luther, "The Estate of Marriage," *LW* 45: 13–15.

28. Luther, "Table Talk," *LW*, 54: 7–8, no. 49; 54: 222–23, no. 3528; 54: 444, no. 5524; 54: 160–61, no. 1658.

29. Ibid., 54: 8, no. 55.

30. Luther, "Lectures on Genesis," *LW*, 1: 198–203 (Gen. 3:16).

31. Luther, "Table Talk," *LW*, 54: 8, no. 55.

32. Douglass, "Women and the Continental Reformation," p. 298.

33. Luther, "A Sermon on the Estate of Marriage," *LW*, 44: 12–13.

34. Luther, "Lectures on Genesis," *LW*, 1: 198–203 (Gen. 3:16); Luther, On "The Estate of Marriage," *LW*, 45: 13–15; Luther, "Temporal Authority: To What Extent It Should Be Obeyed, 1523" *LW*, 45: 83–117; John Dillenberger, ed., "Freedom of a Christian," in *Martin Luther: Selections from His Writings* (Garden City: Doubleday, 1961), p. 78: John Dillenberger, ed., "Commentary on Galatians," in *Martin Luther: Selections from His Writings* (1961) p. 159.

35. Martin Bucer, *De Regno Christi*, ed. François Wendel, in *Martini Buceri Opera Latina*, ed. Wendel, 25 vols. (Paris: Presses universitaires de France, 1954 ff.) 15, 2, chap. 45, pp. 226–31.

36. François Wendel, *Le mariage à Strasbourg à l'époque de la réforme, 1520–1692* (Strasbourg, Imp. alsacienne, 1928). For an excellent discussion of the handling of marital problems and divorce in Lutheran Zwickau see Karant-Nunn, "Women of Zwickau," pp. 32–35.

37. Phyllis Stack, *Better Than Rubies: A History of Women's Education* (New York: G.P. Putnam and Sons, 1978); Lowell Green, "The Education of Women in the Reformation," *History of Education Quarterly* 19 (Spring 1979): 93–116.

38. Luther, *An die Rayherren aller Stadte deutsches Lands dass sie christliche Schulen aufrichten und hatten solle, und Eine Predigt, dass man Kinder zur Schule halten solle*, as cited in Douglass, "Women and the Continental Reformation," p. 317, n. 69.

39. Karant-Nunn, "Women of Zwickau," p. 19; Zophy, "Luther's Attitudes Toward Women," pp. 7–9.

40. Chrisman, "Women and the Reformation in Strasbourg," p. 152.

41. Wyntjes, "Women in the Reformation Era."

42. For what follows on Katherine von Bora, see works cited above, n. 1.

43. Luther, "Table Talk," *LW*, 54, no. 6320.

44. This approach to the development of feminine consciousness is suggested by Janet Giele, "Centuries of Childhood and Centuries of Womanhood, An Evolutionary Perspective on the Feminine Role," *Women's Studies* 1 (1972): 97–110.

45. Bainton, *Women of the Reformation in Germany and Italy*, pp. 79–95.

46. Ibid., pp. 55–76; Chrisman, "Women and the Reformation in Strasbourg," pp. 152, 156–57.

47. Bainton, *Women of the Reformation in Germany and Italy*, pp. 97–109.

48. Ibid., pp. 111–24.

49. Ibid., pp. 125–44.

50. Calvin's ideas on women, the relationship between the sexes, and marriage are spread throughout his works. Much of what follows is based upon John H. Bratt, "The Role and Status of Women in the Writings of John Calvin," and the response by Charmarie Jenkins Blaisdell, both in *Proceedings of a Colloquium on Calvin and Calvin Studies*, ed. Peter der Klerk (Grand Rapids: Calvin College and Seminary, 1976), pp. 1–17, 19–30; John Calvin's *Commentaries* on the first three books of Genesis, his commentaries on the epistles of St. Paul, especially 1 Corinthians 11:2–3 and 14:34–35, and the sermon on Deuteronomy. Calvin, *Commentaries on the First Book of Moses, Called Genesis*, trans. John King (Grand Rapids: W.B. Eerdmans, 1948); Calvin, *Commentary on the Epistles of Paul the Apostle to the Corinthians*, trans. John Pringle (Grand Rapids: W.B. Eerdmans, 1948); Calvin, *The Sermons of M. John Calvin upon the Fifth Book of Moses, Called Deuteronomie*, trans. Arthur Golding (London, 1583). There are also numerous references spread throughout other sermons. See François Wendel, *Calvin: The Origin and Development of His Religious Thought*, trans. Philip Mairet (New York: Harper and Row, 1963). For a comprehensive study of Calvin's ideas on this subject see Biéler, *L'homme et la femme dans la morale calviniste*, which contains many citations from Calvin's works and full documentation. The standard edition of Calvin's works is G. Baum, E. Cunitz, and E. Reuss, eds., *Ioannis Calvini Opera*, 59 vols. (Brunswick, Germany: C.A. Schwetschke, 1863–1900), hereafter cited as *CO*. Where possible I have used the English translations of Calvin's sermons and commentaries.

51. Roelker, "The Role of Women in the French Reformation," p. 192.

52. John Bratt makes this idea the thesis of his paper cited above. I am indebted to him and to Biéler, *L'homme et la femme dans la morale calviniste*, for this perspective.

53. John Calvin, *Commentary on the First Book of Moses Called Genesis*, trans. J. King (Grand Rapids: Wm. B. Eerdmans, 1964), pp. 92, 95, 129, 131, 135.

54. John Calvin, *Commentary on the First Book of Moses*, p. 129; John Calvin, *Sermons on the Epistles of St. Paul to Timothy and Titus*, trans. Laurence Tomson (London, 1579), p. 212.

55. John Calvin, *Commentary on Timothy*, trans. J.W. Fraser (Grand Rapids: Wm. B. Eerdmans, 1965), pp. 217–18; Calvin, *Commentary on I and II Peter*, trans. J.W. Fraser (Grand Rapids: Wm. B. Eerdmans, 1958), p. 282. For another statement that man was already the head of woman before the Fall, see John Calvin, *Sermons on the Epistle to the Ephesians*, trans. Arthur Golding (Edinburgh: Banner of Truth Trust, 1973), p. 567.

56. Calvin, *Sermons on Timothy and Titus*, pp. 209, 228; Calvin, *Commentary on Timothy*, p. 217.

57. Calvin, *Commentary on the First Book of Moses*, pp. 170, 183.

58. John Calvin, *The First Epistle of Paul the Apostle to the Corinthians*, trans. J. W. Faser (Grand Rapids: Wm. B. Eerdmans, 1960), p. 233.

59. Ibid., p. 232.

60. Ibid., p. 234.

61. John Calvin, *Sermons on Timothy and Titus*, pp. 216, 221; John Calvin, *Commentary on Corinthians*, trans. J.W. Fraser (Grand Rapids: Wm. B. Eerdmans, 1960), p. 234.

62. Calvin, *Sermons on Ephesians*, p. 565.

63. Biéler, *L'homme et la femme*, pp. 65–69. Biéler draws on a variety of Calvin's commentaries on books of the Old and the New Testament for this discussion, and the reader would do well to begin with him.

64. Biéler, *L'homme et la femme*, pp. 62, 65, 67. Calvin bases his argument on Deuteronomy 24:5, where a young man was excused from military service and permitted to stay with his wife for a year after marriage.

65. Biéler, *L'homme et la femme*, pp. 44–88.

66. Ibid., pp. 89–104.

67. Calvin's exegesis on the two versions of the creation story will be found in his *Commentary on the First Book of Moses*, pp. 92, 95, 129, 131; *Commentary on Corinthians*, pp. 135, 231, 232; *Commentary on Timothy*, pp. 217–19; *Sermons on Timothy and Titus*; *Commentary on I and II Peter*, p. 282.

68. Bainton, *Women of the Reformation in France and England*, pp. 87–88; Richard Stauffer, *The Humanness of Calvin* (Nashville: Abingdon Press, 1971); Emile Doumergue, *Jean Calvin*, 7 vols. (Lausanne: G. Bridel, 1899–1927), 2, passim.

69. For further discussion of this point see Roelker, "The Appeal of Calvinism to French Noblewomen in the Sixteenth Century," pp. 404ff.

70. Biéler, *L'homme et la femme*, pp. 69–72; Duffield, ed., "Calvin on Marriage," in *John Calvin*; Graham, *The Constructive Revolutionary*, pp. 151–60.

71. Calvin à une dame, 4 June 1559, *CO*, 17, col. 519, no. 3064; Calvin à Madame de Cany, 7 June 1553, *CO*, 14, col. 556–58, no. 1751; Calvin à Madame de Rentigny, 8 December 1557, *CO*, 16, col. 726, no. 2772; 10 April 1558, *CO*, 17, col. 131, no. 2848.

72. *CO*, 10: 41.

73. The research of René Stauffenegger has shown that, in fact, divorces were rarely granted in Geneva in the late sixteenth century. Pastors and the Consistory, like Calvin, always pressed the couple to

solve their problems without rupturing the marriage. René Stauffenegger, "Le Marriage à Geneve vers 1600," *Mémoires de la société pour l'histoire du droit* 27 (1966): 327–28; Keith Thomas, "The Double Standard,"
Journal of the History of Ideas 20 (1959): 200–202. For a fresh perspective
on the traditional position and the fact that under canon law individuals
had long been allowed to instigate proceedings against an adulterous
partner, see John T. Noonan, Jr., *Power to Dissolve* (Cambridge: Harvard
University Press, 1972). Davis makes the case that the shift in attitude
toward divorce had little or no impact on the position of women in
Davis, "City Women and Religious Change," p. 90.

74. John Calvin, *Commentary on a Harmony of the Evangelists, Matthew,
Mark, and Luke*, trans. William Pringle, 3 vols. (Grand Rapids: Wm. B.
Eerdmans, 1949), 3: 339; John Calvin, *The Deity of Christ and Other Sermons*, trans. Leroy Nixon (Grand Rapids: Wm. B. Eerdmans, 1950), pp.
184–85.

75. Calvin, *Sermons on Timothy and Titus*, p. 225; *Second Epistle to
Corinthians, and Epistles to Timothy, Titus and Philemon*, p. 217, as quoted
in Bratt (who has an excellent discussion of this point), "The Role and
Status of Women," p. 5.

76. Bratt, "The Role and Staus of Women," p. 7; Calvinus à Eliza-
bethae Reginae, 15 January 1559, *CO.*, 17, col. 413–15, no. 3000.

77. Calvin, *Commentary on a Harmony of the Evangelists*, 3: 385; John
Calvin, *Institutes of the Christian Religion*, ed. John T. McNeill and trans.
Ford Lewis Battles, The Library of Christian Classics, vols. 20–21 (Philadelphia: Westminster Press, 1960), IV, xv, 20, 21; see Blaisdell, "Calvin's Letters to Women," p. 83, for a discussion of Calvin's quarrel
with a noblewoman over the extent to which she could control the
Reformed congregation in her land.

78. Davis, "City Women and Religious Change," p. 87; Christopher
Hill, *The World Turned Upside Down: Radical Ideas during the English Revolution* (New York: Viking Press, 1972), p. 248.

79. Pierre Viret, *Instruction chretienne en la doctrine de la loy et de
l'evangile* (Geneva, 1564), 2: 721–28, as cited in Davis, "City Women and
Religious Change."

80. Robert M. Kingdon, *Geneva and the Consolidation of the French Protestant Reform Movement* (Madison: University of Wisconsin Press, 1967),
pp. 46–62.

81. Ibid.

82. Morel to Calvin, 3 August 1561, *CO*, 18, col. 589–91, no. 3466;
Morel to Calvin, 25 August 1561, *CO*, 18, col. 641–45, no. 3491; Renée
to Calvin, 17 December 1561, *CO*, 18, col. 483–84, no. 4206, incorrectly
dated 1551; Calvin à la Duchese de Ferrare, February 1562, *CO*, 19, col.

307–8, no. 3727; Morel to Calvin, March 1562, *CO*, 19, col. 372–73, no. 3761; Renée to Calvin, 1562, *CO*, 19, col. 612–14, no. 3890; Morel to Calvin, 1562, *CO*, 19, 614–17, no. 3891; Calvin to Morel, 1562, *CO*, 19, col. 617–18, no. 3892; Morel to Calvin, January 1563, *CO*, 19, col. 628–31, no. 3895; Morel to Calvin, January 1563, *CO*, 19, col. 631–32, no. 3896; Calvin à la Duchesse de Ferrare, 10 May 1563, *CO*, 20, col. 15–18, no. 3951; Morel to Calvin, 6 December, 1563, *CO*, 20, col. 207–9, no. 4055.

83. Roelker, "The Role of Noblewomen in the French Reformation" and "The Appeal of Calvinism to French Noblewomen in the Sixteenth Century." For a slightly different perspective see Davis, "City Women and Religious Change."

84. Jean Jules Le Coultre, *Maturin Cordier et les origines de la pédagogié protestante dans les pays de langue française* (Neuchatel: Secrétariat de l'Université, 1926), p. 117; Henri Naef, *Les origines de la réforme à Genéve* (Geneva: Droz, 1968), 1: 297, as quoted in Douglass, "Women and the Continental Reformation," p. 304.

85. Thérèse Pittard, *Femmes de Genève et les origines de la pédagogié protestante* (Geneva: n.d.), pp. 147–48, 151–52.

86. Elizabeth K. Hudson, "The Colloquies of Maturin Cordier: Images of Calvinist School Life," *Sixteenth Century Journal* 9 (1978): 57–78.

87. Pittard, *Femmes de Genève*, pp. 148, 151–52.

88. The best treatment of this event is in N. Weiss, "L'Assemble de la Rue St. Jacques," *Bulletin de la société de l'histoire du protestantisme français* 65 (1916): 195–235, hereafter cited *BSHPF*; see also *BSHPF* 5 (1856): 382 ff.

89. Eugène Haag, *La France protestante*, 9 vols. (Paris: J. Cherbuliez, 1846–59), 7: 172–73; G. Baum and E. Cunitz, eds., *Histoire Ecclésiastique*, 3 vols. (Paris: Librairie Fischbacher, 1883–89), 1:141; *Les Mémoires de Messire Michel de Castelnau, Seigneur de Mauvissiere*, J. Le Laboreur, ed., 3 vols. (Brussels: Jean Leonard, 1731), 2: 753; *CO*, 17, no. 3113; *CO*, 18, no. 3532; Henri Meylan, et al., eds., *Correspondence de Theodore Bèze*, 6 vols. (Geneva: E. Droz, 1960–70), 3: 89, 184, 202, 236, 237, 240; 4: 101, 102, 107, 125, 135, 141–43, 194; Roelker, "The Role of Noblewomen in the French Reformation," pp. 177–78, and "The Appeal of Calvinism to French Noblewomen", p. 401.

90. R. de Perrot-Bovet, "Jacqueline de Rohan, Marquise de Rothelin," *Musée Neuchatelois*, 20–21 (1883–84); R. de Perrot-Bovet, "La Marquise de Rothelin en Suisse," *BSHPF* 32 (1883): 385ff.; *CO*, 17, no. 3059, 3702; *CO*, 19, no. 3928; H. de la Ferrière and B. de Puchesse, eds., *Lettres de Catherine de Médicis*, 11 vols. (Paris: Imprimerie Nationale, 1880–1943), 3: 80, 82, 128. See also the articles by Roelker.

91. Charmarie J. Blaisdell, "Royalty and Reform: The Predicament of Renée de France" (Ph.D. diss., Tufts University, 1970); Charmarie J. Blaisdell, "Renée de France between Reform and Counter Reform," *Archiv für Reformationsgeschichte* 63 (1972): 196–226; Charmarie J. Blaisdell, "Calvin's Letters to Women," *Sixteenth Century Journal* 12 (1982): 77–84.

92. Nancy Lyman Roelker, *Queen of Navarre: Jeanne d'Albret* (Cambridge: Belknap Press of Harvard University Press, 1968).

93. See the discussion in Roelker, "The Appeal of Calvinism to French Noblewomen," pp. 403–13. For a different point of view at least as regards middle-class women, see Davis, "City Women and Religious Change."

94. Davis, "City, Women and Religious Change."

95. Wyntjes, "Women in the Reformation Era," pp. 180–81.

96. Evelyn Read, *Catherine, Duchess of Suffolk* (London: Cape, 1962); Bainton, *Women of the Reformation in France and England*, pp. 253–77; Constantin Hopf, *Martin Bucer and the English Reformation* (Oxford: Clarendon Press, 1946).

97. Patrick Collinson, "The Role of Women in the English Reformation Illustrated by the Life and Friendships of Anne Locke," *Studies in Church History* 2 (1965): 258–72.

98. Giele, "Centuries of Childhood, Centuries of Womanhood," pp. 97–110.

2

God's Powerful Army of the Weak: Anabaptist Women of the Radical Reformation

Keith L. Sprunger

A maxim of Anabaptist history appeared in T.J. van Braght's *Martyrs Mirror*: "The army of God, which at this time prepared itself for the conflict and the sufferings of Jesus Christ, consisted not only of men, who are sometimes judged to be strongest, but also in women, for God's power is made strong in weakness."[1] During the revolutionary tumult of the sixteenth-century Reformation, Anabaptist women were called upon by the church for extraordinary deeds. Their "weakness" became "strong." After the first and second generations, as church and society settled down, less was asked of Anabaptist women and less was accomplished.

Anabaptism belonged to the Radical Reformation, the most extreme of the sixteenth-century religious movements. In its call for "restitution" Christianity, Anabaptism in many respects exceeded the demands of the Lutheran and Calvinist Reformations. Anabaptism was, in the words of J.A. Oosterbaan, a "Reformation of the Reformation."[2] Not only theological, Anabaptism was a powerful and sweeping socio-religious movement, according to Walter Klaassen, that "questioned virtually all of the assumptions upon which sixteenth-century society, culture, and church rested." In the main, Anabaptists challenged Catholic and Protestant society religiously, by practicing voluntarism and believer's baptism; economically, by attacking usury and placing limitations on use of private property; and politically, by withdrawing from the magistracy and refusing participation in wars. Authorities of church and state saw Anabaptism as "a conspiracy against the social order."[3] Drastic as the Anabaptists' program seemed, a few assumptions were left nearly unchallenged. There was no sixteenth-century Anabaptist women's or sexual revolution, nor did Anabaptist women seem to be calling for one.[4]

To refer to the Anabaptist program or vision of the sixteenth century puts the historian at risk. Anabaptism splintered into a great variety of factions: some with one emphasis, some with another. Anabaptism, for the purposes of this chapter, included such diverse sixteenth-century groups as the Swiss Brethren of Zurich who broke from Zwingli, the south German Anabaptists, the Melchiorites of Strasbourg, the Hutterites, the notorious Munsterites, and the Dutch Mennonite followers of Menno Simons. "Anabaptist" is the general term referring to the original movement. When Menno Simons took over as leader, "Mennonite" became the more common term. "Radical Reformation" is a broader term encompassing Anabaptists, Mennonites, and other non-Lutheran, non-Reformed radicals. All Anabaptists stressed the necessity of believer's baptism, rather than infant baptism; but beyond that, uniformity was not achieved. Many Anabaptists, however, supported the religious, economic, and political propositions summarized above by Klaassen.

Whether or not recognized in their theology, sixteenth-century Anabaptist women, in fact, had a prominence unparalleled in the later history of Anabaptism-Mennonitism. Their homes and congregations were the centers of a dynamic religious movement. Women helped to carry the momentum. Almost from the start, a fierce repression descended on Anabaptists, which indiscriminately put men and women to torture and execution. Two historical sources have collected the story of Anabaptist women. The earliest was the *Martyrs Mirror* of Thieleman Jansz van Braght (published in 1660). This Mennonite martyr book recorded the story of over 900 Anabaptist martyrs; approximately 278 of the martyrs were women. The other comprehensive source is the twentieth-century *Mennonite Encyclopedia* (four volumes, published 1955–59). The *Encyclopedia* has entries for 459 Anabaptist women of the sixteenth and seventeenth centuries. Although many were repeated from the *Martyrs Mirror*, over 250 were new names. These two sources together make accessible in narrative form the stories of some 525 early Anabaptist women (not all of them specifically identified by name).[5] More recently, social historians of Anabaptism, following the lead of Claus-Peter Clasen, have produced lists and analyses of ordinary Anabaptist men and women.[6]

Anabaptism's Heroic Era was the sixteenth century. After that, as Harold S. Bender noted, "the settled communities and congregations reverted more to the typical patriarchal attitude of European culture."[7] The *Mennonite Encyclopedia* itself reflects this reduced role of women. Of its 459 female Anabaptist entries (1500–1700), nearly every one came from the sixteenth-century martyr period. Only fifteen of the women came from the seventeenth century, and these primarily because a few martyrdoms were still occurring in Switzerland. For the post-martyrdom period, the encyclopedia editors included only a handful of seventeenth-century women.

DAUGHTERS OF EVE: WOMEN IN ANABAPTIST THEOLOGY

Anabaptists produced little systematic theology, but through the years a considerable body of religious writings emerged. It is hard to find in the Anabaptist writings any distinctive or innovative trend regarding women. The leadership of the movement, who preached, baptized, and wrote the books, were men. The wives of the early leaders, the founding women of the Anabaptism movement, received very little coverage in the early Mennonite histories, unless they happened to become martyrs. Anabaptist theology was rooted in the Bible, and the leadership and rank-and-file alike immersed themselves in the Bible, being "simply students of the Scriptures and hardly of anything else." Anabaptist "Biblicism" set the course for writing and preaching on women.[8] As they preached from the Bible, Anabaptist leaders unquestioningly repeated the New Testament themes of women being silent in the church and obedient in the home. These were true because they were in the Bible. In spite of female zeal in evangelism and heroism in the face of persecution, the written theology never acknowledged much of the contribution of women.

Among the Anabaptists of Switzerland and south Germany, Michael Sattler (1490–1527) gave some thoughts on women. He helped draft the first Anabaptist Confession of Faith, the "Bruderlich Vereinigung" or Schleitheim Confession of 1527. It was addressed to the "Beloved brothers and sisters in the Lord" but otherwise did not expound on women in the fellowship. Sattler also wrote a short tract on *Divorce*, which will be discussed later. Sattler suffered martyrdom in 1527, one of the featured stories of the *Martyrs Mirror*. Sattler's wife died along with her husband. Her account is extremely brief, tacked on at the end of Michael's longer story: "His wife, also, after being subjected to many entreaties, admonitions and threats, under which she remained very steadfast, was drowned a few days afterwards."[9] Another early leader of the southern Anabaptists was Conrad Grebel (1498–1526). He was humanistically educated and made some clever Latin literary puns about his wife Barbara, his "Barbarity," and some sharp complaints about his mother, "she governs the home, she sleeps, arises, scolds, takes breakfast, brawls frightfully, lunches, wrangles, dines and ceases not to plague us."[10]

Anabaptist theologian Balthasar Hubmaier (1480–1528), one of the most learned, a Th.D., wrote about women under the topic of Adam and Eve in his treatise *On Free Will*. Eve must bear the blame for bringing sin into the world. Man in general is composed of three substances: flesh, soul, and spirit. Hubmaier believed that Adam and Eve were allegorical representations of mankind, with Adam standing for the highest in man and Eve, for the lowest and basest. Adam was "a type of the soul (as is Eve, of the flesh)." Gloriously, however, flesh, soul, and spirit, ruined by the fall of Adam and Eve, will be restored in Christ.[11] In his *Form of the Lord's Supper*, Hubmaier instructed "women to be silent in the church" (1 Cor. 11).[12] Hubmaier and his spouse, Elsbeth Hugeline, suffered martyrdom. Reports say she was more resolute in the face of death than her husband.[13]

Hutterites gave women a lowly place. Peter Riedemann (1506–1556), married to Katarina, produced an important Hutterite book, *Account of Our Religion, Doctrine and Faith* (1545). Under the topic of marriage, he wrote:

We say, first, that since woman was taken from man, and not man from woman, man hath lordship but woman weakness, humility and submission, therefore she should be under the yoke of man and obedient to him, even as the woman was commanded by God when he said to her, "The man shall be thy lord."[14]

The Hutterite woman was taught that she was a very weak vessel (1 Peter 3:7).

In the writings of Menno Simons (1496–1561), the chief Anabaptist theologian, the picture was not much different. Menno was far from encouraging a sisterhood of unmanageable, charismatic females. His model of womanhood was a chaste, demure sister in the Lord:

I, therefore entreat and desire all women through the mercy of the Lord to take this sorrowful, sorrowing woman [the woman who washed the feet of Jesus with her hair] as a pattern and follow her faith. Humble yourselves before the Lord. . . . Do not adorn yourselves with gold, silver, costly pearls and embroidered hair. . . . Be obedient to your husbands in all reasonable things. . . .

Remain within your houses and gates unless you have something of importance to regulate, such as to make purchases, to provide in temporal needs, to hear the Word of the Lord, or to receive the holy sacraments, etc. Attend faithfully to your charge, to your children, house, and family, and to all that is entrusted to you. . . .[15]

Menno's wife, Frau Geertruydt (Gertrude), was perhaps such a woman. However, as the wife of a hunted refugee, there was little of a home for her to remain in, and she followed him through endless exiles.[16] Menno's writings touched on women at another place, the controversial doctrine of the incarnation. Several Anabaptist leaders, beginning with Melchior Hofmann (1495–1543) of Strasbourg, believed that the infant Jesus did not take his fleshly body from the Virgin Mary but rather received heavenly flesh from God the Father. If the body had even partially come from Mary, then, the fear was, Jesus must be tainted with sinful flesh. If bound by traditional theology, Anabaptists judged that the problem would be insoluble. How could Jesus be sinless if he were born from a human woman?[17] The Melchiorite answer, adopted later by Dirk Philips and Menno Simons, surmised that Jesus slipped through Mary uncontaminated, like water through a pipe or through a funnel. Other Protestant theologians condemned this view of the incarnation, smacking of Docetism, as one of the gravest Anabaptist errors.

In describing Christ's incarnation through Mary, Menno expounded on human generation as a whole. The man's role in conception is active, and the woman's role is always passive. In the *Reply to Gellius Faber* (1554), Menno wrote that the father is the only creator of the child and that the woman is passive soil to be planted with the seed. Both man and woman have their ordained place: "the man a sower and the woman as a receptive field."[18] By this kind of biological supposition, Menno and his fellow Dutch Anabaptists attempted to resolve their theological problem. Jesus was born out of Mary, not from Mary (*uit* Mary, not *van* Mary).[19] Menno's incarnation theology bears considerable resemblance to Aristotle's biology of animals, still current in the sixteenth century—did Menno read Aristotle? Menno Simons, however, for theological purposes went further than Aristotle's science required. Aristotle taught that the female was passive in biological generation but still substantively involved. Menno minimized the female role to both passivity and nullity. She was the "field" in which the father's children grew. An alternative scientific theory, the Galenic theory, was also circulating in the sixteenth century. Galenic science stated that women as well as men added an active seed to conception, but such teachings did not serve Menno's theological purposes.[20]

Although Menno Simons' incarnation theology implied an intentional anti-feminism, this was apparently not his goal. The theory, moreover, never gained acceptance universally among Anabaptists, especially in Switzerland; even in Holland it faded away within a few decades. Recent studies have taken a fresh look at the Melchiorite-Mennonite theory, long dismissed as an Anabaptist embarrassment, and they suggest that Menno's incarnation theology may set forth some neglected insights into Christology and the nature of man and woman. The supernatural origin of Jesus Christ made his human body, like the first Adam's, sinless and innocent. Just as Anabaptism sought the restitution of the church, so Anabaptists also longed for the restitution of human nature and "the recovery of human perfectability." Sjouke Voolstra has written, "The restoration of the original human nature as created through faith in Christ as the New Adam, through whom fallen man is recreated to a new creature in whose heart the law is written, is the focus of his faith."[21]

The consolidation of Anabaptist-Mennonite theology occurred with the Dordrecht (Dort) Confession of Faith of 1632. The creed of eighteen articles became authoritative among many Mennonites. Two articles are relevant to the topic. Article IV on the incarnation vaguely slid over the question of "how and in what manner," thus sidestepping the Melchiorite-Mennonite theory. Article IX on officers in the church for the first time in Mennonite theology made a recognized place for women officers, the deaconesses.[22]

Although theology and the writing of books were mostly in the hands of the brethren, some sixteenth-century Anabaptist women also authored books for the service of the church. Only a few are known. Anneken Jans (Anna of Rotterdam), martyred at Rotterdam in 1539, wrote an inspiring will and testament for her son. This was posthumously printed as a little book in 1539 and several times thereafter, eventually being incorporated into *Het Offer des Heeren* (1562 edition) and the *Martyrs Mirror*. She was a supporter of David Joris. It has been suggested that she might qualify as "our first duly recognized Anabaptist woman theologian."[23] Maeyken Boosers, a martyr of 1564, wrote letters which were published in 1566. Soetken Gerrits, a blind songwriter of Rotterdam, had her devotional hymns collected into a hymnbook (first published in 1592).[24]

SISTERS IN THE LIFE OF THE CHURCH

In line with written Anabaptist theology, women of the Reformation era took a second place in the congregational life of the churches. They were forbidden to preach, teach, and baptize; and they did not participate by voting to choose church officers. An early leader, Conrad Winkler of Zurich, in 1529 reported that "they prohibited women to preach or baptize."[25] According to the *Mennonite Encyclopedia* article by Harold S. Bender, "no women are known to have been chosen as preachers or deacons" in early Anabaptism.[26] Some rumors about female preachers among the "continental baptists," especially in seventeenth-century Holland, circulated, but such was not the practice. The English exile congregations in the Netherlands also excluded women preachers. If we widely define the Radical Reformation to include Quakers of the mid-seventeenth century, then the English Quakers first begin to offer examples of frequent female preaching.[27]

Women helped to found and spread the Anabaptist churches. In the first Anabaptist congregation, at Zollikon near Zurich, one woman and thirty-four men were baptized during the first week of its existence (22–29 January 1525).[28] Every Anabaptist congregation had a share of women members. Claus-Peter Clasen, using the methodology of social history, however, has discovered a curious fact about the numbers of Anabaptist women. In his analysis of Anabaptism in Switzerland, Austria, Moravia, and south and central Germany (1525–1618), women made up only 31.6% of known members, about one out of three.[29] Charles Eby discovered a similar situation among the Anabaptists of the Archbishopric of Cologne; about one-third were women.[30] The reasons for this statistic are unclear, nor is it known if the same ratio would prevail among the Dutch Anabaptists. The *Martyrs Mirror*, however, has a remarkably similar ratio of women to men martyrs, about one out of three. These percentages of women contrast with the situation among sixteenth- and seventeenth-century English Separatist and dissenting churches where women often outnumbered the men.[31]

If formal teachings and creeds did not permit women's leadership, other factors worked to give considerable participation to women. One factor was the cohesiveness and warmth of Anabaptist congregational life. In the congregation (the *Gemeente*, the *Gemeinde*) the fellowship and commitment of believers brought all members warmly together. This was the goal across the spectrum of Anabaptists. "Every brother and sister should utterly devote himself to the community (*Gemain* or *Gemeinde*) body and soul in God," taught the communalistic Hutterites.[32] Menno held forth the goal of the church as the "assembly of the righteous and a communion of saints"; Bernhard Rothmann of Munster, after joining the Anabaptists, urged that the church become the Christly fellowship of the believers.[33] Anabaptists cherished fellowship and peoplehood.[34] Women, of course, were drawn into fellowship and distinguished themselves in deeds of evangelism, witnessing, and caring within the family of the congregation. Many a woman gave her wealth to the church, opened her home to house meetings, or entertained itinerant evangelists. Historian C.H. Wedel, in fact, picked out the community and fellowship concept as the most distinctive characteristic of Anabaptism. Anabaptists created the *Gemeindekirche*, as opposed to the authoritarian *Priesterkirche* and *Staatskirche*.[35]

During revolutionary times, like the sixteenth-century Reformation, the ordinary rules and policies cease to function. The unsettledness of the times and the persecution of the male leadership required that Anabaptist women—those weaker vessels—had to work all the harder and carry a larger share of the work of the church. Conrad Grebel, Felix Manz, Georg Blaurock, Hans Denck, Hans Hut, Balthasar Hubmaier, Jacob Hutter, and Michael Sattler were all executed or died within the first years, as was the case with the wives of Sattler, Hubmaier, and Hutter. Menno Simons favored an orderly and definitely "called" ministry and leadership, but these could not always be maintained.[36]

The history of Anabaptism contains many stories of women who appointed themselves to places of leadership. No one asked them. They sometimes became apostles, prophetesses, and visionaries. Their messages were unpredictable. A notable example of lay leadership was Elizabeth of Leeuwarden (Lijsbeth Dirks), martyred in 1549. She was a leading figure in north Dutch Anabaptism, frequently travelling and working with Menno Simons. When the police at last captured her, they exclaimed: "We have the right man, we have now the teacheress." (*Wy hebben de rechte Man, we hebben nu de Leeraresse.*) They mistook her for the wife of Menno, the *Leeraer* (the teacher). The term

Leeraresse or teacheress implies someone who spoke or taught publicly. The interrogators pressed her about her teaching and leadership functions:

Lords: "We say that you are a teacher, and that you seduce many. We have been told this, and we want to know who your friends are."

Elizabeth: [She refused to give any names.] "I will not tell you who my parents are. . . . I hope through the grace of God that he will keep my tongue, so that I shall not become a traitoress, and deliver my brother into death."

Lords: "What persons were present when you were baptized?"

Elizabeth: "Christ said: Ask them that were present, or who heard it." John 18:21.

Lords: "Now we perceive that you are a teacher; for you compare yourself to Christ."[37]

Other women were extraordinary lay witnesses of the gospel. At Augsburg in 1528, the Anabaptist women were so fiercely zealous that they nearly dragged their relatives and neighbors into the meetings.[38] In the Netherlands many women organized meetings and home conventicles, although they did not do the main preaching. Aeffgen Lystyncx, a wealthy woman of Amsterdam, organized Anabaptist conventicles at Limmen in 1533 but was not the preacher. The next year she travelled to the Kingdom of Munster and functioned as a "prophetess."[39] At Schleiden, near Aachen, Germany, three women were reported to be "apostles," perhaps itinerant preachers (Bernhartz Maria of Niederrollesbroich, Maria of Monjou, and Marie Broechers). The first Maria had ecstatic experiences which carried her into the third heaven. Maria of Monjou was executed by drowning at Monschau in 1552. A hymn in the *Ausbund*, "Ach frohlich will ich singen" (no. 25), was dedicated to her.[40] These examples are the exception rather than the usual.

In spite of outbursts here and there, ordinary Anabaptist assemblies were not charismatic sessions where anyone could take the floor to expound the Spirit. Menno Simons treasured the written Word of God, "the true scepter and rule by which the Lord's kingdom, house, church, and congregation must be ruled and governed."[41] Carefully chosen and set-apart leaders were

to have charge in the congregations. In spite of Anabaptist suspicions of spiritual ecstasy, self-proclaimed prophets and prophetesses of the Spirit could not be completely prevented. At
Strasbourg, uncontrollable women, Ursula Jost and Barbara Rabstock, and Ursula's husband Lienhard Jost, prophesied so pow-
erfully, like Isaiah and Jeremiah, that they moved the heart of
Melchior Hofmann. Their revelations helped him to discern his
own great apocalyptical prophecies about the coming New Jerusalem. Ursula's and Barbara's fame spread so splendidly, partly
through Ursula's book, *Die prophetische Gesicht* (1530), that disciples came from as far north as the Netherlands to hear the
prophetesses' wonderful words.[42]

At the fringes of Anabaptism, where established leadership
failed, prophets and prophetesses with ever stranger gospels
popped up. Such luxuriant fanaticism was no female monopoly.
"And for every notorious female fanatic, several men could be
named," observed Joyce L. Irwin.[43] A few Swiss Anabaptist
women turned prophetess extraordinary around St. Gall in the
1520s. Margarita Hattinger of Zurich and Magdalena Muller,
Barbara Murglen, and Frena Bumenin of St. Gall gained particular attention. They proclaimed shocking messages: "I am God,"
and "I am Christ, the way, the truth and the life." Frena Bumenin (Verena Bauman) gathered twelve disciples for her Christly
work, then announced that she was really the "great whore of
Babylon" and "must give birth to the Antichrist" and much
more. Frena sat naked in the street to teach certain lessons. In
the midst of these swift-moving dreams and visions, competition
arose "that whoever could say the most or do anything strange
that no one could understand or decipher was to be considered
the most deified and immersed in God." Not surprisingly, Conrad Grebel and Felix Manz, Anabaptist leaders at Zurich, denounced these unedifying St. Gall "errors and fantasies."[44]

To return to the more settled congregations, what place in the
later sixteenth- and seventeenth-century church was found for
women? The Hutterites of Moravia appointed "sisters" to serve
as teachers and schoolmothers.[45] Dutch congregations in the late
sixteenth century began the office of deaconess. Although not
on the same prestigious level as the preacher of the Word, the
deaconess office recognized some gifts of women. The Dort

Confession, using verses from St. Paul and St. James, described the Mennonite deaconess:

And that also honorable aged widows should be chosen and ordained deaconesses, that they with the deacons may visit, comfort, and care for, the poor, feeble, sick, sorrowing and needy, as also the widows and orphans, and assist in attending to other wants and necessities of the church to the best of their ability. (1 Tim. 5:9; Rom. 16:1; James 1:27)[46]

Women's participation in the decision making of the Anabaptist congregation first appeared about 1609–10 in the English Anabaptist church of John Smyth, a congregation-in-exile in Amsterdam. Smyth declared that women in his church had a share in the congregation's discipline and censures. However, he did not allow women to preach. So far as is known, this example was not soon copied by other Anabaptist churches.[47]

Women also brought other gifts to the service of the church. Some Anabaptist women wrote hymns, sometimes sufficient for a collection or even a full hymnbook (especially Soetken Gerrits and Judith Lubbertsdochter).[48] There is an early example of an Anabaptist woman printer, Margarette Pruss of Strasbourg. She married an Anabaptist, Balthasar Beck, and supported Anabaptist writers. The Pruss-Beck press during the early 1530s printed books by Melchior Hofmann, Ursula Jost, and Sebastian Franck.[49] During the seventeenth century, some Mennonite women entered areas of public life related to the church. They became members of director boards of orphanages and charitable homes. Elysabeth van Damme of Haarlem with her husband founded the Zuiderhofje for old people in 1640. Catharina Schaeff (d. 1692) of The Hague was a benefactress of her congregation and a notable collector of Mennonite books.[50]

Much more time passed until women gained positions of equality as leaders of Mennonite churches. Some Netherlands churches led the way by extending the vote to women in the nineteenth century. Dutch women served on church boards in 1905, and about the same time women began preaching occasionally from Dutch pulpits. Anna Mankes-Zernike was the first female proponent to study at the Mennonite Seminary at Amsterdam (1911), and then as the first Mennonite woman minister of a congregation she served at Bovenknijpe.[51] Among Mennonites in other countries, the process of women's ordination and participation has moved very much slower.

FAMILY, SEX, AND MARRIAGE

The mature Anabaptist woman was, if God prospered, a married woman. Anabaptists, with the exception of the Munsterites, assumed that marriage of one man and one woman was the God-ordained order to Christian family life. To the general Protestant grounds for marriage, namely, preventing fornication, the procreation of children, and the mutual companionship of man and woman,[52] Anabaptists added another compelling doctrine: the spiritual union of believers. Anabaptist marriages were made in heaven.

Anabaptists believed that marriage, under the covenant of God, was an ideological action. The common faith of believers in Christ must create a bond far outweighing mere earthly, fleshly concerns. Marriage was not a two-sided relationship of male and female, but a three-sided relationship of believer and believer and Christ, the heavenly bridegroom. Menno Simons defined "heavenly marriage" as the marriage bond between Christ—the eternal bridegroom—and human souls. "Therefore, a man may not in deference to father, mother, son, daughter, husband, or wife, life or death, yield or compromise in any disobedience to His Word, even in the smallest matter."[53] In this spirit, Jelis Bernaerts, from his death cell at Antwerp in 1559, exhorted his wife sternly in the faith: "I console myself with the Word of the Lord. . . . And when I also consider that the union of the flesh which we have formed together, cannot last forever. . . ." The physical marriage must be secondary to the spiritual marriage of Christ and his believers, which "Union shall endure forever, if we remain faithful to Him." Jelis' wife was "dear wife and sister in the Lord."[54] Adriaenken Jansdochter from prison greeted her husband, still at liberty, "I your dearly beloved wife and sister in the Lord."[55] When the marriage became a brotherhood-sisterhood in the Lord, the church could become a controlling force.

The Dort Confession, 1632, summarized the doctrine of heavenly marriage as "marriage in the Lord." "So the believers of the New Testament have likewise no other liberty than to marry among the chosen generation and spiritual kindred of Christ, namely such, and no others, who have previously become united with the church. . . . "[56] Marriage must be judged primarily by the depth of spiritual commitment between the couple. Affection and companionability did not rank very high as a factor in Anabaptist marriage. The last words of Jan Waitier, tied to the stake, to his wife were austere: "Greet my wife, and tell her to fear God."[57]

The Anabaptist family, religious at base, was the church in miniature. Its heavenly head was Christ; its earthly head was the father; and the wife and children were the devoted members. Although Anabaptism challenged many of the social and economic principles of sixteenth-century society, the patriarchal family was hardly questioned. In the Netherlands, Menno Simons and his strict disciples admonished Christian women that they must be obedient to their husbands.[58] Peter Riedemann of the Hutterites bluntly kept Hutterite wives in their God-ordained submissive corners: "She should heed her husband, inquire of him, ask him and do all things with and naught without his counsel."[59] In spite of enormous fatherly power, most Anabaptists opposed a family dictatorship or husbands beating their wives. A husband should discipline his children but not physically chastise his wife. Wife beating was going out of style among Protestants of the sixteenth century, and Anabaptists followed this trend.[60]

The subordination of wives was accepted throughout Europe, but subordination counted less in lower-class families and in revolutionary or crisis situations. For economic or religious necessity, husband, wife, and children had to work together. They formed a close-knit unit, "like the crew of a ship, in which the role of the wife was critical."[61] This describes early Anabaptist family life. Husbands and wives in pre-industrial times worked side by side in many occupations, including farming. If the husband was seized and taken to jail, the wife was left to manage the house, land, and children.

The education level of the wife helped to determine her ability to participate in family and church life.[62] If she could read and write, she took her place beside the husband in Bible knowledge and other family affairs. The *Martyrs Mirror*, in its pious pages, gives much information, apart from details of martyrdoms, about women and family life. A substantial number of the women were literate and produced letters which were carefully preserved by family and friends. Felistis Jans, an elderly woman, learned to read and write "in order to know the truth" of the Bible.[63] Claesken of Workum (1559) was better educated than her husband who could not read or write, and gave a much better account of her faith before execution. Her prosecutors accused her, because of her good education, of seducing her husband into Anabaptism.[64] Claudine le Vettre's husband, himself a minister of the Word, praised her astonishing knowledge of Scripture. "For whenever he could not find a passage, he would ask his wife Claudine, who would at once clearly indicate to him what he sought."[65]

The picture of sixteenth-century family life revealed in the *Martyrs Mirror* is thoroughly structured and traditional, surprisingly so for people in such tumultuous crisis. Letters of husbands and wives—most with revolutionary spiritual views—described a traditional male-female relationship, and their child-rearing goals for their sons and daughters aimed to prepare them for a quiet, orderly place in society. Where was the revolutionary fire for a new order? Of course, the letters and documents likely have been highly edited by the sixteenth- and seventeenth-century historians of the martyr books. Many kinds of unacceptable radicalism were edited away, and certain extremist persons and views were simply omitted.

A minister's family would be a model Anabaptist family. Lijsken Dircks described what an Anabaptist minister's family should be: "A teacher must be the husband of one wife, blameless, having his children in subjection; no drunkard, winebibber or whoremonger." (1 Tim. 3:2)[66] Every father and mother awaiting death desired that their sons would grow up to be godly, industrious, and hard working and that the daughters would be demure and obedient. Joos Verbeeck, in prison at Antwerp in 1561, had this instruction for his daughters: "Bring them up in the nurture of the Lord, and behave yourself as becomes holy women, in order to teach the young women to be sober, to love their husbands, to be discreet, chaste, and obedient to their husbands; and firmly persevere in the same rule in which you stand." Maeyken Boosers (1564) warned her children to avoid worldly pride, dancing, gossip, and rather to adorn themselves like the holy women of old.[67]

Chastening must not slacken. Jacob de Roore (1569) told his wife to bring up the children "with good instruction and chastening while they are still young, for with the rod their back is bowed, and they are brought into obedience to their parents."[68] They would grow up to become worthy citizens of the commonwealth and to be dedicated Christians.

Parents strongly urged education for both girls and boys, in order that they might read the Scripture. Soetgen van den Houte (1560) admonished her son David "to beware of bad company, and of playing in the street with bad boys; but diligently learn to read and write so that you may get understanding." To daughters Betgen and Tanneken, she wrote, they must learn obedience and be "kind, honorable, and quiet as behooves young girls." They also should learn to read and write. Soon after writing her letter, mother Soetgen was executed at Ghent.[69]

The ascetic, almost puritanical spirit of family life was all inclusive. Sexual relations were the inferior part of marriage, necessary for the procreation of children and prevention of adultery, but not to be carnally desired or enjoyed. Ulrich Stadler, a Hutterite leader, warned married men against lust and evil desire in marriage, which could accompany sexual intercourse. God, however, "winks at our marital work," based on Tobit: "Thou knowest that I have not taken this my sister for a wife for the sake of evil lust but only that I may beget children by whom Thy holy name may be praised and extolled." Most Anabaptists, if not so explicit, had a similar attitude about sex.[70] Many of the martyr women were threatened during torture with sexual molestation or had their clothes stripped from them. Modest and chaste, they "were greatly ashamed," but they always resisted the shameful acts and preserved the sexual honor and modesty of Anabaptist women.[71]

The strength of the Anabaptist family came from its intense group ideological commitment. As Jan de Swarte was arrested and pulled out of his house, he called to the family: "Children, do you want to go along to the New Jerusalem?" They replied, "Yes, father," and went captive with him. Eventually Jan, his wife Klaesken, and their three sons were all burned at the stake—swiftly dispatched to their New Jerusalem.[72] However, if the religious commitment within the family was weak, the family was threatened.

What was the married Anabaptist to do, if his spouse backslid? During the first years of Anabaptism it often happened that one was converted and the other refused to join the Anabaptist church. Church teaching insisted that Christ must always take precedence over loyalty to spouse or children. Practical questions about divided or mixed marriages troubled the early Anabaptist-Mennonites almost more than any other issue. In the first onrush of Anabaptist evangelism, the 1520s, the burning *täufer* convictions split families apart as new converts rushed forth "into the entire world" to preach and baptize. After hearing Hans Hut preach, several husbands of Nürnberg deserted their wives and material possessions to live "like the birds in the air" (Matt. 6:26) and "see the world."[73] The notorious Claus Frey from Windsheim fled from his home because of religious persecution, leaving behind his wife and eight children. Frey's wife refused to uproot herself to follow him into exile. He went to Strasbourg and lived with Elizabeth Pfersfelder, a fellow Anabaptist, as man and wife. It was surely one of the heavenly marriages, but even his fellow Strasbourg Anabaptists rejected him for his bigamy and family desertion. The magistrates in 1534 executed Frey for bigamy, the only Anabaptist executed at Strasbourg.[74]

The reverse situation—the husband compelling the Anabaptist wife to stay—happened at Wurttemberg. When an Anabaptist wife was married to a non-Anabaptist husband, she was liable for punishment. The law called for banishment or prison. When the non-Anabaptist husbands were left with uncared for children and messy homes, they earnestly petitioned to have their wives returned to them, regardless of Anabaptist opinions. A Wurttemberg ordinance of 1584 declared the policy of handing over the wives to the custody of the husbands on the condition that they be kept chained in the house. The chained Anabaptist housewives were allowed a tether long enough to carry on the housework.[75]

The oldest Anabaptist writing on marriage is predominantly about divorce and mixed marriages of believer and unbeliever, the anonymous 1527 treatise, *On Divorce*, thought to be by Michael Sattler. In the case of mixed marriages, obedience to God takes priority over the marriage bond. "Thus one should forsake rather the fleshly than the spiritual, and not slave one's conscience with the marriage bond, by honoring more the fleshly duty and obligation than the spiritual." The believer was admonished to "separate" from the unbeliever, if faith was threatened, but not to remarry. Separation did not necessarily mean seeking a formal divorce. Divorce and remarriage were permitted only because of the spouse's adultery.[76]

Evil consequences could be prevented by believers marrying only within the church. Where a mixed marriage existed, a separation was likely; and some Anabaptists believed that spouse unbelief was grounds for divorce. Hutterites allowed divorce from unbelievers, because those married in the world (i.e., outside the church) had not been united by God.[77] Although recommending separation, the majority of Anabaptist leaders did not permit formal divorce in mixed marriages or subsequent remarriage. By suggesting that Christian commitment, or lack of it, might allow for separation and divorce, Anabaptism raised some new issues in the history of marriage and divorce.

Even where marriage took place within the Anabaptist church, the discipline of the ban created many tensions in marriage. Banning meant that the offenders were excluded from communion until they repented, and other church members were to avoid contact with them. Did this mean that within a marriage the offending spouse was to be "avoided" by the faithful spouse? Should the household be broken up temporarily as a part of the discipline? Dirk Philips and Menno Simons of the northern Mennonites held a very strict position that required marital avoidance. A famous case occurred in the Rutgers family of Emden, Germany, in 1556. Elder Leenaert Bouwens banned Mr. Rutgers for some offense and ordered wife Swaen Rutgers to avoid her husband. She refused, and Bouwens banned her as well. Menno eventually supported Bouwens' action as a necessary Christian discipline. Sometimes the strict-ban advocates broke into homes, where marital avoidance was not functioning as it should, and took away the wife, leaving behind the children and banned husband.[78]

Anabaptist marriage policies were always controversial, even among faithful church members. Shortly before Menno Simons died in 1558, he wrote that he personally knew of "not much less than three hundred spouses" who refused to practice banning in their own families. The strict Mennonite position prevailed in the north for a long time, but the Swiss and south German Mennonites were more lenient and did not break up marriages. "Marital avoidance among Mennonites is one of the most peculiar events in the history of Christianity," states the *Mennonite Encyclopedia*.[79]

REVOLUTIONARY WOMEN

The quietistic examples of the non-resistant Anabaptists, patiently suffering persecution, did not suit all Anabaptists. Spiritual radicalism translated easily into political, social, and economic radicalism. Why not bring in the New Jerusalem here and now? Thousands of Anabaptists became temporarily caught up in violent revolutionary schemes in the 1530s. The largest center of revolutionary Anabaptism was Munster, and offshoots of radical action broke out at various Dutch cities. The driving force behind militant Anabaptism was Melchior Hofmann of Strasbourg, who taught the doctrine of millennialism. In the last days 144,000 apostles were to be saved.[80] He won many converts in the Low Countries.

Through special revelations, the Melchiorites calculated that Melchior Hofmann's predicted apocalyptic kingdom of Christ would unfold at the city of Munster in Westphalia. Munster there and then would become the New Jerusalem. Under the charismatic leadership of Jan Matthijsz (d. 1534) and then Jan Beuckelsz (better known as Jan van Leiden, d. 1536), Munster was occupied by Anabaptists in 1534–35 and transformed into a dramatic new society. The Munsterite social revolution included the use of military force—hitherto mostly refused by Anabaptists—as well as community of goods, polygamy, and new family structures. At its revolutionary height, Anabaptist Munster was populated predominantly by women (about 5000 to 6000 women and 2000 men).[81]

Ordinary Christian sexual and family standards were thrown to the winds. King Jan van Leiden set the example by marrying sixteen wives. The new day of sexual liberation had arrived. Still, the sexual and feminist revolution, which often accompanied extreme revolutionary groups of the sixteenth and seventeenth centuries, failed to materialize. All leadership positions at Munster were monopolized by men, and the new marriage and family policies proved to be completely male-dominated. The Munsterites "turned the world upside down" but not for women.[82]

The heart of the new social order was the polygamous family, which was very popular with the men of Munster. The edicts on polygamy initially required that a woman must accept any proposal of marriage, even if she did not like the man or even if she would become his second, third, fourth wife, or more. Later, because of considerable resistance to the law, the woman was allowed to refuse a proposal. Plural marriage was restricted to men, however, and the male prophets made laws punishable by death against female free love or adultery. The magistrates executed one woman for bigamy, another for refusing sex with her husband.[83] The motivations for instituting polygamy at Munster were various and confusing. Publicly, the Munster leaders based their polygamy on the Bible, following the examples of the godly patriarchs. Much of the Munsterite program, polygamy included, might also be explained as a desperate war measure of a community squeezed by a long siege. There was a disproportionate number of women to men; the population was dropping. Or was it a case of misogyny?[84]

Preacher Bernhard Rothmann (1495–1535), Jan van Leiden's favorite theologian, wrote in the *Restitution* (1534) about the new role of women. In family, sex, and marriage, "God was doing a new thing."[85] One of Rothmann's chapters was entitled "Duty and Dominion of the Man in Marriage;" the next was "Duty and Submission of the Woman in Marriage." Revolutionary polygamy meant freedom, but freedom for the man. "The freedom of the man in marriage means that he may have more than one wife at a time." No longer would he be dependent upon the whims of one woman. The God-given order is that the man is subject to Christ, and then the woman is subject to man, and thereby she shall be saved. Contrary to most appearances, Rothmann feared that women as a whole had become too powerful in the world. "Women almost everywhere have taken control, and they lead men around like bears on a chain."[86] Polygamy was wonderfully biblical and at the same time it would help to press the women back into place. Rothmann married nine wives.

Jan van Leiden, King of the Zion, declared that, as a public policy, "the wife must give honor to her husband and call him lord." His approach was more down to earth than Rothmann's. In the new kingdom, old and burdensome Christian taboos would give way to a new freedom of the Christian man. Jan pronounced: "It is better that I have many wives than many prostitutes."[87] One of his wives he publicly executed as a punishment for disobedience. For radicals like Jan van Leiden and Rothmann, brotherhood love in the church and sexual love were not far apart. George H. Williams has commented, "The Radicals almost inevitably at times approached the border where *agape* and *eros* became confused."[88]

The Munster Kingdom was crushed by an invasion of Catholics and Protestants in 1535, and all the leaders and many rank-and-file citizens were executed. The tortured bodies of King Jan and his chief lieutenants were stuffed into three iron cages, still hanging on the tower of St. Lambert's Church.

Several little Munsterite revolutions broke out in 1535 and 1536, with women predominantly participating. Van Braght's *Martyrs Mirror* recorded many women's stories, but he almost completely eliminated the revolutionary Munsterite women, even if martyred, or any associated with violence at Amsterdam, Oldeklooster, or Poeldijk. Many unarmed women were arrested or perished at Bergklooster in 1534 on the way to Munster. At Amsterdam in 1535 twelve naked Anabaptist men and women streaked through the streets in February (the *Naaktlopers*); others attempted an uprising in May.[89] After the Munsterite Kingdom fell, some of the male and female refugees regrouped in the Netherlands under the leadership of Jan van Batenburg (1495–1538). A considerable number of women were drawn to David

Joris (1501–1556), not a violent revolutionary but a bitter rival of Menno Simons. Nearly all of the female Munsterites, Batenburgers, and Davidjorists were cut out of the sixteenth- and seventeenth-century Mennonite histories. The *Mennonite Encyclopedia* has helped to bring some of them back to light. About seventy of the 459 Anabaptist women fall into the radical categories. At Munster Hille Feicken from Sneek aimed to play a heroic "Judith" (to seduce and kill the Bishop of Munster), but was herself executed.[90] Aeffgen Lystyncx of Amsterdam became a prophetess at Munster, but her message and influence are unknown.[91]

HEROIC WOMEN OF THE *MARTYRS MIRROR*

The most complete records about Anabaptist women were preserved in the *Martyrs Mirror* by Thieleman Jansz van Braght (1625–1664). First published at Amsterdam in 1660, its full title in English reads *The Bloody Theater or Martyrs Mirror of the Defenseless Christians* (in Dutch, *Het Bloedigh Tooneel der Doops-Gesinde*). This built upon the earlier Dutch martyr book, *Het Offer des Heeren* (1562, 1567, 1570, etc.). For over 400 years, these books, along with the Bible, have been treasured by Mennonites.

The women of the *Martyrs Mirror*, about 278 in number, made up nearly one-third of the Anabaptist martyrs (over 900 in all). Their deaths were gruesome. They were drowned, burned, tied crooked, gagged, strangled, and buried alive; but their spirits were heroic.[92] Apostates and backsliders there must have been, but van Braght eliminated such failures from his book. This early Mennonite historian arranged his stories to make the point that God needs both women and men. Women, to be sure, are the "weaker vessels," but in God's power they too can stand firm in the faith. Again and again, a woman displayed surprising valor, "valiant manliness," and "manful courage." "Though women, they were manful and valiant in God, so that many were amazed at their steadfastness."[93]

Although a large number of the women martyrs were merely mentioned as dying with their husbands, others received several pages of narrative and had letters and speeches printed. Several pairs of sisters or mothers and daughters went to death together. Women showed themselves to be resolute and biblically grounded against the priests and interrogators. They quoted Scripture like theologians. The first martyr book, *Het Offer des Heeren* (1562 edition), used the story of Anneken Jans immediately after Michael Sattler, and the 1570 edition added the very early history of Weynken Claes, a Sacramentarian woman, not an Anabaptist, burned at The Hague in 1527.Weynken had a sharp tongue and quick mind, as these samples of her confession show:

Ques. "What do you hold concerning the sacrament?"

Ans. "I hold your sacrament to be bread and flour, and if you hold it as God, I say that it is your devil."

Ques. "What do you hold concerning the saints?"

Ans."I know no other Mediator than Christ." (1 John 2:19)

Ques. "What do you hold concerning the holy oil?"

Ans. "Oil is good for salad, or to oil your shoes with." (1 Tim. 4:4)

Naturally, with these kinds of answers she was found to be full of error, and she was sentenced to the fire. "She then went gladly, as though she were going to a marriage."[94]

Along with questions of infant baptism, the sacrament, and the authority of the church, many of the women were quizzed on the topic of the incarnation, which they defended as a Mennonite doctrine.

Ques. "Whether she did not believe that Christ had assumed His flesh from Mary?"

Pierijntgen: "But she confessed that He was from above, and had come down from the Father; that the Word had become flesh, even as John says."

At the place of her execution in 1573, Pierijntgen Looseveldt inspired the crowd to "Go, buy Testaments, and read therein." And like Weynken above, Pierijntgen, a spinster, viewed death as her wedding day. She met the Bridegroom.[95]

The imagery of marriage, bride, and bridegroom, ancient in the Christian church, was widely used by Anabaptists. George H. Williams called this Anabaptist theme a "nuptial theology" or "bridal theology."[96] The church is the bride of Jesus Christ and like the wise virgins (Matthew 25) eagerly awaits his coming for the great churchly wedding celebration. Melchior Hofmann and Menno Simons drew upon this rich love imagery from the Song of Solomon and the New Testament. The amorous Bernhard Rothmann of Munster taught that the true congregation is the "Chaste bride of Christ." Believers of the church, wrote Menno Simons, "are the new Eve, the pure chaste bride."[97] The meaning of the bride and bridegroom applied to the whole company of the church, both male and female. In the *Martyrs Mirror*, however, the bride-bridegroom imagery, in a fascinating way, was used almost exclusively for the women. The women resolutely gave up husband, children, and possessions for the sake of the faith, but like earlier women saints and virgins of the church, they entered into a relationship far better—mystical marriage with Christ.[98]

The love of a man and children, the condemned women said, was not enough, but the earthly love experience prepared the way for the heavenly marriage. In earthly marriages, the virgin prepared herself beautifully and chastely for her bridegroom; the martyr women had the same desire. Like the bride adorns herself for the earthly bridegroom, "Oh, how ought we then to adorn ourselves, to please our bridegroom."[99] Spiritual beauty perhaps, but it was deeply real for Felistis Resinx, who went to her burning dressed in a white apron to show how purely and uprightly a Christian virgin ought to appear "before her beloved heavenly bridegroom, Jesus Christ."[100]

Many temptations threatened their physical and spiritual chastity. Leering prison masters tore off the prisoners' clothes. Certain suave priests tempted them with bland words. Men tried to mislead them with "carnal sympathy." Hadewijk of Leeuwarden was sexually threatened by a half-witted fellow, but she warded him off with Scripture about how adulterers and adulteresses had to burn forever in hell. He took off saying, "The jade is too wise in the Scriptures."[101] At least two Anabaptist maidens, not yet having experienced married love, were tempted in prison with promises of love and marriage if they would recant. "You are young yet," a monk told one, "you shall be married and receive a large dowry." She merely shook her head.[102]

Maria of Monjou (1552) well expressed the connection between Anabaptist love, marriage, and martyrdom. On her way to the execution, she said, "I have been the bride of a man; but today I hope to be the bride of Christ, and to inherit His Kingdom with Him." Maria became the subject of one of the martyr songs in the *Ausbund*, the old Mennonite-Amish hymnbook.

> Today my marriage will be broken,
> The wife of a man I have been.
> New vows I have now spoken
> To Christ who does me redeem.[103]

The story of Anabaptist women of the Reformation varied from time to time and place to place. Anabaptism was both legalistic and spiritualistic. Where legalistic doctrines prevailed, Anabaptist women were the quiet sisters; but in communities where the Spirit broke forth abundantly, women grasped many opportunities.

Following the heroic Reformation era, the "Mennonite sister" (*Menniste zusje*) settled into an unprominent place in church and home. In most branches of the Mennonite Church, she wore a simple, distinctive costume and on her head a covering or veiling. She excelled as wife, mother, housekeeper, and sometimes as lay worker or teacher in the church. She was the model of decorum and modesty—almost too good to be true. In the early twentieth century the way for women in church leadership once again began to open.

NOTES

1. T.J. van Braght, *Martyrs Mirror* (Scottdale: Herald Press, 1972 ed.) p. 1120; in *Het Bloedigh Tooneel* (Dordrecht, 1660), Bk. 2, p. 876. The author gratefully acknowledges helpful suggestions from Dale R. Schrag and Rachel Waltner Goossen, colleagues at Bethel College, and from Mary Matthijsen-Berkman, Amsterdam.

2. J.A. Oosterbaan, "The Reformation of the Reformation: Fundamentals of Anabaptist Theology," *Mennonite Quarterly Review* 51 (July 1977): 171–95, hereafter cited as *MQR*.

3. Walter Klaassen, "The Nature of the Anabaptist Protest," *MQR* 45 (Oct. 1971): 291–311. See also Walter Klaassen, *Anabaptism: Neither Catholic nor Protestant* (Waterloo, Ont.: Conrad Press, 1973); and Michael

Mullett, *Radical Religious Movements in Early Modern Europe* (London: George Allen & Unwin, 1980), p. 65.

4. Historical views are rather mixed about the amount of change which Anabaptism brought to women. See George H. Williams, *The Radical Reformation* (Philadelphia: Westminster Press, 1962), who saw great gains for women; and Claus-Peter Clasen, *Anabaptism: A Social History, 1525–1618* (Ithaca: Cornell University Press, 1972), who concluded that Anabaptism "showed no inclination to grant women a greater role than they customarily had in sixteenth-century society" (p. 207).

5. Based upon my count in the *Martyrs Mirror* and *The Mennonite Encyclopedia*, ed. Harold S. Bender and C. Henry Smith, 4 vols. (Hillsboro, Kans: Mennonite Brethren Publishing House, 1955–59), with help from Kendal Warkentine. I also wish to acknowledge Wayne Plenert, "Anabaptist Women" (Unpublished student paper, Bethel College, Kansas, 1974).

6. In addition to Clasen's book, see David M. Hockenbery, "The Radical Reformation in Nürnberg, 1524–1530" (Ph.D. diss., Ohio State University, 1973); and Charles Eby, "Social Aspects of Anabaptism in the Archbishopric of Cologne, 1550–1700" (Ph.D. diss., Notre Dame University, 1978).

7. *Mennonite Encyclopedia*, 4: 972, hereafter cited as *ME*.

8. Robert Friedmann, *The Theology of Anabaptism: An Interpretation* (Scottdale: Herald Press, 1973), p. 37; (Christian Hege and Christian Neff, eds., *Mennonitisches Lexikon* (Frankfurt Am Main and Weierhof: Pfalz, 1913), 1: 692, s.v. "Frau" by B. Unruh.

9. Van Braght, *Martyrs Mirror*, p. 418.

10. Harold S. Bender, *Conrad Grebel, c. 1498–1526* (Scottdale: Herald Press, 1950), p. 4; on his mother, Grebel to Vadian, 1521, Epp. Greb. 126, Goshen College Library.

11. George H. Williams, *Spiritual and Anabaptist Writers* (Philadelphia: Westminster Press, 1957), pp. 116–24; Joyce L. Irwin, *Womanhood in Radical Protestantism, 1525–1675* (New York and Toronto: Edwin Mellen Press, 1979), pp. 3, 8–11.

12. Balthasar Hubmaier, *Schriften* (*Quellen zur Geschichte der Taüfer*, Gütersloher: G. Mohn, 1962, no. 9), p. 356.

13. Henry C. Vedder, *Balthasar Hubmaier* (New York: Knickerbocker Press, 1905), p. 243.

14. Peter Riedemann, *Account of Our Religion, Doctrine, and Faith*, 2nd English ed., (Rifton: Plough Publishing House, 1970), p. 98.

15. Menno Simons, *Complete Writings of Menno Simons* (Scottdale: Herald Press, 1956 ed.), p. 383, hereafter cited as *CW*.

16. Cornelius Krahn, *Menno Simons* (Newton: Faith and Life Press, 1936; repr. 1982), pp. 97–98.

17. William E. Keeney, *The Development of Dutch Anabaptist Thought and Practice from 1539–1564* (Nieukoop: B. de Graaf, 1968), pp. 89–94.

18. Simons, *CW*, p. 768.

19. Keeney, *Dutch Anabaptist Thought*, pp. 91–92.

20. Joyce L. Irwin, "Embryology and the Incarnation: A Sixteenth-Century Debate," *Sixteenth Century Journal* 9.(Fall 1978): 96–97, 99; Ian Maclean, *The Renaissance Notion of Woman* (Cambridge: Cambridge University Press, 1980), pp. 29–30.

21. Sjouke Voolstra, "The Word Has Become Flesh. The Melchiorite-Mennonite Teaching on the Incarnation," *MQR* 52 (April 1983): 159–60; Oosterbaan, "Reformation of the Reformation", pp. 182–92.

22. Van Braght, *Martyrs Mirror*, pp. 40–41.

23. *ME*, 1: 126–27; Dorothy Yoder Nyce, "Are Anabaptists Motherless?" in *Which Way Women?* (Akron, Pa.: MCC Peace Section, 1980), p. 125.

24. Maeyken Boosers' letters in *Het Offer des Heeren*, in *Bibliotheca Ref. Neerlandica*, ed. S. Cramer, 2 (1904): 411–20; *ME*, 3:437; 4:570.

25. Leonhard von Muralt and Walter Schmid, eds., *Quellen zur Geschichte der Täufer in der Schweiz* (Zurich: S. Hirzel), 1 (1952), p. 313; Clasen, *Anabaptism*, p. 207.

26. *ME*, 4: 972.

27. Irwin, *Womanhood*, pp. 179–99.

28. Fritz Blanke, *Brothers in Christ* (Scottdale: Herald Press, 1961), p. 41.

29. Clasen, *Anabaptism*, pp. 334–36.

30. Eby, "Anabaptism in Cologne," pp. 117–19.

31. Michael R. Watts, *The Dissenters* (Oxford: Clarendon Press, 1978), p. 319.

32. Williams, *Radical Reformation*, p. 232.

33. Simons, *CW*, p. 99; Wim Kuipers, " 'Der gleib ist nicht idermans dinck': De ontwikkeling van Bernhard Rothmanns denken over de christelijke gemeente," *Doopsgezinde Bijdragen*, N.R. 5 (1979): 28.

34. Dale Brown, "Communal Ecclesiolgy: The Power of the Anabaptist Vision," *Theoloqy Today* 36 (April 1979): 25.

35. Coendius H. Wedel, *Abriss der Geschichte der Mennoniten* (Newton, Kans.: Schulverlag von Bethel-college, 1900–1904), 2: 147–59; 4: 206–8.

36. Cornelius J. Dyck, "The Place of Tradition in Dutch Anabaptism," *Church History* 43 (March 1974): 40–41; Russell L. Mast, "Menno Simons Speaks Concerning the Ministry," *MQR* 54 (April 1980): 106–8. See also Friedman, *Theology of Anabaptism*, pp. 115–18.

37. Van Braght, *Martyrs Mirror*, p. 481; and 1660 ed., Bk. 2, p. 161. However, a rather recently published record of her case shows that she recanted before execution: A.F. Mellink, *Documenta Anabaptistica Neerlandica*, pt. 1, *Friesland en Groningen (1530–1550)* (Leiden: E.J. Brill, 1975), p. 85.

38. Wolfgang Schäufele, "The Missionary Vision and Activity of the Anabaptist Laity," *MQR* 36 (April 1962): 108.

39. A.F. Mellink, *De Wederdopers in de noordelijke Nederlanden 1531–1544* (Groningen: J.B. Wolters, 1953), pp. 44, 343; *ME*, 1: 18–19.

40. Ernst Crous, "Anabaptism in Schleiden-in-the-Eifel," *MQR* 34 (July 1960): 189; Eby, "Anabaptism in Cologne," p. 177.

41. Simons, *CW*, p. 160.

42. Miriam U. Chrisman, "Women and the Reformation in Strasbourg 1490–1530," *Archiv für Reformationsgeschichte* 63 (1972): 160; James M. Stayer, *Anabaptists and the Sword* (Lawrence: Coronado Press, 1972), p. 223.

43. Irwin, *Womanhood*, p. 201.

44. Ibid., pp. 203–10; Clasen, *Anabaptism*, p. 127.

45. Clasen, *Anabaptism*, pp. 266–67.

46. Van Braght, *Martyrs Mirror*, p. 41 (Art. IX).

47. John Smyth, *Paralleles, Censures, Observations* (n.p., 1609), p. 63; Johannes Bakker, *John Smyth* (Wageningen: H. Veenman & Zonen, 1964), p. 125.

48. *ME*, 3: 410; 4: 570.

49. Chrisman, "Women in Strasbourg," pp. 159–60.

50. *ME*, 2: 5; 4: 438.

51. N. van der Zijpp, *Geschiedenis der Doopsgezinden in Nederland* (Arnhem: Van Loghum Slaterus, 1952), pp. 128, 222.

52. Roland H. Bainton, *Women of the Reformation in Germany and Italy* (Minneapolis: Augsburg, 1971), pp. 10–13; Lawrence Stone, *The Family, Sex and Marriage in England 1500–1800* (New York: Harper Colophon Books, 1979), p. 101.

53. Simons, *CW*, p. 970; Williams, *Radical Reformation*, pp. 506–8, 513–14.

54. Van Braght, *Martyrs Mirror*, pp. 627, 624.

55. Ibid., p. 926.

56. Ibid., p. 42 (Art. XII).

57. Ibid., p. 759.

58. Simons, *CW*, p. 383; also Pieter Jansz Twisck's confession of faith (1617), in Van Braght, *Martyrs Mirror*, p. 377.

59. Riedmann, *Account of Our Religion*, p. 98.

60. Irwin, *Womanhood*, p. 55; Friedrich Roth, *Augsburgs Reformations-*

geschichte (Munich: Theodor Ackermann, 1901–11), 4: 614–15; for contemporary Protestant views, see Charles and Katherine George, *The Protestant Mind of the English Reformation* (Princeton: Princeton University Press, 1961), p. 284.

61. Stone, *Family*, p. 139.

62. Ibid., pp. 142–44.

63. *ME*, 2: 63.

64. Van Braght, *Martyrs Mirror*, p. 616.

65. Ibid., p. 737.

66. Ibid., p. 517.

67. Ibid., pp. 652, 668.

68. Ibid., p. 798.

69. Ibid., p. 649; for other examples, see pp. 642, 982, 985.

70. Kenneth R. Davis, *Anabaptism and Asceticism* (Scottdale: Herald Press, 1974), p. 198; Friedmann, *Theology of Anabaptism*, p. 65; and Robert Friedmann, *Hutterite Studies* (Goshen: Mennonite Historical Society, 1961), p. 123.

71. Van Braght, *Martyrs Mirror*, pp. 494, 502, 569.

72. Ibid., p. 665.

73. Hockenbery, "Nürnberg," pp. 146–49.

74. Chrisman, "Women in Strasbourg," p. 161; *ME*, 4: 159.

75. Irwin, *Womanhood*, pp. 63–65; Clasen, *Anabaptism*, p. 387.

76. John H. Yoder, ed., *The Legacy of Michael Sattler*, (Scottdale: Herald Press, 1973), pp. 100–107; John C. Wenger, "Concerning Divorce," *MQR* 21 (April 1947): 114–19.

77. Clasen, *Anabaptism*, pp. 203–7.

78. *ME*, 4: 665–66.

79. Simons, *CW*, p. 972; Keeney, *Dutch Anabaptist Thought*, pp. 125–27; *ME*, 3: 507.

80. Stayer, *Anabaptists and the Sword*, pp. 217–22; Cornelius Krahn, *Dutch Anabaptism* (The Hague: Nijhoff, 1968), pp. 112–17.

81. Hans Ritschl, *Die Kommune der Wiedertäufer in Münster* (Bonn: Kurt Schroeder, 1923), p. 43.

82. For examples of sexual revolution in the seventeenth-century English Revolution, see Christopher Hill, *The World Turned Upside Down: Radical Ideas during the English Revolution* (New York: Viking Press, 1973), chap. 9.

83. Stayer, *Anabaptists and the Sword*, p. 258.

84. James M. Stayer, "Vielweiberei als 'innerweltliche Askese,' " *Mennonitische Geschichtsblatter* 37 (1980): 32, 34.

85. Bernhard Rothmann, *Restitution* (Halle: Max Niemeyer, 1888), p. 91. Also on Rothmann, see Jack W. Porter, "Bernhard Rothmann

1495–1535, Royal Orator of the Münster Anabaptist Kingdom" (Ph.D. diss., University of Wisconsin, 1964).

86. Rothmann, *Restitution*, pp. 83, 89–91.

87. Otthein Rammstedt, *Sekte und soziale Bewegung: Soziologische Analyse der Täufer in Münster (1534/35)* (Koln: Westdeutscher Verlag, 1966), pp. 96, 100.

88. Williams, *Radical Reformation*, p. 508.

89. Mellink, *Wederdopers*, pp. 122–24.

90. Ibid., pp. 41–43.

91. Ibid., p. 44; *ME*, 1: 18–19.

92. Wayne Plenert, "The Martyr's Mirror and Anabaptist Women," *Mennonite Life* 30 (June 1975): 13–18.

93. Van Braght *Martyrs Mirror*, pp. 437, 441, 759.

94. Ibid, pp. 422–23.On the topic of suffering and recantation, see Alan F. Kreider, " 'The Servant Is Not Greater Than His Master': The Anabaptists and the Suffering Church," *MQR* 58 (Jan. 1984): 9–10.

95. *Martyrs Mirror*, pp. 962–65.

96. Williams, *Radical Reformation*, pp. 307–9, 513.

97. Porter, "Rothmann," p. 160; Simons, *CW*, p. 94.

98. For the long history of mystical ecstatic love and its importance to the female saints and virgins of the church, see Marina Warner, *Alone of All Her Sex: The Myth and the Cult of the Virgin Mary* (New York: Alfred A. Knopf, 1976), pp. 121–33, 299–300.

99. Van Braght, *Martyrs Mirror*, p. 517.

100. Ibid., p. 539.

101. Ibid., pp. 547, 1091.

102. Ibid., pp. 872, 887.

103. Ibid., p. 525; see *Ausbund* or *Ethliche Schöne Christliche Geseng*, 1st ed. 1564. Maris's hymn is no. 25 in *Ausbund*, 13th ed. (Lancaster, PA: Verlag von den Amischen Gemeinden in Lancaster County, 1970).

3

Foundation Builders: The Role of Women in Early English Nonconformity

Richard L. Greaves

The involvement of English women in the radical Protestant movements of the 1640s and 1650s has attracted the attention of a number of modern historians. Some recent studies suggest that these women built on a tradition of active involvement in Nonconformity that began well before the 1640s.[1] Although certain aspects of this participation have been noted in passing in the works of modern historians, no systematic effort has been made to grasp the total extent of female activity. In part this is due to the nature of the surviving records, which reflect the pronounced male biases of the early modern period. As late as the eighteenth century such an enlightened author as James Boswell was convinced that the inequality of women would continue even in heaven; to hope otherwise, Samuel Johnson informed the Quaker Mrs. Knowles, was to expect too much.[2] Sometimes such biases are sufficiently manifest as to be readily discounted, as in the case of the Bishop of London's slur against the Independent minister John Lathrop before the High Commission in 1632, when Lathrop was implicitly accused of deriving lurid sexual gratification by preaching to women who sat cross-legged on a bed. But it is far more difficult to deal with the fact that women, commonly regarded as inferior, were sometimes simply ignored in the historical records. When, for example, a list of the members of the Separatist congregation of Francis Johnson and John Greenwood was compiled by the High Commission in 1593, some wives, including Greenwood's, were overlooked.[3]

Even for the 1640s and 1650s, when information on the religious activities of women is more plentiful, the emphasis on men is undoubtedly disproportionate to their role in the radical Protestant movements. In the course of editing a biographical dictionary of British radicals in the seventeenth century with Robert Zaller, an intensive search was made for female subjects, but of the 1014 entries, only 41 (4%) are of women due to the paucity of adequate information. All but one of these were selected because of their involvement in religious Nonconformity: twenty-six Quakers, eight sectaries, four Fifth Monarchists, and two Independents.[4] Yet despite the relative dearth of data for female Puritans and Separatists prior to the 1640s, a general overview of their activities is possible.

Numerically, women were significant in strengthening the Nonconformist churches, especially those of a Separatist persuasion. Edmund Grindal, Bishop of London, asserted in 1568 that most Separatists in one London church were females from the lower social orders, an observation that is indeed true with respect to some other congregations. Of the thirty-two members of John Smyth's Baptist church who initially applied for admission to the Waterlander Mennonites in the Netherlands, seventeen were women. The signatories of "A Short Confession of Fayth" prepared by those who refused to join the Mennonites in 1610 included twenty-four women and seventeen men. In 1645 the Independent church in Norwich, Norfolk, had eighty-three women but only thirty-one men; and of the twenty-eight Separatists living in Great Yarmouth, Norfolk, in 1630, twenty or twenty-one were women. Eight of them were described as "poor." There were, of course, undoubtedly numerous churches where males predominated, as in the case of Richard Blunt's Particular Baptist congregation in London in 1641, which claimed thirty men and twenty-three women. Of the twelve people who seceded from Lathrop's congregation in 1633 to establish a Particular Baptist church, at least three or four were women.[5]

Not only were women often prominent numerically, but they also bore their share of suffering for spiritual ideals. Of the twelve parishioners at Ormskirk, Lancashire, charged in 1630 with frequenting conventicles, five were women, and the number increased in 1637 to twelve of nineteen. Close scrutiny of the lists reveals that in addition to widows and wives of male members some of these ladies had joined Nonconformist congregations without their spouses. The divisive effects on the family were even greater when wives left their husbands to follow ministers overseas, as in the case of John Lathrop's emigration to New England in 1634.[6]

One of the most critical spheres in which women furthered Nonconformity was the home, where they had a specific responsibility to catechize children and servants. A marginal note to Deuteronomy 21:18 in the Geneva Bible insisted that "it is the mothers dutie also to instruct her children," and Puritan clergy reiterated this duty to their flocks. On each workday, no less than two hours were to be devoted to catechetical instruction in families according to Josias Nichols, a Presbyterian pastor. The demand was such that approximately one hundred catechisms were published for household use in the half century after 1550. To aid parents in teaching their children, the Puritan Robert Allen compiled a special collection of alphabetized Proverbs with brief expository comments. One of the most well-known practitioners of this catechetical instruction was Lady Margaret Hoby of Hackness, Yorkshire, who listened each evening as her chaplain catechized the servants, and who herself instructed "the poore and Ignorant" as well as neighbors, and on at least one occasion provided spiritual advice to a woman living in incest.[7] Mrs. Margaret Corbet took notes at sermons and then used them to catechize her servants. They in turn were examined by her husband.[8] The significance of such activity has been aptly recognized in R.C. Richardson's important study of Puritanism in the diocese of Chester:

It was mainly this stress on the value of household religion which gave to women a role of acknowledged importance in the development and organization of Puritanism. It was in the home that women had the greatest scope not only for participating in, but for actually shaping, the religious life of the family."[9]

Because this teaching had to supplement—and sometimes correct—what was learned in the parish church, the woman's pedagogical role could be critical in shaping the spiritual ideals and loyalties of her children and her servants.

Women also used their homes to advance the cause of the saints by providing hospitality to Nonconformist clergy and sometimes even by allowing their homes to be used for Separatist religious services. Elizabeth Crane "kept what was virtually a puritan salon in her London house," whereas Lady Margaret Hoby, while in London in late 1600, welcomed the great Puritan casuist, William Perkins, and the author of the infamous Marprelate tracts, Job Throckmorton. Lodgings at Stepney were provided for the Separatist minister, John Penry, by Mrs. Thomas Settle, herself a Separatist; and at Newbury, Berkshire, several women furnished him not only with hospitality but with an occasion to expound his message to others in that region. Lady Bowes of Coventry allowed deprived ministers, including Arthur Hildersham and John Smyth, to use her home in 1606 to discuss the state of the Church of England; a minority, including Smyth, thereupon opted for Separatism. In 1638 Henry Jessey's Independent Church was meeting in the London home of Mrs. DeLamar in Barnaby Street when the authorities apprehended members, and while the Short Parliament was in session two years later, members of the same church fasted in Mrs. Wilson's house at Tower Hill. Such women helped Separatist leaders create the kind of underground spiritual network so effectively utilized by English Catholics in this period, though the latter operated primarily among the aristocracy, not the lower and middling social orders where the Separatists found their strength.[10]

In some cases women actually helped found new churches. Women as well as men were present for the organizational meeting which established Francis Johnson's Separatist church at Southwark in September 1592. Accompanied by four men, Mrs. Dorothy Hazzard seceded from her husband's parish church in

1640 to establish the Separatist congregation later known as Broadmead Bristol. Meeting at first in her own home, the church quickly grew until it had 160 members by June 1643. Mrs. Hazzard herself was largely responsible for selecting the church's second minister, Mr. Pennill. The Independent Church founded at Bury St. Edmunds, Suffolk, in August 1646 was largely the doing of Katherine Chidley, and the church at Bedford to which John Bunyan later ministered was begun in 1650 by eight women and four men. The full extent to which women were responsible for establishing Nonconformist churches has yet to be determined.[11]

No less significant was the patronage provided by women to both Puritan and Separatist ministers. One of the most direct manifestations of such patronage was the provision of ecclesiastical benefices to Puritan clergy. Lady Ann Bacon, one of the most active patrons, presented the vicarage of Redburn, Hertfordshire, to Edward Spendlowe in 1580 and later to Humphrey Wildbloud, who subsequently became a chaplain in her household at Gorhambury, Hertfordshire. Through her influence her son Anthony presented the vicarage of Hemel Hempstead to William Dyke. The leader of the Northampton Classis, the Presbyterian Edmund Snape, was appointed city preacher of Exeter in 1600 through the efforts of Anne Dudley, countess of Warwick, and Lady Margaret Paulet, widow of Sir Amyas Paulet, Mary, Queen of Scots' jailer. Such activities sometimes thwarted the efforts of ecclesiastical authorities to curtail Nonconformity, as when Margaret Fosbrooke presented William Kitchin to the living of Cranbrook St. Andrew despite the opposition of the Bishop of Peterborough. When benefices could not be found for Puritans, they could still receive appointments as chaplains in private households, such as that of Lady Anne Bacon. Lady Sundamore's Puritan chaplain, John Wilson, used her home as a base from which to launch preaching forays into Essex and Suffolk, during the course of which he influenced such key future Independent leaders as Thomas Goodwin, Jeremiah Burroughs, and William Bridge.[12]

Patronage sometimes took the form of direct grants of money to further the saints' cause. To enable Anthony Thomas to preach in Wales, Lady Jane Barnardiston donated £50 to the Feoffees for Impropriations in 1637, along with another £150 to support the ecumenical efforts of John Dury to unite Continental Protestants. Approximately £100 was given by Lady Bowes of Coventry to support Puritan clerics. Margaret Clifford, countess of Cumberland, and her husband, the third earl, contributed to a fund to purchase the living of Guiseley, Yorkshire, for the Puritan Robert Moore, who had been preaching in the region around Skipton Castle for a year and a half with their support. Again, such assistance diminished prelatical control over the clergy. When Dame Dorothy Leigh of Worsley, Lancashire, gave £400 in 1638 to support a minister at Ellenbrook Chapel, it was on the condition that "the bishop should have no hand in the putting in, placing or displacing of the minister there." Women sometimes pooled their resources to achieve their ends, as when a group of Independent women subscribed to support like-minded clergy in the chapelry of Birch, Lancashire, in the 1640s.[13]

Patronage could even be extended beyond one's death by using bequests to assist Nonconformist clergy. Judith Fox, a Puritan widow in Manchester, left funds to five Puritan ministers in 1624, and her example was not unique among Lancashire and Cheshire women. In London, Dame Mary Weld donated £300 to establish a lecture to be preached by a Puritan at St. Mary Olave, and she bequeathed an additional £2000 to establish a revolving fund to purchase impropriations with which to acquire benefices for Puritan ministers. In comparable fashion, Lady Elizabeth Camden bequeathed £600 to St. Mary Magdalen, Milk Street, London, to purchase land, the rents from which would provide £30 a year to fund a weekly lecture. But undoubtedly the most substantial bequest was that of Lady Frances Radcliffe, dowager Countess of Sussex and a friend of the prominent Puritan Edward Dering, which provided £5000 to found Sidney Sussex College, Cambridge, primarily to educate more preaching ministers.[14]

Puritan and Separatist ministers alike looked to patrons to plead their causes at the royal court. In February 1585 Lady Anne Bacon wrote to William Cecil, Lord Burghley, requesting that Puritan ministers be allowed to defend their cause before the Queen and Privy Council, for they "Labour for right reformation in ye ministery of ye Gospel." In the 1590s she prevented the

Star Chamber from interrogating some Presbyterian clergy. The dowager countesses of Huntingdon and Cumberland were also among the protectors of Puritan ministers. Imprisoned in the Fleet in 1591, the Presbyterian leader Thomas Cartwright responded warmly to Lady Elizabeth Russell's offer to intercede with Lord Burghley on his behalf. In the early 1620s the Independent John Davenport looked to Lady Mary Vere to obtain help at court from her brother, Sir Edward Conway, a Secretary of State, in obtaining admission to the vicarage and lectureship of St. Stephen, Coleman Street, London. Even the Separatists had a friend at court in Anne Dudley, Countess of Warwick, who appealed to Archbishop Whitgift and Bishop Cooper on behalf of John Udall. Henry Barrow and the extremist Edmund Copinger also hoped for her assistance. For the Puritans in particular, having such supporters at court partially alleviated the increasingly hostile attitude of the government toward Nonconformity after 1588.[15]

Patronage was also significant in furthering the publication of works by Nonconformist authors. Due to the influence of Lady Catherine, wife of Lord John St. John of Bletsoe, the Presbyterian Edward Bulkeley published a sermon on the Lord's Supper. Publication in 1593 of the collection of Puritan documents known as *A Parte of a Register*, compiled by John Field, was probably financed in part by Lady Anne Bacon. Lucy Russell, countess of Bedford, commissioned Thomas Tymme to render an English translation of Dudley Fenner's Puritan classic, *Theologia Sacra* (1585), an exposition of covenant theology. The support of Puritan women for Nonconformist literature is also reflected in epistles dedicatory. William Perkins devoted two works to the countess of Bedford; Henry Peacham dedicated a sermon on Job to the countesses of Cumberland and Warwick; the latter had a collection of sermons dedicated to her by George Gifford and lectures on Exodus 20 by John Knewstub. William Fulke published a sermon on faith at the request of the widow Mary Harris.[16]

But women did more than encourage and subsidize Nonconformist works; they contributed directly to the corpus of religious writings by composing their own books and translating the works of others. Before the mid-seventeenth century, most literary efforts of a religious nature by women were limited to translations, though Lady Margaret Hoby was surely not alone in writing out sermons and keeping a common-place book containing religious extracts. According to Nicholas Udall, a number of women, including some of aristocratic status, helped translate Erasmus' *Paraphrase* of the New Testament. Anne Locke Prowse, who at one time was married to Edward Dering, published a translation of John Calvin's sermons in 1560 and three decades later a translation of Jean Taffin's *Of the Markes of the Children of God*. In the latter she acknowledged the constraints upon her religious activities because of her sex but insisted that

> euerie one in his calling is bound to doo somewhat to the furtherance of the holie building; but because great things by reason of my sex, I may not doo, and that which I may, I ought to doo, I haue according to my duetie, brought my poore basket of stones to the strengthning of the walles of that Ierusalem, whereof . . . wee are all both Citizens and members.

English translations of Bernardino Ochino's sermons and John Jewel's *Apologie* were made by Lady Anne Bacon, while her sister, Lady Elizabeth Russell, translated John Ponet's tract on the Lord's Supper into English. One of the greatest patrons of the Elizabethan Age, Mary Sidney Herbert, countess of Pembroke, joined her brother, Sir Philip Sidney, in translating the Psalms into English lyrics.[17] She also made a translation of De Mornay's *A Discourse of Life and Death* which she published in 1592.

Among the earliest female authors in the Nonconformist tradition was Sara Jones, a member of John Lathrop's Independent Church in London. Imprisoned in 1632 for her nonconformity, she wrote several documents, including her "Grievances," which she read before the High Commission, and her "Cronicle of Gods Remarkable Judgments & Dealings That Year [1632]." She undoubtedly was a co-author of the petitions submitted by her fellow religious prisoners to the Commissioners, as well as of "The Answers of Mrs Jones & Some Others."[18] When Thomas Edwards, a Presbyterian, issued his *Reasons Against the Independent Government of Particular Congregations* in 1641, congregational polity was defended by Katherine Chidley in *The*

Justification of the Independent Churches of Christ (1641). In the context of the collapse of censorship occasioned by the Civil War, religious writings by Nonconformist women became more frequent and ranged from the moderate tracts of the Independent Elizabeth Warren to the radical works of women such as the Fifth Monarchist Mary Cary.

The role of women in printing Nonconformist literature has hardly been noticed. Of the approximately 383 publishers and patentees in Elizabethan England, seventeen—all widows—were females. Of them, at least one, Mrs. Joan Aldee, was active in the Nonconformist cause, for in 1632–33 she was one of the printers of William Prynne's *Histriomastix, the Players Scourge*, a well-known Puritan attack on the theater. Two of her apprentices, Gregory Dexter and William Taylor, were cited before the High Commission in 1637 for attempting to publish Prynne's *Brief Instructions for Church Wardens*; and four years later Dexter and Richard Oulton, her son or son-in-law, published John Milton's *Of Prelatical Episcopacy*, a castigation of the bishops.[19]

Printing, writing, and translating religious works were manifestations of the growing desire by women to participate more fully in the life and work of the church. So too was the potentially volatile question of their participation in the government of the church, though many Nonconformists were extremely chary of giving a real voice to women, normally coupling them with children in any discussion of this issue. John Smyth was not typical in proposing that women have a say in the selection of a pastor, the excommunication of wayward members, and other "public affairs" of the congregation, but even he excluded women from preaching and prophesying. Women were denied a vote in church affairs by the Separatists Francis Johnson and John Robinson, though the latter allowed the ladies to address issues which came before the church and, in cases of necessity when men failed to act, to reprove the church for its errors. In Henry Ainsworth's Separatist congregation, women had to be content as quiescent observers of church business, "the Apostle [Paul] and nature it self requiring women to be *silent* in the church." Some Nonconformist congregations permitted widows aged sixty or more to care for the ill in the capacity of deaconesses, and the Presbyterians favored the creation of the office of church widow for this purpose. But although some Nonconformist churches increased the scope of women's participation in church affairs, by no means was this true of all. Women, for example, had neither the right to prophesy nor a voice in the government of John Goodwin's radical congregation of London Independents.[20]

The question of women's right to preach was even more controversial. Before the Reformation some Lollard women had preached and read Scripture in worship services. Radical Protestant women must have been preaching in the 1590s, for the conservative apologist Leonard Wright warned them that they were imitating Eve by usurping the office of teacher. Conformists and Puritans alike were convinced that women must not preach, except in those rare instances where they were "extraordinarily called thereunto, and have certain signs of their calling." The words are those of that staunchly conservative prelate, John Whitgift, Queen Elizabeth's "little black husband." Essentially, he insisted that females could preach only where there were none but infidels and where other means to take them the message of God were lacking—"which is nowhere in this church" of England. This, in effect, was the position of such Continental divines as John Calvin, Peter Martyr, and the Dutch Calvinist Gisbertus Voetius. Because women were unskilled as preachers, their attempt to prophesy, according to the Puritan Henry Smith, rendered that noble calling "vile and despised." The crux of the issue was probably best expressed in a marginal note to 1 Timothy 2:12 in the Beza-Tomson Bible: Women could not preach because this would make them masters over men.[21]

Fears for the preservation of male dominance and the Pauline admonition for women to be silent in church made it difficult indeed for females to preach. In 1584 the Presbyterians of the Dedham Classis even raised the question of "whether it were convenient a woman shuld pray having a better gift than her husband," but they backed off without answering it. Women apparently preached among the Baptists in the Netherlands, and there were reportedly female preachers among the Baptists in Massachusetts by 1636. Thomas Lamb's General Baptist congregation in London permitted women to gather for their own religious services, and out of this there developed in 1645 public lectures on spiritual matters by women. Meeting on Tuesday afternoons, these gatherings allegedly attracted as many as 1000 persons, thus testifying to the substantial interest in an active role for women in preaching and teaching. In 1641 women were preaching in London, at Ashford and Faversham in Kent, at Ely in Cambridgeshire, and at Salisbury. Some of the hostility to the women was fanned by the controversial views they were alleged to propagate. According to an anonymous critic, Joan Bauford of Faversham taught that "husbands being such as crossed their wives wils might lawfully be forsaken," while Susan May of Ashford supposedly proclaimed that "the Devill was the Father of all those which did not love Puritans." Of the major sectarian groups, only the Quakers really provided women with the unquestioned right to preach. In 1656 the Midland Particular Baptist Association allowed women only the right to make a profession of faith before the congregation. Although there were probably more women who preached to Nonconformist congregations than has been realized, the practice did not win the general acceptance of most Nonconformists.[22]

In addition to preaching and writing, there were other prominent ways for women to demonstrate their convictions to an often unreceptive society. In an age when symbolism was still critically important, some ladies proclaimed their faith through actions that were at once symbolic and substantive. The Separatist Margaret Maynard, arrested for recusancy in 1587, proclaimed that she had not gone to her parish church in a decade because "there is no church in England." Her fellow sectary, Katherine Unwin, caused a minor scandal by refusing to have her son baptized by one of the "false" ministers of the Church of England. Several Lancashire women pulled the hands of ministers away rather than let them use the sign of the cross in baptism. Because kneeling in the Eucharist might imply adoration of the elements or the Real Presence, many refused to genuflect; of the thirty-six persons in Manchester cited for this offense in 1617, fourteen were women. Because Mrs. John Traske insisted on keeping the sabbath on Saturday, she was imprisoned for more than a decade. With other ladies of St. Chad's parish, Shrewsbury, Katherine Chidley refused to be churched following childbirth in 1626. Such actions by these women were manifest testimony of their religious convictions and were taken so seriously by the authorities that imprisonment sometimes resulted.[23]

A willingness to defy the laws of the state in obedience to divine law, as they perceived it, led the more radical women into the Nonconformist underground. The most striking example of this kind of activity was the publication of the viciously satirical and anti-prelatical Marprelate tracts in the late 1580s. Elizabeth Crane, who married the Puritan M.P. George Carleton in 1589 and who was a friend of the Separatist minister John Penry and the radical printer Robert Waldegrave, was one of those involved in the Marprelate controversy. For harboring the Marprelate press in her home at East Molesey, Surrey, she was taken before the Star Chamber, fined 1000 marks for contempt and another £500 for concealing the press, and imprisoned in the Fleet. Similarly, the wife of the squire Roger Wigston was arraigned in Star Chamber, fined £1000, and imprisoned for allowing the Marprelate printers to use her home in Wolston, Warwickshire. Claiming that his wife was the real instigator of this activity, Wigston was fined only one-third as much. Among the others involved in the Marprelate affair were Waldegrave's wife, who helped distribute the tracts, and Widow Adams, whose house at Banbury, Oxfordshire, was used to store 1600 copies of the tracts. There were other instances of similar activity— probably more than we suspect. The maid of the Separatist minister John Greenwood smuggled copies of illegal religious tracts to imprisoned sectaries, just as she or Greenwood's wife probably smuggled the manuscript copies out to the printers in the first place. A published collection of letters by Greenwood and his colleague Henry Barrow was secretly conveyed to the latter in prison by Ellyn Bowman. Such surreptitious activities were not restricted to the Separatists. The stationer for Thomas Cartwright's secretly published *Replye* to John Whitgift in 1573 was the wife of Richard Martin, Master of the Mint. When the authorities were about to seize this tract, the wife of John Strowd, the book's probable printer, burned most of the 1000 copies of the second edition. Clearly, then, the role of women in the Nonconformist underground cannot be ignored.[24]

More dramatically, Nonconformist women participated in

public demonstrations on behalf of the godly cause. When Edmund Grindal, Bishop of London, suspended John Bartlett from his lectureship at St. Giles Cripplegate and then confined him to his house for refusing to stay silent, some sixty ladies protested at the bishop's palace. Because Grindal "would not in such case deal with such numbers of women," he asked them to send half a dozen of their husbands instead. Not until another Puritan, John Philpot, himself suspended, asked the women to leave did they disband—in tears. Women publicly ridiculed Grindal when he wore his square cap—a "popish" vestment—in the parish church of St. Margaret, Fish Street, London. When Philpot and John Gough were banned from London for their Puritan preaching, several hundred women lined London Bridge, offering them provisions and "animating them most earnestly to stand fast in their doctrine." Others acted less provocatively, such as Dame Elizabeth Golding of Kent, who confined her protest to signing a testimonial in defense of the Puritan cleric John Strowd.[25]

The Separatists too did some demonstrating. Following the death of Roger Rippon in Newgate prison in February 1593, the Separatists staged a procession to Cheapside, carrying Rippon's coffin replete with inscriptions castigating the Archbishop of Canterbury as a "great ennemy of the saints" and attacking the Romish Antichrist, prelacy, and the priesthood. Among those arrested for taking part in this demonstration was Mrs. Nicholas Lee. In the crackdown that ensued, numerous Separatists were incarcerated, prompting John Penry to draft a petition—"The Humble, Most Earnest and Lamentable Complaint"—protesting the imprisonment of fifty-six Separatists. Copies were presented to the Lord Keeper of the House of Lords and the Speaker of the House of Commons by a contingent of Separatist women that included Penry's wife Helen, but for their efforts the ladies themselves were locked up. Their appeal to Parliament foreshadows the demonstrations of the 1640s, such as that in February 1642 when "great Multitudes" of women petitioned Parliament for religious reform. Should Parliament refuse to hear their demands, they threatened that "where there is one Woman now here, there would be Five hundred To-morrow; and that it was as good for them to die here, as at home." In addition to demanding the abolition of episcopacy, the sequestration of the Catholic peers, and the punishment of Archbishop William Laud, they justified their activism by insisting that Christ died for women as well as men, that women too must be happy if the church and commonwealth are to flourish, and that women as well as men have suffered for their religion under the persecuting prelates.[26]

Women had indeed earned a place on the roll of those persecuted for their faith. Among the Separatists imprisoned in Bridewell in 1568, there were more women than men. The list of Elizabethan Separatists who died in prison includes Margaret Maynard and Alice Roe, both elderly widows, and Judith Myller, Anna Tailour, and Margaret Farret, apparently younger women. During Archbishop Laud's dominance, women frequently appeared before the notorious High Commission. When members of John Lathrop's London congregation, including at least a dozen women, were imprisoned in April 1632, they were taken before the Commission, "even ye weake Women as their Subtill & malicious Adversarys ware not able to resist but ware ashamed." While in jail, Lathrop's people won fourteen converts to their cause, of whom eight or nine were women. The same year five members of a Separatist conventicle which met near Christ Church, London, were taken before the Commission; two were females, and all five, in typical Separatist fashion, refused to take the oath *ex officio mero*. When eight women of John Spilsbury's London congregation were cited before the Commission in April 1640, they were turned over to the quarter sessions because "these were poor women, schismatics." The psychological and physical perils of incarceration were severe enough, but in 1641 members of Henry Jessey's congregation were beaten as well as jailed, and one—the pregnant Mrs. Berry—was thrashed so severely that she miscarried and died. But the persecutions only intensified the determination of the Nonconformists to overturn their oppressors, and in this the women were indeed instrumental, particularly through their participation in the demonstrations of the early 1640s that helped overthrow Laudian repression.[27]

Thus, women contributed substantially to the growth of the Puritan and Separatist movements, not only in terms of their active participation in the spiritual life of the congregation but by providing religious instruction as well as patronage and hospitality to ministers. Women helped found new churches, participated in public demonstrations and acts of symbolic defiance, and wrote, translated, and printed religious literature. Some women even became directly involved in the government and ministry of the church. But because they were generally barred from the ministry and most positions of leadership in the church, discouraged from writing, and sometimes even overlooked as mere women, their total contribution to Nonconformity prior to the early 1640s has been substantially neglected.

NOTES

1. See for example Claire Cross, " 'He-Goats Before the Flocks': A Note on the Part Played by Women in the Founding of Some Civil War Churches," *Studies in Church History* 8 (1972): 195–202; Patrick Collinson, "The Role of Women in the English Reformation," *Studies in Church History* 2 (1965): 258–72. An earlier version of this chapter was first published in *Church History* 52 (September 1983): 299–311.

2. James Boswell, *Boswell's Life of Johnson*, ed. George Birkbeck Hill and rev. by L.F. Powell, 6 vols. (Oxford: Clarendon Press, 1934), 3:287–88.

3. Champlin Burrage, *The Early English Dissenters in the Light of Recent Research (1550–1641)*, 2 vols. (Cambridge: Cambridge University Press, 1912), 2: 313; Leland H. Carlson, ed., *The Writings of John Greenwood and Henry Barrow 1591–1593* (London: George Allen and Unwin, 1970), p. 307.

4. Richard L. Greaves and Robert Zaller, eds., *Biographical Dictionary of British Radicals in the Seventeenth Century*, 3 vols. (Brighton: Harvester Press, 1982–84). The remaining female radical is Katherine Boyle, Lady Ranelagh. Many of the men, of course, were included for reasons other than religious radicalism.

5. Hastings Robinson, ed. and trans., *The Zürich Letters*, (Cambridge: The Parker Society, 1842), p. 202; Burrage, *Early English Dissenters*, 1: 244, 326; 2: 199–200, 303–4, 309–10; John Browne, *History of Congregationalism and Memorials of the Churches in Norfolk and Suffolk* (London: Jarrold & Sons, 1877), p. 254 n.

6. Burrage, *Early English Dissenters*, 1: 325; R.C. Richardson, *Puritanism in North-West England: A Regional Study of the Diocese of Chester to 1642* (Manchester: Manchester University Press, 1972), pp. 109–10.

7. [Josias Nichols], *An Order of Hovshold Instrvction* (London, 1596), sigs. B7ᵛ-Clᵛ; Lawrence Stone, "The Rise of the Nuclear Family in Early Modern England: The Patriarchal Stage," *The Family in History*, ed. Charles Rosenberg (Philadelphia: University of Pennsylvania Press, 1975), p. 30; Robert Allen, *An Alphabet of the Holy Proverbs of King Salomon* ([London], 1596); Dorothy M. Meads, ed., *Diary of Lady Margaret Hoby 1599–1605*, (London: George Routledge & Sons, 1930), pp. 48, 62, 66, 80. Cf. John Carpenter, *Time Complaining* (London, [1588]), sig. A3ʳ, for an acknowledgment of the work of Jane and John Walrond, esq., in "the exercising of your family in godlines."

8. Samuel Clarke, *A Collection of the Lives of Ten Eminent Divines* (London, 1662), pp. 506–7.

9. Richardson, *Puritanism*, p. 179; cf. pp. 91, 105. Catholic women likewise played a major role in household religion. See John Bossy, "The Character of Elizabethan Catholicism," *Past and Present* 21 (April 1962): 40; Richard L. Greaves, *Society and Religion in Elizabethan England* (Minneapolis: University of Minnesota Press, 1981), pp. 307–9.

10. Patrick Collinson, *The Elizabethan Puritan Movement* (Berkeley: University of California Press, 1967), p. 393 (quoted); Meads, *Diary of Lady Margaret Hoby*, p. 153; Leland H. Carlson, *Martin Marprelate, Gentleman* (San Marino: Huntington Library, 1981), p. 129; Carlson, *Writings of Greenwood and Barrow*, p. 299; Albert Peel, ed., *The Notebook of John Penry 1593*, Camden Society, 3rd Series, 67 (1944), p. 38; Claire Cross, *Church and People 1450–1660* (Atlantic Highlands, N.J.: Humanities Press, 1976), pp. 167–68; Burrage, *Early English Dissenters*, 2: 300–301.

11. Carlson, *Writings of Greenwood and Barrow*, p. 307; Roger Hayden, ed., *The Records of a Church of Christ in Bristol, 1640–1687*, (Bristol: Bristol Record Society, 1974), pp. 13, 87–91; Cross, " 'He-goats Before the Flocks' " 8:195–98; Geoffrey F. Nuttall, *Visible Saints: The Congregational Way 1640–1660* (Oxford: Basil Blackwell, 1957), pp. 27, 29; *The Church Book of Bunyan Meeting 1650–1821*, intro. by G.B. Harrison (London: J.M. Dent & Sons, 1928), p. 2.

12. Paul S. Seaver, *The Puritan Lectureships: The Politics of Religious Dissent 1560–1662* (Stanford: Stanford University Press, 1970), pp. 106, 217, 226; Collinson, *Puritan Movement*, pp. 439–40, 442; Rosemary O'Day, *The English Clergy* (Leicester: Leicester University Press, 1979), p. 91; T.W. Davids, *Annals of Evangelical Nonconformity in the County of Essex* (London: Jackson, Walford, and Hodder, 1863), pp. 166–67. Cf. also the role of Sir Thomas Knyvett's wife as a patron: Egerton MSS 2713, fols. 220ʳ, 223ʳ, British Library.

13. *Calendar of State Papers Domestic, 1636–37*, p. 545; Richardson, *Puritanism*, p. 138; Patrick Collinson, *Archbishop Grindal 1519–1583*

(Berkeley: University of California Press, 1979), pp. 211–12; Robert Halley, *Lancashire: Its Puritanism and Nonconformity*, 2 vols. (London: Hodder and Stoughton, 1869), 2: 153.

14. Richardson, *Puritanism*, pp. 137–38; Seaver, *Puritan Lectureships*, pp. 149, 158–60; Lansdowne MSS, 61/34, British Library.

15. Lansdowne MSS, 43/48; 68/58; 115/55 British Library (quoted); Cross, *Church and People*, pp. 159–60; *Calender of State Papers Domestic, 1623–25*, pp. 354–57; Carlson, *Writings of Greenwood and Barrow*, pp. 239–40.

16. Edward Bulkeley, *A Sermon Preached . . . at Bletsoe* (London, 1586), sig. A5ʳ; Albert Peel, ed., *The Seconde Parte of a Register*, 2 vols. (Cambridge: Cambridge University Press, 1915), 1: 12–14; Greaves, *Society and Religion*, p. 309.

17. Meads, *Diary of Lady Margaret Hoby*, pp. 62–63, 67; Nicholas Udall, preface to *The First Tome or Volume of the Paraphrase of Erasmus vpon the Newe Testamente* (London, 1548); Anne Prowse, epistle to Jean Taffin, *Of the Markes of the Children of God* (London, 1590), sigs. A3ᵛ-A4ʳ (quoted); Marjorie Keniston McIntosh, "Sir Anthony Cooke: Tudor Humanist, Educator, and Religious Reformer," *Proceedings of the American Philosophical Society* 119 (June 1975): 240, nn. 38–39; Greaves, *Society and Religion*, p. 310.

18. Burrage, *Early English Dissenters*, 1: 324.

19. Edward Arber, *A List . . . of 837 London Publishers . . . Between 1553 and 1640* (Birmingham: For the Author, 1890); Stephen Foster, *Notes from the Caroline Underground* (Hamden, Conn.: Archon Books, 1978), pp. 62–63.

20. W.T. Whitley ed., *The Works of John Smyth*, 2 vols. (Cambridge: Cambridge University Press, 1915), 1: 256; Francis Johnson, *A Christian Plea Conteyning Three Treatises* ([Leyden], 1617), p. 309; Robert Ashton, ed., *The Works of John Robinson*, 3 vols. (London: J. Snow, 1851), 2: 158, 215–16; Walter H. Burgess, *John Robinson* (London: Williams and Norgate, 1920), p. 292; Henry Ainsworth, *An Animadversion to Mr Richard Clyftons Advertisement* (Amsterdam, 1613), p. 34; B.R. White, ed., *Association Records of the Particular Baptists of England, Wales and Ireland to 1660*, 1 (London: Baptist Historical Society, 1971): 11; Hayden, *Records of a Church of Christ in Bristol*, pp. 33, 51. I owe the observation on Goodwin's congregation to Dr. Ellen More. The Conformists permitted women to baptize in private homes in cases of necessity and sometimes to serve as churchwardens. John Ayre, ed., *The Works of John Whitgift*, 3 vols. (Cambridge: The Parker Society, 1851–53), 2: 505; Pearl Hogrefe, *Tudor Women: Commoners and Queens* (Ames: Iowa State University Press, 1975), p. 27.

21. Keith Thomas, "Women and the Civil War Sects," *Past and Present* 13 (1958): pp. 337–38; Leonard Wright, *A Summons for Sleepers* ([London?], 1589), p. 55; Ayre, *Works of Whitgift*, 2: 499–502, 504; 3: 5; Henry Smith, *A Frvitfvll Sermon* (London, 1591), pp. 16–17.

22. Roland G. Usher, ed., *The Presbyterian Movement in the Reign of Queen Elizabeth as Illustrated by the Minute Book of the Dedham Classis, 1582–1589*, Camden Society, 3rd Series, 8 (1905), p. 35; Thomas, "Women and the Civil War Sects," p. 339; Robert Barclay, *The Inner Life of the Religious Societies of the Commonwealth*, 2nd ed. (London: Hodder and Stoughton, 1877), pp. 155–56 n.; Richard L. Greaves, "Mrs. Attaway," in *Biographical Dictionary of British Radicals*, ed. Greaves and Zaller, 1: 28; anon., *A Discoverie of Six Women Preachers* (London, 1641), pp. 4–5; White, *Association Records*, 1: 28.

23. Leland H. Carlson, ed., *The Writings of John Greenwood 1587–1590*, (London: Geoge Allen and Unwin, 1962), pp. 298–99, 308; Richardson, *Puritanism*, pp. 79–80, 110; *Calendar of State Papers Domestic, 1639*, pp. 466–67.

24. Carlson, *Martin Marprelate*, pp. 22, 24, 36, 38, 42–45, 50, 75, 78, 137, 311; Carlson, *Writings of Greenwood*, pp. 106–7, 176; Carlson, *Writings of Greenwood and Barrow*, pp. 223–24; Collinson, *Puritan Movement*, p. 140.

25. William Nicholson, ed., *The Remains of Edmund Grindal, D.D.* (Cambridge: The Parker Society, 1843), pp. 288–89; Collinson, *Puritan Movement*, pp. 82, 140–41 (cf. p. 93).

26. Carlson, *Writings of Greenwood and Barrow*, pp. 295, 367, 407, 411; Peel, *Notebook of Penry*, pp. 54–55; *Commons' Journals* (London: H.M. Stationery Office, 1742 ff.), 2: 407; Ellen A. McArthur, "Women Petitioners and the Long Parliament," *English Historical Review* 24 (October 1909): 699–700.

27. Burrage, *Early English Dissenters*, 1: 204, 322–23, 327; 2: 9–11, 297 (quoted), 300, 301, 311, 314–20, 322; Carlson, *Writings of Greenwood*, pp. 280, 308, 333–34.

4

Shaking Patriarchy's Foundations: Sectarian Women in England, 1641–1700

Dorothy P. Ludlow

In 1641, on the eve of the English Civil War, a popular tract reported the alarming news that six women preachers were openly holding religious meetings throughout England and discussing the Scriptures, doctrine, and church practice.[1] This report marked the beginning of twenty years of unusually intense and visible religious activism by English women, the range of which is documented in contemporary newsletters, pamphlets, ballads, sermons, and assize and quarter sessions records. By 1646, "petticoat preachers" and "apron apostles" had become so plentiful that London officials felt compelled to petition Parliament for repressive action,[2] and in the 1650s swarms of Quaker women missionaries forced local magistrates to interpret strictly the Elizabethan vagabondage laws against their incessant interruptions of neighborhood congregations.[3] In both city and countryside, prophetesses or female visionaries were a common occurrence, and obstreperous behavior by women parishioners became a regular feature of the religious controversies which agitated the entire nation. Women harangued prelates and country priests, tore down altar rails, smashed stained glass windows, and cut up surplices with their sewing shears. More positively, they were instrumental in "gathering" Independent Churches and in taking up their pens to defend their doctrinal beliefs or to publicize the special insights their spiritual experiences had given them. They demonstrated before the doors of Parliament, and thousands signed petitions demanding the release of popular dissident leaders or protesting the traditional collection of tithes.[4]

This sustained activity has been variously explained by modern historians who disagree on the specific dynamic of women's restiveness while agreeing that intense spiritual feelings and convictions were a primary cause. Some scholars believe that by exalting and secularizing the married state, Protestant dissent and sectarian practice subjected English family life to far-reaching changes indirectly beneficial to women. Public speaking, writing, and church-organizing were expressions of these changes.[5] Others link women's activities to incipient feminism[6] or to the currents of radicalism which surfaced during this period.[7] According to these views, women were encouraged by the Reformation to rebel against the societal, political, and religious restrictions which had hitherto repressed them.[8]

Another line of thought denies the "revolutionary" impact of Protestantism upon women, arguing that Puritan attitudes actually could be deleterious to women's status since they were now permitted no alternative roles apart from the family ones of marriage and motherhood. These historians question the uniqueness of women's conduct during the 1640s and 1650s and insist that women had been assuming increasingly innovative and independent religious tasks years before the unrest of the mid-seventeenth century and were redefining and extending their ordinary religious activities as part of a widespread evolutionary process among women, which was not peculiar to the Reformed Churches, to the sectaries, or even to England.[9]

Interpretation of female religiosity becomes even more diverse and difficult for the period following the upheavals of 1640–60, when, except for the Quakers, women activists all but vanished from historical sight as sectaries. Men, as well as women, found themselves forced into low-visibility survival strategies for nearly thirty years.[10] The most recent scholarship, focusing on the emergence of feminist tracts in the later decades, suggests that female independence of thought and action during this period owes more to Anglican women than to Nonconformists and that sectarian attitudes over the long run were less conducive to changes in women's religious roles than were those of the *laissez-faire* Established Church.[11]

A truly comprehensive approach to women's contributions to Protestant development in the seventeenth century needs to go beyond the details of their activities, motivations, and the immediate consequences of their behavior to look at issues of power and control, the ambiguities of female religiosity and its socially disruptive potential, as perceived by both men and women. Historians need also to consider the emancipating and restricting effects of untoward female behavior on the participants, before trying to trace the connections (if any) between female consciousness and religious activism over a period of some fifty years.

THE REVOLUTIONARY ERA

One of the most distinctive roles seized by women during the turbulent 1640s and 1650s was that of lay preacher. Although modern research has suggested that formal or informal preaching by women may have begun with the earliest Lollards, it was not until the later years of the sixteenth century that the growth of the Anabaptist and other reformed doctrines brought a significant number of women into the ranks of religious dissent and a few of them into the glare of publicity which allows one to classify them definitely as women preachers.[12] Apart from such notorious sixteenth-century "preachers" as Anne Askew[13] and Joan Boucher[14] and the most famous woman preacher of the seventeenth century, Anne Hutchinson,[15] there is very little concrete evidence to support the numerous accounts of women preaching in private or public—accounts which are invariably emotional, hostile, inexact, banal, and polemical. Labels were automatically applied to women who stood up in public: "ignorant," "proud," "weak," "vain," "ambitious," "insolent." The distinction between women teaching at home and their preaching in public was often blurred: thus the indiscriminate sneers at "catechising women" in the family and "prattling hus-wives" in the pulpit.[16] Nevertheless, with all due allowance for contagious suspicion and excited exaggeration, it is certain that a good many women all over the country were publicly preaching.[17] Generally, these sermons or exhortations seem to have been spontaneous orations, under the irresistible urging of the Holy Spirit—or so the women claimed. A few, at least, may have preached on a regular basis, since Thomas Edwards claimed he knew of women preachers "who keep constant Lectures, preaching weekly to many men and women."[18] Often the sermon was delivered at private, even clandestine assemblies, perhaps in a barn or field. Except for the Quakers, some of whose family backgrounds are known, the women preachers themselves are simply names or descriptions tossed casually into a letter or tract. The content of their sermons is also unknown for the most part. A few silly or trivial texts are given, reflecting the contempt some men held for them. Only Thomas Edwards, incapable of the slightest touch of satire, made deadly serious charges: a woman in Norfolk taught the heretical belief that the Bible was not the word of God and that miracles had never occurred; an Anabaptist "shee-sectary" boastingly proclaimed that "she was every whit as good as Christ, no way inferiour to him, but equal to him, and if she were not so the Scripture was a liar"; another woman took as her text Romans 8:2, "For the law of the Spirit of life in Christ Jesus has set me free from the law of sin and death," a verse frequently brought in accusation against women in the radical sects.[19]

Thanks to Edwards' malignant obsession with Mrs. Attaway, "the mistress of all the she-preachers in Coleman Street," we know more about her than any other woman preacher. A Cheapside lace-seller and a member of Thomas Lamb's Baptist Church, she was one of three women who jointly conducted weekly religious meetings in Bell Alley, London. If Edwards' account can be trusted, she expounded commonly held tenets of the General Baptists, arguing, for example, the case against infant baptism, adroitly managing to avoid precise definitions of the sacrament itself. Her commendation of John Milton's *Doctrine and Discipline of Divorce* (first published in 1643) to two gentlemen of the Inns of Court horrified Edwards and his contemporaries, but her only recorded comment—that "she for her part would look more into it, for she had an unsanctified husband, that did not walk in the ways of Sion, nor speak the language of Canaan"—scarcely bespeaks an intimate knowledge of Milton's complex web of arguments.[20] It seems far more likely that Edwards was simply preparing his readers for the *denouement* of the Attaway story: her elopement with "another woman's husband" and their melodramatic escape to Jerusalem, using funds fraudulently obtained from members of her own congregation— an escapade which, as Edwards tells it, has all the elements of a medieval morality play.

How much of Edwards' reports about Mrs. Attaway and other women preachers can one believe? Many women accused of being preachers undoubtedly were just continuing the anti-clericalism which began decades before the Civil War period. Distinctions between interruption, exhortation, and actual preaching were seldom clear and certainly not consistent. Nevertheless, many of Edwards' contemporaries were quite ready to believe him. The most significant response was that taken by the London Aldermen and Common Council on 15 January 1646, when they sent a delegation to the House of Commons to petition for the "speedy Settling of Church Governement" and to complain of "private Meetings of Women Preachers," where strange new doctrines and blasphemies were vented.[21] Several females were arrested as a result of the petition, and others were summoned for interrogation: Mrs. Attaway may well have been one of these since Edwards reports that she was questioned by the "Commission of Examinations."[22] Thus it seems probable that Edwards' alarm had an actual basis; and perhaps the prompt Parliamentary action had a dampening effect on preaching by women, since it was shortly after her interrogation that Mrs. Attaway purportedly ran off with her paramour.

The treatment accorded to women preachers depended mainly on four factors: the religious prejudices of local magistrates and clergymen against sectaries and against women; the amount of public attention the woman was able to draw; her attitude when haled before the authorities; and occasionally the male protection and influence she could call upon. The importance of local feeling is best seen in the sentences passed on women Quakers who interrupted worship services and "exhorted" in the streets, market places, churchyards, and other public areas. Because of the widespread suspicion and fear of these "inner Light" advocates, women Friends were often condemned to humiliating public whippings and long, inhumane imprisonments. Never given to tergiversation and bold to the point of foolhardiness, these women brought down upon themselves the combined wrath of civil and religious leaders, along with the resentment of local citizens who saw them as obnoxious, hypocritical troublemakers.[23] Some women, like the Fifth Monarchist Anna Trapnel, were so well known that they had to be handled with discretion and moderation, even in the face of their steely refusal to be submissive. On the other hand, the notorious Mary Gadbury, who also mixed prophecy and preaching, was sentenced to Bridewell and repeated whippings for a period of months. When she protested the severity of her sentence, she was told that the "punishment was too light for such a lewd woman; and her offence was the greater, because she so committed it under the cloak of Religion."[24]

The appearance during this period of persons like Mary Adams,[25] Mary Gadbury, and a number of others who claimed to be with child by the Holy Spirit or to have been told in a vision that the child in her womb would be the second Messiah were probably not examples of the perpetuity of medieval ecstatic "free spirit" tradition, of a "sexual revolution" brought on by the Reformation, or of a new interest in freedom by women[26] but illustrations of pathetic responses to images and mores advanced by men about women. These images included, on the one hand, women as silly, shallow, blindly enthusiastic followers of charismatic leaders (2 Tim. 3:6–7) and, on the other hand, as needing mentors and guides because they were too simple to understand the complexities of Scripture by themselves. Despite their emphasis on individual spiritual responsibility, the sectarians believed just as firmly in the intellectual inferiority of women as did their more orthodox brethren. Another popular image and a real and present danger was "Woman as Heretic Temptress," especially to those men foolish enough to listen to her. The alarming fact was that such men existed. If women were particularly vulnerable to the machinations of evil forces and false teachers, men were perilously vulnerable to women.

"Preaching" women were held up as objects of scorn and ridicule, not only because they were seen as contemptible or ludicrous but also because they were feared.[27] The jeering abuse often found in the tract literature had two aims: to intimidate forward women into silence and to block the ears of men—by amusement or by sheepishness. It mattered little what a woman preacher was saying; the important thing was to insure that no one paid much attention to her. Even the most talkative of women needs an audience, and the authorities hoped to limit her auditors to other "silly" women like herself.[28]

A sort of naive and instrumental seduction into error was not the only element involved in the male perspective of female religious activism. As Keith Thomas points out, many men believed that some women actively and ambitiously sought the power which men in their caution and God in his wisdom denied them.[29] Because they were inherently restless and fickle, John Brinsley wrote, women sought an outlet for their frustrated energies by expressing their discontent with any ecclesiastical system which kept them on short tether. This negative attitude made them a ready prey to Satan's delusions, especially the notion that they could usurp the authority and assume the independence of men.[30] Such a usurpation obviously had dangerous overtones when exercised publicly.

Less threatening, perhaps, but still viewed with some trepidation, were women prophets and visionaries, who, like men acting under a similar spiritual mandate, were plentiful during these two decades.[31] The special danger accruing to a woman mystic was that she tended to be drawn out of her sheltered environment by the actions of the Holy Ghost and thus escaped the immediate surveillance and control of the male members of her family. No man could control the workings of the Inner Spirit and in many cases could not even satisfactorily determine whether a woman was evilly intentioned or instructed. A general rule of thumb held that if she was infringing on "male authority"—i.e., behaving like a man—she could not be acting under divine direction. But so many ambiguous questions arose in particular circumstances that this criterion was not always reliable. Were such women to be prized, admired, and listened to? Could they be ignored without imperilling one's salvation? Where were the limits of acceptable prophecy and how could these be enforced? Although the most learned men declared that prophecy was a matter for scorn, they could not deny that popular credulity was widespread and hardly confined to the ignorant masses.[32] This credulity is understandable when one remembers the long Judaeo-Christian and Classical traditions associating women and prophecy: the women vatics in the Old and New Testaments, Greek and Roman sibyls, heretical Montanists, Rhineland mystics, the Beguines—all contributed to a legend of feminine sensitivity to divine visitations. In the religiously troubled sixteenth century, a series of English "Holy Maids" demonstrate that women were not excluded because of their gender from being regarded as valid instruments and messengers of the divine will. Government officials and clergymen may have been skeptical about particular individuals, but not because they were women. The truly pious among the early Holy Maids either were already bound to convent life or soon entered it, an environment which both tested and controlled their spiritual gifts.[33] Such trials and rules were impossible to impose upon the seventeenth-century women visionaries.

Although Christopher Hill has suggested that much irrational behavior—trances, visions, and the like—may have been "a deliberate form of advertisement," especially in lower-class radicals,[34] Alfred Cohen insists that "there was real madness involved" in most of the visionaries' behavior, even if the "madness" was only temporary.[35] Whatever the psychological component—and it is difficult to evaluate psychopathology in terms meaningful to twentieth-century categories and definitions—women prophets did indeed command serious attention, both from their lay audiences and from the authorities. As Phyllis Mack recently put it, their appearance "must have been comprehensible to a very wide audience, because most people believed that ecstatic behavior was especially appropriate to woman's essential being."[36]

A more useful basis for evaluation than saintliness or insanity is that of function. During the period 1640–60, women visionaries fall into two general categories: those who had a political or politico-religious message to impart and those who were purely mystical or spiritual seers. Among women of the first type, the degree of political sophistication, the means of attracting attention, and the public impact of the prophecies varied considerably. Lady Eleanor Douglas predicted the death of the duke of Buckingham, a dark fate for Bishop Laud, and even hinted at the demise of Charles I. Grace Cary, a middle-class Bristol widow, had nothing more specific to tell the King than to urge him to suppress "all idolatry, superstition and prophanity" in the kingdom, dismiss his wicked advisors, convert the Queen from Popery, and offer liberty of conscience to a carefully selective list of Puritan Nonconformists. An obscure Surrey wife named Elinor Channel commanded Oliver Cromwell to bring about peace, while Elizabeth Poole had words for the Army Council in 1649 about the sinfulness of executing the King. Anna Trapnel, the noted Fifth Monarchist prophetess-preacher, foresaw that God would soon "batter" Cromwell and his evil cohorts.[37]

Government response to these messages varied according to their content and the publicity they received. The poor prophetess, wandering aimlessly about with a vague message of peace or even of disaster, was hardly perceived as a threat to national security. If, however, she had money, friends, or connections with the press, it was well to pay closer attention to her. Arrest, as in the case of Trapnel, might stir up a hornet's nest. Attempting to discredit her message by making scurrilous sexual accusations was the method used on Mistress Poole. Despite the best efforts of successive governments, Lady Eleanor was irrepressible, and her many incarcerations in every prison in London, as well as Bedlam, had little dampening effect on her energies and activities. Psychotic though she undoubtedly was, her high social rank protected her from serious injury.

While it is true that most women prophets were acting independently of accepted societal norms for women and sometimes against the advice of family or friends, there is no evidence that they urged other women to do likewise or that their practice of moving about freely was linked to notions on freedom of thought. Perhaps, in making claim to extraordinary gifts, women were in fact indicating a desire to dominate, but that seems an extravagant assumption in view of the lack of proof that they attempted to act as leaders of groups or to do anything more than try to persuade men in positions of authority to listen to them.[38]

The non-political visionary posed fewer problems for government officials: it was usually the clergy who were the most skeptical and critical about the woman mystic's claim. Ministers of all denominations worried incessantly about the gullibility of their flocks and their acceptance of even the most unlikely tale of visions, locutions, trances, or ecstasies. Several "mystics" appear to have been silly, vain, and rather egocentric girls who enjoyed attention and were aided and used by male sectaries for their own purposes.[39] Some probably were frauds but most seem to have been God-intoxicated adolescents who saw themselves (and were viewed by others) as evidence of God's use of the "weaker vessel" to fulfill his mysterious purposes. The best known of these was fifteen-year-old Sara Wight, whose prolonged trances aroused the curiosity and respect of hundreds of Londoners, many of them "persons of note."[40] Some had suspicions about the authenticity of her divine "visionations" or thought her fastings were "a forgery or pretense," but she adroitly evaded theological entrapment by examining ministers and even avoided any specific claim of prophecy. Her motivation, she insisted, was solely the compulsion to express the ineffable. Unlike Trapnel, who was also a mystic, Sara offered no political message, so she was never a threat to the civil authorities. No doubt some surveillance was maintained over her because of the large crowds who attended her; had she ventured any sort of political remark, it would have been all over London in a matter of hours. Sara apparently did not seek influence (as opposed to attention) and certainly made no attempt to exercise power. Had she combined action with spirituality, she might have had the impact of a George Fox. Yet her non-controversial nature was probably one of the most important factors in her contemporary fame: people—even well-known London personalities—could visit her without embarrassment, loss of reputation, or suspicions of political deviancy. She was the embodiment of a feminine visionary, filled with special grace, devout, and humble, without any of the inconvenient, uncomfortable qualities of the prophetess. Men like the Baptist Henry Jessey could allow their wives and daughters to visit her without fear that she would teach them anything alarming. Men could live with the presence of women visionaries, provided that their dreams and trances were politically innocuous or exclusively spiritual. Intrusion into the male preserve of politics, however, was considered dangerous or suspicious. Women preachers were not only dangerous, they were monstrosities. Both preachers and prophetesses asserted a warrant beyond earthly laws and customs, and thus implicitly expressed contempt for man-made contrivances. For this they were ridiculed and feared. The evidence does not permit an estimate of how wide or deep or lasting the influence of these women actually was. Many in their audiences almost certainly came out of curiosity or malice. Those who listened sincerely were probably members of the preacher/prophet's own small religious community, and thus she was speaking to the already converted. There is even a strong possibility that their impact was largely negative—i.e., they antagonized more people than they converted.

The same might also be said of women writers of this period. During the sixteenth century, writing had become an accepted medium through which educated women could express their intellectual talents or religious commitment without inviting criticism for "unseemly" behavior. Royal and noble women produced books of devotion, epitaphs, and translations of religious and philosophical works. From the beginning of the seventeenth century, gentlewomen also appeared in print with collections of meditations and prayers and treatises of advice for the godly upbringing of children.[41] With the abrogation in 1641 of the strictures imposed upon the press, however, women from even lower social orders began publishing on a wide variety of topics.

This marked increase was closely related to the enormous overall proliferation of pamphlet literature during the 1640s and 1650s, a substantial amount of it by uneducated men. But one cannot make a simple analogy between increased men and women writers. Even barely literate men had always considered themselves entitled to write about whatever they pleased, provided they were willing to face the wrath of authorities. No doctrinal sanctions prevented them from entering their ideas into the public forum. Women, on the other hand, were not conceived to have opinions at all; and if they did, they were not expected to voice them in print. Thus, when some women suddenly broke with their traditional role of silent non-involvement, the historical significance is quite different.

Instead of avoiding controversy, some women writers seemed to welcome it, even to seek it out. Pen and paper became a practical weapon for pressuring all those against whom the author had a religious, economic, or political grievance. It was as Christians that these women were moved to call attention to social wrongs, to complain about economic hardships, to suggest political policies, and, above all, to debate doctrinal interpretation and church discipline. One reason why women were suddenly writing on more controversial issues is opportunity. The Long Parliament had allowed royal and ecclesiastical censorship to fall into abeyance in 1641—an action they quickly regretted, but not soon enough to recapture the initiative seized by clamorous writers and their printers, publishers, and booksellers. If a woman wished to publish her work, she only needed cash or connections to do so. Mary Pope, for example, paid the costs of her tracts herself; Anna Trapnel's were published with Fifth Monarchist funds; Katherine Chidley and her son had friends in the printing business even before they became Levellers. Only Elizabeth Warren went through the formality of having her tracts licensed by the government censors.[42] Women were frequently arrested for hawking pamphlets by known dissidents, but there are very few instances of a woman actually being thrown in prison for writing such tracts.[43] It was reasonably safe to write, therefore, although one might expect verbal or written abuse and ridicule for doing so.

Opportunity also existed in the sense that women, even some of the "meaner" sort, were educated enough to put down their thoughts on paper. Through listening or reading they were familiar with the Bible, printed sermons, and many of the current doctrinal disputes.[44] They were also conscious of the power of public opinion to bring about political and religious change. The desire to persuade or pressure assumes a cause worth espousing, and in the 1640s and 1650s such causes were plentiful. For the first time, women became involved, in part because the need seemed so urgent and in part because they felt that men were not working hard enough to resolve the important crises facing the nation. Thus, a group of women's tracts discussed the disposition of the King in 1649; petitions demanded an end to tithing; dire warnings told of the apocalypse to come if God's will was not immediately carried out.

Perhaps the most significant feature of these works is that they were intended to be read by men—by important and powerful men at that. Women addressed the King, the Lord Protector, Parliament, the army, and influential clergymen. They disputed doctrine with trained theologians, apologizing profusely to be sure, but nevertheless tackling the task.[45] For a feminine audience, more conventional works of devotion and spiritual autobiographies seem designed not only to inspire and comfort other women in spiritual distress but also to convert them.

Often reticent about revealing their personal lives in print, women writers usually displayed a suitably feminine modesty when speaking in the first person. A repeated theme is instrumentality: the Fifth Monarchist Elizabeth Avery, for example, considered herself, as a woman, to be a "weak and contemptible instrument of God's power." Mary Pope, whose *Treatise of Magistracy* was flaunted at the very doors of Parliament, regarded herself as a "contemptible woman;" and Susannah Parr wrote, "Weakness is entailed upon my sex in generall," although her own *Apologie Against the Elders* is characterized by a shrewd, hard-hitting style that is anything but weak.[46] Using the language of meekness and subordination, other women called themselves "handmaids" or "poor vessels." Undoubtedly, some of this rhetoric is an expedient bow to convention; nevertheless, many women—even most women—seem to have accepted their inferior status with resignation. Subordination defined them, but did not completely inhibit them.

Another unique aspect of the 1640s and 1650s is the opportunities women found to play a substantial role in politico-religious groups such as the Levellers and Fifth Monarchists. One of the most unexplained facets of Leveller history is the lack of detail about women's internal organization and functions, even though women undeniably were very active in the movement. Historical knowledge of their activities is largely confined to the

"Women's Petitions" and demonstrations at Westminster, which attracted a great deal of attention in the hostile press. Nevertheless, the reader is left with the impression of a very extensively organized network of women, capable of mobilizing thousands of signatures or markers on fairly short notice. Since there is no mention of women regularly attending the men's meetings, it seems likely that they met separately, exchanging their ideas and plans in shops, private homes, and sectarian churches.[47]

Both men and women members were swayed by the charismatic leadership of John Lilburne, and women appear constantly throughout his career as distributors of his tracts, testifiers at his several trials, and petitioners for his release from prison. Other women became involved because they were servants or relatives of Leveller activists, and this is especially true of the leaders' wives, some of whose lives were nightmares of sudden invasions of privacy in the dead of night. The impact of their stories, exploited by their husbands in the press, must have had a powerful effect upon other Leveller women, reinforcing their commitment to the party's political aim of justice for "free-born subjects." Although no demand for "women's rights" was ever formalized, even the most uneducated woman could understand and identify with the Leveller appeal and manifest her sense of grievance, not as a woman, but as a citizen. As Patricia Higgins observes, "The religious and political crisis caught up women, stimulated them into undertaking unconventional actions and into forming their own opinions on religion and politics."[48] The women's petitions reflect this intense interest and assert their equal interest in the welfare of the nation, their equal responsibility to call their attention to wrongs, and their equal obligation to support the army.[49] There is no evidence to establish whether men Levellers initiated the female petitions or whether they were generated by the women themselves. Whatever the relationship, women were without question treated as valuable allies in the cause. Their participation was permitted, even encouraged and solicited. They may have been auxiliaries, but they were also activists who carried their full weight and suffered persecution accordingly. At the very least, their involvement afforded them a constructive outlet for their grievances and enabled them to acquire some political experience and sophistication—a notable gain in a climate which denied both to women of all classes.

Like the Levellers, the Fifth Monarchy movement also involved a contingent of women in its activities. Two of its best known and most industrious members were the theorist, Mary Cary, and the prophetess/mystic/preacher, Anna Trapnel, but even on these two the biographical material is sketchy at best. For the rank-and-file female membership, the only insight comes from an odd notice here and there or from the spiritual testimony of John Rogers' Dublin congregation in 1650–52, a Baptist/Independent group which may have embraced some of the concerns and orientation of the Fifth Monarchists.[50] Intense religiosity and long spiritual battles, often going back to childhood, were characteristic of these testimonies, and women seem to have found in the Fifth Monarchist movement's millenarian tenets the religious peace of mind they had sought for so long. A program of preparation, of militant action, was extremely enticing to individuals who had suffered from feelings of uncertainty and helplessness for years and who could not find in this organization concrete assurance of their "election," together with the companionship and help of like-minded people engaged in work worth doing.[51] The actual roles women played are obscure. Trapnel was not only a seer, but a writer and an evangelist. Mary Cary, one of the group's most articulate writers, offered a comprehensive outline of the world they envisaged and even formulated a twelve-point corrective of current social ills, which included wage ceilings, a post office, and a stamp tax. She seems to have enjoyed the esteem of prominent sectaries, even if they did not necessarily endorse all her ideas and plans. If she played any part in the party other than her writing, the evidence does not indicate it.[52] Some of the freedom permitted to women in Rogers' congregation—they were allowed to vote and to contribute to debates on church matters—may have carried over into the Fifth Monarchist meetings, where women are known to have had their own assemblies. Close liaison between men and women is suggested by references to "the sisters," who served as custodians of documents, agents, and spies. They spoke in public and went to jail along with men rioters.

In both these movements, and in the Quakers as well, a certain "emancipatory" effect among women members very probably can be assumed, however limited their actual roles were. Working for a common cause made both men and women more tolerant, less suspicious and antagonistic of each other, at least within the group. Their shared sufferings gave them a commonality of experience and may have increased men's respect for their female colleagues, although the women were probably admitted in the first place because men perceived a use for them. Fulfilling that need, and perhaps going on to others, would have given women a sense of their own capacities and expanded their consciousness of the world outside the home and their personal stake in its affairs.

In sum, then, sectarian women of the 1640s and 1650s were enabled and emboldened by a unique sense of Christian mission to move into untraditional modes of religious expression. Within the sects, they found benefits unavailable to them in the conventions of the established churches: a demanding outlet for their energies, mental stimulation, excitement and adventure, a sense of belonging, self-confidence, recognition, and gratification at doing God's work.

THE RESTORATION ERA

What happened to this dynamism and these motives after the Restoration? The answer to this question seems to be that although visible changes in women's activities did take place soon after the return of Charles II in 1660, a good deal of continuity is also apparent. Ample evidence suggests that when the provisions of the Clarendon Code began to be felt painfully all over England, women Nonconformists supported their faiths as loyally as did men and bore the inevitable consequences as bravely.

In many dissenting congregations, the numerical preponderance of women members, noted in the earlier periods,[53] continued unabated. For example, eight women and four men were in the original founding group of the Bedford church of which John Bunyan was a later member; the 1673 and 1693 membership rosters indicate that there were still twice as many females as males.[54] Some of the respondents to the Episcopal Returns of 1669 (specifying the location and numbers of local "conventicles") may have had their own reasons for fudging on their size, composition, and ubiquity; but the figures strongly suggest that women not only attended these meetings in large numbers but also instigated them in the sense of opening up their homes to the outlawed sects.[55] This service was also in the tradition of earlier dissent, when willing hospitality was an important factor in perpetuating Puritan congregations.[56] In the Diocese of Bath and Wells, to cite a few examples, there were nine conventicles known to be meeting in the homes of women; in Norwich, eleven women offered their residences. Other women are listed as "great abettors," "principals," and in some instances "teachers." The congregations, whether Quakers, Baptists, Independents, Presbyterians, or simply "Fanatiques," are frequently described contemptuously as "of the common sort" or "vulgar" or "mostly silly women." At the end of the London lists (none mentioning a woman householder), there appears the laconic comment, "the generality of these Meetings consists of Women, & persons of meane ranke"—a composition echoed by the Winton Diocese compiler who estimated that "there are for the most part three or four women and children for one man."[57]

Women sectarians had unflinchingly suffered persecution in the early decades of the seventeenth century and even in the middle period, in the case of the Quakers, Ranters, and other radical groups. This kind of commitment continued in full measure. The torments of the Quakers have been graphically and amply described in a number of contemporary and modern accounts.[58] Suffice it to say here that women shared hardships completely with their brothers, fathers, and husbands—as indeed they had since the inception of the Society of Friends. The "weaker sex" was strong enough to face months, even years, in prison; loss of children, health, and property; and even death on the scaffold in order to testify to their faith. Social status meant nothing: Margaret Fell Fox went to jail as willingly and as matter-of-factly as did Quaker servant girls.

But women in the other sects also encountered great hostility "for maliciously and seditiously assembling in unlawful conventicles under pretext of religion." In the Baptist stronghold of Abingdon, Berkshire, one of the first to feel the heavy weight of government authority was Thomasine Pendarves, widow of the dynamic preacher, John Pendarves, and possibly a friend of the visionary Elizabeth Poole, who found that her past connections with Fifth Monarchists had made her a very visible focus of suspicion. Less prominent Abingdon women were also under surveillance—in the case of Katherine Peck, for many years.[59]

London women also had good reason to be apprehensive. A few females had been active in the Fifth Monarchist uprising of 1661, and the authorities did not soon forget the Cheapside termagant who spoke "most horrible and malicious speeches" against the King, or the woman reportedly taken "all in Armour," or the three women arrested and sent to the Poultry Counter with almost forty male rebels.[60] Suspected women supporters of the movement were still being arrested years later, including Ursula Adman, sister of prophetess Anna Trapnel, who was apprehended holding meetings at her Middlesex home in 1669.[61] Many of those arrested in London had had prior convictions, but heavy fines and months in prison apparently did not daunt them. Transportation to Jamaica for seven years was a new (and desperate) form of punishment, apparently reserved exclusively for intransigent Quakers, and women were not spared this extremely harsh form of repression. Responsibility for children or pregnancy did not prevent a woman Nonconformist from being fined exorbitantly or thrown into crowded prisons. While it was true that men also endured great hardships in jail, the effect of such an environment upon pregnant or nursing women must have been particularly grueling.[62] If a wife was not arrested herself, she sometimes spent weeks or months of frustration, anxiety, and humiliation trying to get the authorities to release her husband. If she could not obtain this, she might join her spouse in prison, sharing miseries but also alleviating the depression and loneliness which plagued long-term prisoners. Men such as Richard Baxter and Oliver Heywood gratefully acknowledged the comfort and spiritual support their wives brought into their bleak prison sojourns by actually sharing their quarters with them.[63]

Membership in the outlawed sects was an especial burden to women taught all their lives to be obedient and submissive. Family and community rules of affection and courtesy were often trespassed under the stress of religious intolerance. Agnes Beaumont's irate father locked her out of her home when she joined Bunyan's congregation against his will. So invidious was Bunyan's influence viewed by her neighbors that she was accused of murdering her father at Bunyan's urging; and although the coroner's jury exonerated her of encompassing his sudden death, she encountered continued family and community harassment and hostility.[64] Anne Wentworth, a visionary of the 1670s who was given to apocalyptical verse, suffered grievously for her religious convictions. Not only did her husband try to hinder her ecstatic writings by seizing her manuscripts, but he also made known his feelings about her dreams and revelations by his "fierce looks, bitter words, sharp tongue, and cruel usage." According to Anne, he was encouraged and abetted in this harsh treatment by his ministers and their London congregations, who diligently maligned her virtue, sanity, and spiritual health. Wentworth literally forced his wife out of their home and refused to take her back "unless I deny the Lord, and His Message, and avow to be deluded by a lying Spirit."[65] Anne's outburst was not directed against an orthodox Anglican congregation, as one might expect, but rather against the Particular Baptist Church to which she had formerly belonged. She insisted that she was being judged and condemned not only for differences in religious belief but also because she was not properly subservient to her husband and his ministers.

In some cases, even common decency went by the boards. The body of a newly dead Baptist woman was exhumed from the local burying ground in 1664 and reinterred at the crossroads, like a suicide or common criminal. Another woman was sent to prison for attending a conventicle even though her neighbors testified that she had given birth to a child early in the morning of the day of the assembly. Women in the throes of childbirth were turned out to lie on straw while all their linens and bedsteads were confiscated for overdue tithes and fines.[66]

Besides the continuity of membership and suffering, the post-Reformation era also saw continued writing, preaching, and missionary work by women Quakers. Margaret Fell Fox, for example, published her best-written work, *Women's Speaking Justified*, in 1666. Although her arguments are not especially original, her beliefs on the responsible role of women in religion do not simply gloss on female instrumentality—the uses to which the "weaker vessel" might be put—but affirm the positive attributes of women which fit them for duty and trust. A number of other Quaker writers of the earlier period persisted in their efforts (Rebecca Travers, Dorothy White, Mary Howgill) and new ones appeared in print (Elizabeth Bathurst, Anne Downer Whitehead, Dorcas Dale, Abigail Fisher, Theophilia Townsend). Like the earlier Quaker tracts, these are also chiefly apocalyptical proclamations, warning inhabitants of a particular area or the national leaders of present or future disaster. Much of this corpus is monotonous in style, unimaginative in content, incoherent in syntax—but worth reading simply because of the insight provided into the mind-set and sincere piety of these women pioneers and their refusal to surrender what they clearly saw as a mission to be "Publishers of Truth."[67]

Preaching by women continued also, although not at quite the feverish level as in the 1650s. One reason why so many women Quakers were thrown in jail was because they persisted in public exhortation; but the general trend during the last decades of the century was towards channeling female energy and enthusiasm into the institution of the Women's Meetings. A great deal has been written about these meetings and their consequences both for the women involved and for the Friends' Society itself;[68] but within the context of women's religious activities as a whole, a few relevant observations might be made. In the first place, even within a movement as radical as the Quakers there obviously were serious differences of opinion about the roles women could and should play. A few "dark spirits" felt that women were getting too much attention and autonomy, despite their active participation in the Society from its earliest days. Most of the duties assumed by the Women's Meetings seem fairly innocuous and well within traditional female nurturant tasks: relief of the sick, poor, and aged; education of children; alleviation of prisoners' needs. Even the instruction of less experienced wives and mothers by the older women was hardly radical or unbiblical. Eventually, however, the women became involved in certification, arbitration, supervision, and investigation duties,[69] which may have struck some male Quakers as giving them too much inappropriate discretionary—and very real—power. The women enjoyed autonomy, for example, in the administration of funds collected by themselves, granted to them by the Men's Meetings, or left to them in legacies. These amounted to a considerable purse of money and property over which the women had absolute and unaccountable control.[70]

Issues of power may also have been behind the objections to women entering into the discussions of the Six Weeks' Meetings (attended by both sexes) and to the separate Women's Meetings. Apparently, the objections to the latter also came from some women, since Fox once reprimanded "some women that denieth womens meetings yet will be at the heel of the quarterly meeting and would order it as they please."[71] From its inception, the Society had disciplinary problems with extravagant, ecstatic women; and since Fox was not notably successful in dealing with them, he probably felt that such matters were best left to other women, within the institutional setting of the Women's Meetings. It is quite possible that few other men were willing to delegate such a basic authority.

Women's preaching also came under criticism. Even in the 1650s there were objections to this activity, not only because of the women's sometimes wild behavior but also because they stirred up local hostility to male Quakers on missionary circuits. "Running out," the term for such shenanigans, was viewed with alarm and disgust by a majority of Quakers, and these feelings did not abate with the years. Perhaps, however, the definition of "inappropriate" was extended to much less frenzied exhortation. Anne Downer Whitehead sent out a lengthy warning against women who insisted upon preaching to win "popularity" or "to be seen or heard of men." Women speakers were advised to be brief—"no more words than the Lord requires"— and to refrain from burdening Friends with large retinues while travelling. Above all, young men and women must not journey together, as they often had in the early years. In 1701, the London Yearly Meeting decided to do away with the Saturday planning meetings of women ministers because they were "taking up too much time" and preventing "several public and serviceable Men Friends" from serving. Women who wished to preach at specific Sunday meetings were to leave their names at the central office—a clear case of "Don't call us, we'll call you," and probably a manifestation of competitive jealousy and assertion of control.[72]

If such changes could occur in a movement with a long history of women's full participation, it is no great surprise that other religious groups should also have suppressed unconventional female activism. The lack of tirades against Baptist or Congregational women preachers suggests that such missionary efforts had come to a halt—as had tracts on doctrine or practice by dissenting women. But if they were no longer writing themselves, Nonconformist women were active in publishing the works of others. Although very little specific research has been done on women printers, publishers, and booksellers, the evidence suggests that there was a group of women in London and elsewhere who carried on a brisk illicit publishing and selling trade. The best known of these was Elizabeth Calvert, widow of Giles Calvert, one of the most prolific publishers of the 1640s and 1650s. From the time of her husband's arrest in 1661, Elizabeth carried on the business and commitment to dissenting literature to which he had devoted his life. Even the deaths of her husband and elder son, the constant harassment of the government censor, the seizure of her presses, frequent imprisonment, and financial ruin did not stop this intrepid Baptist from printing books repugnant to the government and to the reestablished Church of England. Nor was she alone in this defiance. At least two other women had strong connections with Mrs. Calvert. One was Ann Brewster, widow of Thomas Brewster, who had been Giles' apprentice and then collaborator in printing surreptitious tracts. Ann took over the business after his death and suffered government prosecution for fifteen years. The second contact was Mrs. Susannah Moone in Bristol, widow of another former apprentice of Calvert, who received and distributed illegal books from Mrs. Calvert on at least one occasion.[73] Other widows of Nonconformist publishers were Ann Maxwell and Ann Ibbotson, both of whom entered into bonds of £200 not to print seditious material; the widow of Simon Dover (martyred in prison with Brewster and a colleague of Calvert), who was active in the operation of an illegal press in Blue Anchor Alley, a favorite haunt of Quakers and the remnants of the Fifth Monarchy party; and Jane Curtis, who carried on her husband's newssheet, *The True Protestant Mercury*, while he was in exile abroad. Arrested in 1682, Mrs. Curtis disputed the authenticity of the warrant and the authority of the court, refused to divulge her husband's whereabouts, and was thrown into jail. Tace Sowle, daughter of a notorious printer of Quaker tracts, inherited the business at his death and continued his commitment. Another Sowle daughter married her father's apprentice, emigrated with him to America, and set up a Quaker press in Pennsylvania and later in New York.[74]

These vigorous Nonconformist women could look back to the activities of similar women in the Civil War and Interregnum periods. Mary Overton, wife of the Leveller leader, defiantly carried on the party's propaganda machine during her husband's many incarcerations in the 1640s and also suffered imprisonment and humiliation herself.[75] The unknown but spunky Mrs. Edwards dared to publish under her own imprint the tracts of Mary Pope against the magistrates and even advertised that she was selling them. Mary Westwood specialized in Quaker materials. It may well be that the active commitment to their faith of these "ordinary" women of the middling and trades classes is a more remarkable and significant phenomenon than the more outlandish antics of the women preachers and visionaries who have caught and preoccupied the imaginations of contemporary and modern historians. If the seventeenth century was indeed a "man's world," and both men and women knew it, one needs to account somehow for these women who apparently paid little or no attention to the legal, economic, and religious restrictions which made them subordinate to men; who carried on their daily lives independently of these limitations; and who apparently felt there was nothing "unfeminine" or shameful about doing so.

The explanation seems to be that, although the sectarians and other radical politico-religious groups during the Civil War had little concern for or interest in women's issues or status *per se*,[76] their encouragement of women as participants had an unintended effect: women learned to allot their time and energies to tasks outside the home—missionary work, petitions, demonstrations, perhaps only sewing on badges or streamers—and thus to make conscious choices between loyalties and demands.

Even if they only thought of themselves as "God's instruments," they were still enlarging their horizons substantially. They did not have to be motivated by a desire for "equality" or to long for some undefined freedom in order to enjoy and benefit from the opportunity to share in an enterprise larger than themselves.

After the Restoration, loyalty to one's particular faith and desperate attempts to preserve it in the face of a government determined to stamp it out were the primary focus of many individuals, women as well as men. Survival was an all-absorbing occupation, and if it sometimes meant infringement of certain conventional ideas about appropriate behavior for women, as in the case of Elizabeth Calvert and her friends, that was unimportant. On the other hand, if female forwardness could hurt the cause, then it too must be suppressed—and thus the restrictions on Quaker women ministers. A few women protested, others turned to clandestine ways, and the majority, as always, went along with what their spouses, fathers, or ministers asked them to do.

Lower-class Nonconformist women in the later period had role models in their upper-class sisters. The inclusion of Presbyterianism within the general category of "Dissent" meant that a number of gentry and even noble women were now in the ranks of the outsiders. Early Puritanism had also included such women, of course, but during the 1640s and 1650s, as members of the church which replaced the Anglican Communion, they were generally found on the government's side rather than in opposition. Although gentlewomen usually had less to fear from harassment and prosecution than humbler women, they were still kept under constant government surveillance[77] and thus were also very conscious of the choices open to them daily to practice their faith and demonstrate their devotion to a cause that gave meaning to their lives. To poor women prisoners in London, for example, the compassionate visits of Mrs. Homes must have been comforting and persuasive, since state spies reported that "she gaines with her money serverall from ye Church dayly, and under pretence of Charity corrupts many and wanting people."[78] Although she and her colleagues may have pursed their lips and shook their heads over obstreperous women activists in previous decades, they would not soon forget their demonstrations of corporate strength and shared commitment.

In contrast, women in the restored Church of England led much quieter, less anxious (and less exciting) lives. In one of her books, Mary Astell, a devout Anglican, tells all that the Church of England required of a woman: "to know their Catechism and a few good Sentences, to read a Chapter and say their Prayers, though perhaps with as little understanding as a Parrot."[79] The contrast with the demands of the sectarians is striking and may help explain the flurry of proto-feminist books in the 1680s and 1690s by women who obviously found this regime tedious and unrewarding. These works, however, did not seek to overturn the social order and make women anything but the spiritual equals of men. As Joan Kinnaird points out in her study of Mary Astell:

They preached only equality of "souls," and hence, according to the philosophy of the time, equality of the rational faculties God had given to men and women alike that they might achieve personal sanctity. . . . The sexes were different in their equivalence—and so in their appointed tasks.[80]

This view would not have been repudiated by most of the tract-writing women or the petitioners of the 1640s and 1650s, for all their modest protestations of instrumentality and "imbecility." Astell advocated the total destruction of Dissenters as a party[81]— but she owed more to the example of their outspoken women than she would ever recognize or admit.

NOTES

1. Anon., *A Discovery of Six Women Preachers in Middlesex, Kent, Cambridgeshire, and Salisbury* (London, 1641).

2. *Journals of the House of Commons* (London, 1803): 4: 407, hereafter cited as *C.J.*

3. William C. Braithwaite, *The Beginnings of Quakerism* (London: Macmillan and Co., 1912), p. 445.

4. Ellen McArthur, "Women Petitioners and the Long Parliament," *English Historical Review* 24 (1909): 698–709; Patricia Higgins, "The Reactions of Women, with Special Reference to Women Petitioners," in

Politics, Religion and the English Civil War, ed. Brian Manning (London: Edward Arnold, 1973), pp. 178–222.

5. Keith Thomas, "Women and the Civil War Sects," *Past and Present* 13 (April 1958): 42–62; Levin L. Schücking, *The Puritan Family: A Social Study from the Literary Sources*, trans. Brian Battershaw (New York: Schocken Books, 1970); William Haller, *The Rise of Puritanism* (New York: Harper & Brothers, 1957), pp. 120ff.; Louis B. Wright, *Middle-class Culture in Elizabethan England* (Chapel Hill: University of North Carolina Press, 1935), pp. 201ff.; Charles H. and Katherine George, *The Protestant Mind of the English Reformation* (Princeton: Princeton University Press, 1961), pp. 257ff.

6. Ethyn Morgan Williams, "Women Preachers in the Civil War," *Journal of Modern History* 1 (1929): 561–69.

7. Christopher Hill, *The World Turned Upside Down: Radical Ideas During the English Revolution* (New York: Viking Press, 1972), chap. 15.

8. Higgins, "Reactions," pp. 179–82; Roger Thompson, *Women in Stuart England and America: A Comparative Study* (London: Routledge & Kegan Paul, 1974), pp. 12–13.

9. Claire Cross, " 'He-Goats Before the Flocks': A Note on the Part Played by Women in the Founding of Some Civil War Churches," *Studies in Church History* 8 (1972): 195–202; Jane Dempsey Douglass, "Women and the Continental Reformation," in *Religion and Sexism: Images of Women in the Jewish and Christian Traditions*, ed. Rosemary Radford Ruether (New York: Simon and Schuster, 1974), pp. 292–318; Katherine M. Rogers, *The Troublesome Helpmate: A History of Misogyny in Literature* (Seattle and London: University of Washington Press, 1966), pp. 135–59; Natalie Zemon Davis, "City Women and Religious Change," in *Society and Culture in Early Modern Europe* (Stanford: Stanford University Press, 1975), pp. 65–95; Richard L. Greaves, "Foundation Builders: The Role of Women in Early English Nonconformity," chap. 3 of this volume.

10. The standard general works on Restoration religion are C.E. Whiting, *Studies in English Puritanism 1660–1688* (London: Frank Cass & Co., 1968); and G.R. Cragg, *Puritanism in the Period of the Great Persecution 1660–1688* (Cambridge: Cambridge University Press, 1957).

11. Catherine Smith, "Jane Lead: The Feminist Mind and Art of a Seventeenth-Century Protestant Mystic," *Women of Spirit: Female Leadership in the Jewish and Christian Traditions*, ed. Rosemary Ruether and Eleanor McLaughlin (New York: Simon and Schuster, 1979), pp. 184–203; Hilda Smith, *Reason's Disciples: Seventeenth Century Feminists* (Urbana: University of Illinois Press, 1982); Joan K. Kinnaird, "Mary Astell and the Conservative Contribution to English Feminism," *Journal of British Studies* 19 (1979): 53–75.

12. Thomas, "Women and the Sects," p. 46; Greaves, "Foundation Builders," chap. 3 of this volume.

13. The most recent retelling of her story is Derek Wilson, *A Tudor Tapestry: Men, Women and Society in Reformation England* (London: Heinemann, 1972), pp. 155ff.

14. J. Gairdner and R.H. Brodie, eds., *Letters and Papers . . . Henry VIII* (London: HMSO, 1902; Kraus reprint, 1965), 18, pt. 2, p. 353; Irvin B. Horst, *The Radical Brethren: Anabaptism and the English Reformation to 1558* (Nieuwkoop: DeGraaf, 1972), p. 177; John Strype, *Ecclesiastical Memorials* (Oxford: Clarendon Press, 1822), 1, pt. 1, pp. 334–35.

15. For a good summary of the literature on Mrs. Hutchinson, see Lyle Koehler, "The Case of the American Jezebels: Anne Hutchinson and Female Agitation During the Years of Antinomian Turmoil, 1636–1640," *William and Mary Quarterly* 31 (1974): 55–56; Lyle Koehler, *A Search for Power: The "Weaker Sex" in Seventeenth-Century New England* (Urbana: University of Illinois Press, 1980), pp. 219ff.

16. See, for example, anon., *A Spirit Moving in the Women-Preachers* (London, 1646), pp. 3–5; [John Taylor], *The Brownists Conventicle* (London, 1641), pp. 2–3; John Vickers, *The Schismatick Sifted* (London, 1646), p. 34.

17. Thomas Edwards, *Gangraena* (London, 1646), 1: 84, 88, 116; 2: 28; 3: 22, 33–34, 80, 93; see the many references in Patricia Higgins, "Women in the Civil War Sects" (M.A. thesis, University of Manchester, 1965), pp. 99–100.

18. Edwards, *Gangraena*, 3: 170. Edwards had an ecclesiastical grapevine of correspondents.

19. Ibid., 3: 93; also "A Catalogue of Some Blasphemies of the Sectaries, not mentioned in the first nor second parts of Gangraena," unpaginated.

20. Robert Baillie, *Anabaptism, the True Fountaine of Independency* (London, 1646), p. 53; Edwards, *Gangraena*, 2: 116ff., Appendix, pp. 120–23; 2: 10–11; 3: 25–27. See Allen H. Gilbert, "Milton on the Position of Woman," *Modern Language Review* 15 (1920): 7–27, for a résumé of Milton's four divorce tracts.

21. *C.J.*, 4: 407; see Williams, "Women Preachers," p. 564, and Higgins, "Women in the Civil War Sects," pp. 53–67.

22. *A Diary, or an Exact Journal*, 22–29 Jan. 1646; Edwards, *Gangaena*, 1: 120 Appendix.

23. Male lay preachers were treated under the same basic criteria, but since men often could raise bond more readily than women, their imprisonments were shorter. Male Quakers refused bail as resolutely as did women and often supported their female colleagues.

24. Humphrey Ellis, *Pseudochristus* (London, 1650), p. 51. She bore a bastard child.

25. Richard L. Greaves and Robert Zaller, eds., *Biographical Dictionary of British Radicals in the Seventeenth Century*, 3 vols. (Brighton: Harvester Press, 1982–84).

26. Norman Cohn, *The Pursuit of the Millennium* (New York: Oxford University Press, 1970), pp. 298–301; Hill, *World Turned Upside Down*, pp. 200, 255.

27. The power of feminine weakness over masculine strength is a familiar theme in works of far greater literary merit: for example, Milton's views of Eve and Delilah. Cf. Rogers, *Troublesome Helpmate*, chap. 4.

28. See, for example, [Peter Hausted], *A Satyre against Separatists* (London, 1642), p. 3; anon., *Tub Preachers Overturn'd* (London, 1647), p. 15.

29. Thomas, "Women in the Sects," p. 51.

30. Anon., *A Looking-Glass for Good Women* (London, 1645), pp. 8–17.

31. For the origins and nature of these prophecies and visions, see Keith Thomas, *Religion and the Decline of Magic* (New York: Charles Scribner's Sons, 1971), pp. 128–44.

32. For example, Francis Bacon, "Of Prophecies," in *The Essayes or Counsels, Civil and Morall* (London, 1625).

33. Phillis Bird, "Images of Women in the Old Testament," in *Religion and Sexism*, pp. 67ff.; Constance F. Parvey, "The Theology and Leadership of Women in the New Testament," in *Religion and Sexism*, pp. 117–49; Russell C. Prohl, *Women in the Church: A Restudy of Women's Place in Building the Kingdom* (Grand Rapids: Wm. B. Eerdmans, 1957), p. 65; R.A. Knox, *Enthusiasm* (Oxford: Clarendon Press, 1950), pp. 19–20, 29–30; James M. Clark, *The Great German Mystics: Eckhart, Tauler and Suso* (New York: Russell & Russell, 1970); Brenda M. Bolton, "Mulieres Sanctae," *Studies in Church History* 10 (Oxford: Basil Blackwell, 1973): 77–94; Alan Neame, *The Holy Maid of Kent: The Life of Elizabeth Barton, 1506–1534* (London: Hodder and Stoughton, 1971), pp. 83–84; Rufus M. Jones, *The Flowering of Mysticism: The Friends of God in the Fourteenth Century* (New York: Macmillan, 1939), pp. 43–59, 224–33.

34. Hill, *World Turned Upside Down*, pp. 280, 286.

35. Alfred Cohen, "Prophecy and Madness: Women Visionaries During the Puritan Revolution," *Journal of Psychohistory* 11 (Winter 1984): 411, 426.

36. Phyllis Mack, "Women as Prophets During the English Civil War," *Feminist Studies* 8 (Spring 1982): 24.

37. Theodore Spencer, "The History of an Unfortunate Lady," *Harvard Studies and Notes in Philology and Literature* 20 (1938): 43–59; Theophilus Philalethes Toxander, *Vox Coeli to England* (London, 1638); Arise Evans, *A Message from God [By a Dumb Woman]* (London, 1653/4). See also D.P. Ludlow, " 'Arise and Be Doing': English 'Preaching Women' 1640–1660" (Ph.D. diss., Indiana University, 1978), chap. 4.

38. Even Anna Trapnel is best described as a publicist for the Fifth Monarchist cause rather than a leader.

39. James Fisher, *The Wise Virgin* (London, 1653); Geoffrey Nuttall, *James Naylor: A Fresh Approach* (London: Friends' Historical Society, 1954), pp. 9–10, 14; anon., *Satan Deluding by Feigned Miracles* (London, 1655).

40. Henry Jessey, *The Exceeding Riches of Grace Advanced by the Spirit of Grace* (6th ed., London, 1652); anon., *A Wonderful Pleasant and Profitable Letter Written by Mrs. Sarah Wight* (London, 1656).

41. Myra Reynolds, *The Learned Lady in England, 1650–1750* (Boston and New York: Houghton Mifflin, 1920), pp. 1–23; Ruth Hughey, "Cultural Interests of Women in England from 1524 to 1640 Indicated in the Writings of Women" (Ph.D. diss., Cornell University, 1932); Suzanne W. Hull, *Chaste Silent & Obedient: English Books for Women 1475–1640* (San Marino: Huntington Library, 1982).

42. For a larger discussion of these women and their writings, see Ludlow, " 'Arise and Be Doing'," pp. 41–48 and chaps. 3 and 5.

43. Anna Trapnel and Lady Eleanor Douglas are the only two cases.

44. Thompson, *Stuart Women*, chap. 9, is a recent survey of scholarship on women's education for the period.

45. The best known disputant is Katherine Chidley; Elizabeth Warren and Elizabeth Poole also discussed doctrine.

46. Elizabeth Avery, *Scripture-Prophecies Opened* (London, 1647), sig. A3^r; Mary Pope, *A Treatise of Magistracy* (London, 1647), p. 59; *Susanna's Apologie Against the Elders* (London, 1659), sig. A2^r.

47. Ludlow, " 'Arise and Be Doing'," pp. 242–59.

48. Higgins, "Reactions," p. 222. The hunger for charismatic leaders was also manifested in the many women followers of the Quakers George Fox and James Nayler.

49. There were four petitions by women: 24 April and 5 May 1649, and 25 and 29 July 1653.

50. Edward Rogers, *Some Account of the Life and Opinions of a Fifth-Monarchy-Man* (London: Longmans, Green, Reader & Dyer, 1837); John Rogers, *Ohel or Beth-shemesh* (London, 1653), pp. 407–17.

51. B.S. Capp, *The Fifth Monarchy Men: A Study in Seventeenth-century English Millenarianism* (Totowa, N.J.: Rowman and Littlefield, 1972), pp. 16–54, 174–75.

52. Alfred Cohen, "The Fifth Monarchy Mind: Mary Cary and the Origins of Totalitarianism," *Social Research* 31 (Summer 1964): 195–213.

53. Thomas, "Women in the Sects," pp. 44–45.

54. Cross, " 'He-Goats' ,", p. 200.

55. G. Lyon Turner, ed., *Original Records of Early Non-Conformity Under Persecution and Indulgence*, 3 vols. (London: T. Fisher Unwin, 1911–14).

56. See Greaves, "Foundation Builders," chap. 3. of this volume.

57. Turner, *Original Records*, pp. 5–12, 77–83, 90, 95–104, 108–21, 137.

58. J. Besse, *A Collection of the Sufferings of the People Called Quakers* (London: J. Sowle, 1733); Norman Penney, ed., *"The First Publishers of Truth"* (London: Headley Brothers, 1907); William C. Braithwaite, *The Second Period of Quakerism* (Cambridge: Cambridge University Press, 1961), Hereafter cited as *SPQ*.

59. E.A. Payne, *The Baptists of Berkshire Through Three Centuries* (London: Carey Kingsgate Press, 1951), pp. 44–46, 70. For the Pendarves-Poole connection, see Ludlow, " 'Arise and Be Doing'," pp. 228–29.

60. Anon., *The Last Farewell to the Rebellious Sect Called the Fifth Monarchy* (London, 1661), p. 7; anon., *London's Glory* (London, 1661), pp. 14, 16; anon., *London's Allarum* (London, 1661), p. 5; Champlin Burrage, "The Fifth Monarchist Insurrections," *English Historical Review* 25 (1910): 735–36, 744, 746.

61. Capp, *Fifth Monarchy Men*, pp. 239, 262, 264, 268.

62. John Cordy Jeaffreson, ed., *Middlesex County Records*, 4 vols. (London: County Record Society, 1888), vol. 3; Braithwaite, *SPQ*, pp. 40–52.

63. Whiting, *English Puritanism*, p. 107; Cragg, *Great Persecution*, p. 122. Mrs. Bunyan's experiences are reminiscent of Elizabeth Lilburne's lifelong career of interceding for her husband: Cragg, pp. 89–90.

64. Whiting, *English Puritanism*, pp. 122–23.

65. Anne Wentworth, *A Vindication of Anne Wentworth* (London, 1677), p. 5; see also Anne Wentworth, *The Revelation of Jesus Christ* (London, 1679), pp. 19–20. For comments on Anne, see Whiting, *English Puritanism*, p. 123.

66. Stories like this are not rare, unfortunately. See for example, Whiting, *English Puritanism*, p. 114; and Cragg, *Great Persecution*, pp. 44, 58.

67. See Hugh Barbour and Arthur O. Roberts, eds., *Early Quaker Writings 1650–1700* (Grand Rapids: Wm. B. Eerdmans, 1973); Luella M. Wright, *The Literary Life of the Early Friends* (New York: Columbia University Press, 1932).

68. For example, Braithwaite, *SPQ*, pp. 272–74, 286–88; Elaine C.

Huber, "A Woman Must Not Speak: Quaker Women in the English Left Wing," in *Women of Spirit*, pp. 154–81; Arnold Lloyd, *Quaker Social History 1669–1738* (London, New York, Toronto: Longmans, Green & Company, 1950), pp. 107–20; Mabel Brailsford, *Quaker Women 1650–1690* (London: Duckworth & Co., 1915), pp. 282–89.

69. Brailsford, *Quaker Women*, pp. 285–86.

70. Lloyd, *Social History*, p. 109.

71. Ibid., p. 110.

72. Ibid., pp. 113, 118; Braithwaite, *SPQ*, p. 287.

73. Altha E. Terry, "Giles Calvert, Mid-Seventeenth Century English Bookseller and Publisher" (M.L.S. thesis, Columbia University, 1937); Public Record Office, London, S.P. 29/209/75 I, II (Information from Bristol, 13 July 1667).

74. Henry R. Plomer, *Dictionary of the Booksellers and Printers*, vols. 2–3 (London: Bibliographic Society, 1907; Oxford University Press, 1922); George Kitchin, *Sir Roger L'Estrange* (New York: Augustus M. Kelley, 1913), pp. 113, 169, 304–5.

75. Mary Overton, *The Humble Appeale . . . of Mary Overton, Prisoner in Bridewell* (London, 1647).

76. Smith, *Reason's Disciples*, p. 56.

77. Turner, *Original Records*, pp. 178, 190, 248; Whiting, *English Puritanism*, p. 416; G. Lyon Turner, ed., "Williamson's Spy Book," *Transactions of the Congregational Historical Society* 5 (1911–12): 248–54, 301–7. Of the 112 names of "disaffected and dangerous persons" watched by the spies, twelve are women.

78. Turner, "Spy Book," p. 250. She may have been the wife of excluded clergyman Nathaniel Homes *(Dictionary of National Biography)*.

79. Smith, *Reason's Disciples*, p. 128.

80. Kinnaird, "Mary Astell," p. 74.

81. Ibid., p. 73 n.

5

"The Hidden Ones": Women and Religion in Puritan New England

Gerald F. Moran

In the last decade or two the birth and growth of a new genre of historical endeavor, women's studies, has had a profound effect on our understanding of American women in past times, especially in the late eighteenth and early nineteenth centuries. Mary Beth Norton's *Liberty's Daughters*, Linda Kerber's *Women of the Republic*, Nancy Cott's *The Bonds of Womanhood*, Mary Ryan's *Cradle of the Middle Class*, Carl Degler's *At Odds*, and other recent works point to the era of the Revolution and New Nation as a time of great transition for American women.[1] With the birth of the new republic, womanhood acquired a hitherto unknown political and social dimension, while motherhood became endowed with new meaning. To a society whose very survival now depended on the kind of habits and manners first nurtured and cultivated in the home, mothers, as guardians of the home, became indispensable. In the words of Mary Beth Norton:

In the prerevolutionary world, no one had bothered to define domesticity; the private realm seemed unimportant, and besides, women could not escape their inevitable destiny. In the post-revolutionary world, the social significance of household and family was recognized, and simultaneously women began to be able to choose different ways of conducting their lives. As a direct result a definition of domesticity was at last required. The process of defining woman's proper role may well have stiffened the constraints that had always encircled female lives, but that definition also—by its very existence—signaled American society's growing comprehension of woman's importance within a sphere far wider than a private household or a marital relationship.[2]

According to the same recent studies, revolutionary change in the lives of liberty's daughters was a drama that was played out on the stage of religion. At the turn of the eighteenth century, women gained a striking visibility in Protestant churches. Membership in various denominations became feminized, and women emerged as the pillars of the evangelical community, working through voluntary societies to bring about revivals. The American woman became the "guardian of morality, custodian of conversion, and cornerstone of society."[3] In the East, the South, and the frontier West, patriarchy in matters spiritual and educational lost ground to matriarchy, as mothers assumed increasing control of the moral, religious, and intellectual guidance of children. In time, women came to be considered by nature more pious and virtuous than men.

Unfortunately, recent work on the women of the Republic has been undertaken with little, if any, background information on the lives and experiences of their predecessors, the women of the colonies. While early Americanists were innovators in the "new social" history, exploring during the 1960s and 1970s the uncharted seas of communal, demographic, and familial history, they have lagged well behind their colleagues in women's studies. Witness, for example, the absence of women in Philip Greven's *Four Generations*, a book on the early New England family, or the lack of any reference to feminine experience in Patricia Tracy's *Jonathan Edwards*, a book on the social context of Puritan revivalism. Even Lyle Koehler's *A Search for Power*, a remarkably researched study of seventeenth-century New England women, is flawed for its treatment of feminine behavior as deviant, pathological, or proto-feminist in motivation.[4]

The topic of women and religion is thus a promising field of historical investigation for early Americanists. For one region of the colonies, New England, sources of a religious nature, including sermons, diaries, relations of conversion, and church records, seem suffused with a feminine presence. As this essay hopes to show, such sources indicate that in important areas of religion, such as church membership and lay piety, cracks in the foundation of traditional patriarchy were becoming visible by the time of the American Revolution, setting the stage for the transitions of the late eighteenth and early nineteenth centuries.

"The Hidden Ones," Cotton Mather called them. The women of New England, the Boston minister said, were the "People, who make no Noise at all in the World; People hardly Known to be in the World; Persons of the Female Sex, and under all the Covert imaginable."[5] Yet these "Hidden Ones," Mather realized years before he coined the phrase, could prove to be the church's salvation; "as there were three *Maries* to one *John*, standing under the Cross of our dying Lord," he observed, "so still there are far more *godly Women* in the World, then there are *godly Men*; and our *Church Communions* give us a little Demonstration of it."[6] The preponderance of churchly women in New England was a fact revealed to Mather in 1691, at the start of an era that witnessed the gradual discovery, then frequent extolment, of the Puritan woman of virtue. For the period 1668–1735, Charles Evans' *American Bibliography* lists fifty-five elegies, memorials, and funeral sermons for women in addition to fifteen other works of practical piety devoted completely or in part to females, with the bulk of these works appearing in print during the 1710s, 1720s, and 1730s. By the end of this period, New England women had acquired unusual visibility, thanks in large part to the efforts of several generations of Puritan ministers.

Using sermons and other tracts of the period, we can paint a composite picture of the Puritan woman of virtue. According to the New England clergy, a virtuous woman possessed a good mind and intellect, which she expressed in enlightened conversation and in attention to reading and writing. She was also cheerful and pleasant in character yet sober and reserved whenever circumstances demanded it. Though by nature "tender" and "weak," she had "a strong and noble soul." Moreover, she displayed perfection "under all the Characters & Relations of

Life": she was a kind and generous neighbor; a faithful friend; a dutiful wife; reverent and respectful to her husband; a keeper at home, a good manager of the household, "a lover of good Order, neat & cleanly," and mindful of all under her care, especially her children.[7]

But by all accounts, her "greatest glory" was her piety, for piety was "the *Root* and *Source* of all true Virtue" and virtue was the sign of saving grace in the soul. The pious woman, said the preachers, exercised her faith in a variety of ways: she attended the Lord's house on the sabbath and partook of the holy ordinances; she supported the ministry, spent every day in prayer, and read the Bible diligently. But feminine piety found its fullest expression in love of Christ and subordination to his rule. As Charles Chauncy, pastor of Boston First Church, said at the funeral of Mrs. Sarah Byfield in 1730:

Her *chief* Excellency, & what *most* recommended to all that knew her, was her *undissembled* Piety. She had an habitual prevailing Awe and Reverence of GOD upon her Heart: which *early* discovered it self, and *all along* thro' the Course of her Life, not only in an utter Abhorrence of every thing that savour'd of Prophanness & Irreverence; but in a due Treatment of those things, wherein the *Divine Honour* is nearly concern'd. She lov'd the House, & Sanctify'd the Day of God; gave her constant devout Attendance on the Public Worship, and all Gospel Ordinances; paid a singular Regard to the Holy *Scriptures*; valued the Minsters of Religion; and had an universal Regard to all good Men. But above all, CHRIST was the *Object* of her Love, her Faith, her Hope.[8]

One of the primary responsibilities of the virtuous woman was attendance on the Lord's Supper, which was attained only after passage through a rigorous test of regeneracy. As Cotton Mather told his female parishioners:

[The virtuous woman] cannot bear to be shut out from the *Church* of God, any more than *Miriam* from the *Camp* of old. . . . *Christian Women* would count it *Hell upon Earth* to be depar'd (from the church). She is desirous to *eat* and to *drink*, where she may not speak; and having been baptiz'd she is not satisfied until she come to *eat* among the *Friends*, to *drink* among the *beloved*, of the Lord *Jesus Christ*. She will not make Part of that *unworthy Croud*, which throng out of Doors, when the *Supper* of the Lord is going to be administered, as if they were frighted at it; or had Cause to say, *The Table of the Lord* is polluted. . . . Having had her Soul purify'd by *Regeneration*, she brings her *Offerings* to the *Tabernacle*. She presents unto the Church . . . a sensible Account, like another *Lydia*, of some never to be forgotten Things which *God has done for her Soul*; or at least, she makes the Church to understand, like *Ruth* of old, *That she would come to rest under the Wings of the God of Israel.*[9]

In praising feminine piety and proclaiming its importance to the life of the church, second- and third-generation New England ministers were elevating women to a religious status commensurate with that of men. To be sure, they never forgot that there was a darker side to feminine character, that it was the biblical Eve, the temptress, who seduced Adam into eating the forbidden fruit (a sin for which the "eternal pangs of childbirth" were considered a kind of postlapsarian penance) and that Satan often took the shape of a witch (the latter figure constituting one of the most formidable and powerful images of the late seventeenth century).[10] As John Demos has written of New England, "The culture at large maintained a deep and primitive suspicion of women, solely on account of their sex. Some basic taint of corruption was thought to be inherent in the feminine constitution."[11] Even the third generation Cotton Mather, the culture's spokesman for women, harbored suspicions of feminine piety, arguing that religious seducers "have a special Design upon the *Weaker Sex*, who are most easily *gained* themselves, and then fit Instruments for the *gaining* of their Husbands, to such Errors as cause them to *lose* their Souls at last. . . ."[12] Nevertheless, from the 1690s onward, the image of Eve the seductress slipped gradually out of the mainstream of pulpit oratory, only to be succeeded by the contrapuntal figure of the regenerate, virtuous woman, God's instrument for the conversion of men.

On a number of occasions Puritan ministers also came close to granting women equality with men in the area of parenthood. Especially in elegies delivered over the graves of departed mothers, preachers paid women homage for inculcating grace in children. Pious mothers, they said, possessed three attributes. First, they instructed their children in the ways of the Lord, teaching them their catechism and warning them away from sin. Second, they provided good examples to their young, reading the Bible through perhaps twice a year and paying a constant regard to religion. And third, they continually prayed for their offspring, "Travailing for the Conversion and Salvation" of their souls. Pious mothers, Cotton Mather wrote, "had a distressing Sollicitude upon their Minds for the *Conversion of their Children* unto GOD, & their Preservation in the *Right ways of the Lord*," and to illustrate this point he recalled the case of a woman who, according to her diary, had "kept a Day of Fasting and Prayer, That God would bestow special Grace upon all the Family; and that He would keep all our poor children, that not one of them should be Guilty of any *Scandalous Sins*, nor live in any *Secret Sins*." So heavily did the feelings of maternal responsibility weigh upon the soul of this mother, that she "was often afraid in having many children, lest I should have one more than Jesus Christ would accept of: But now I desire to believe for them all."[13] In this and other evidence from sermons and diaries we see the outlines of what might be labelled Puritan motherhood, which in time would be replaced by the more powerful and pervasive cultural ideal of Republic motherhood.

While in doctrinal matters ministers failed to distinguish between the sexes, their discussions of the sociology of piety seem decidedly sex-specific. When preaching about the social context of faith and piety, they tended to differentiate between a feminine and a masculine sphere of activity and devotion. Women, they maintained, exercised their piety in private, in the home or extensions of it, the clan or neighborhood, where they were expected to serve as extensions of the evangelical ministry, urging church membership on all family members, especially unconverted husbands. "Every *Paul* may have *Women that labour with him in the Gospel*," said one clergyman. "Vast Opportunities are those that a Woman has to bring over her Husband unto real and serious Godliness. And a good Woman will use those Opportunities."[14] Male piety, on the other hand, could be found both in private and in public places, in the home and also in the marketplace and workplace. Men were also obliged to work in the world for the support of the established church and its ministry.

At the same time preachers knew full well that the public

domain contained the greatest threats to piety and orthodox faith. In one Jeremiad after another they lamented that the religious ideals of the founders of New England had succumbed to the profane laws of the workplace and marketplace and to greed, materialism, and avarice. They sensed that, by pursuing their callings in public arenas, men were exposing themselves to piety's worst enemies. Wealth, for example, could subvert faith, unless it was put to work for the good of the church. As Thomas Prince said in an eulogy to Samuel Sewall in 1730, "He is put into the early Possession of *Secular Wealth and Dignity*; Nor this as into a Snare to ruin his soul, or make an empty show in the World, but as into a larger sphere and Power of employing his Talents for the Glory of GOD, and Advantage of Men."[15]

As they bewailed the profane distractions of the secular world, Puritan divines began to conclude that, by virtue of their isolation from public places and their confinement to the household, women were more prone to lead a life of piety than men. They also argued that the specter of death in childbirth made women more religiously inclined than men. As Cotton Mather observed in 1692:

It seems that the *Curse* in the Difficulties both of *Subjection* and of *Childbearing*, which the *Female Sex* is doom'd unto, has been turn'd into a *Blessing*, by the *free Grace* of our most gracious GOD. GOD sanctifies the *Chains*, the *Pains*, the *Deaths* which they meet withal; and furthermore, make the *Tenderness* of their Disposition, a further Occasion of serious Devotion in them. . . . And let me tell you, that most of you, have more *Time* to employ in the more immediate *Service* of your Souls, than the *other Sex* is owner of. You are ordinarily more within the *House*, & so may more mind the Work within the *Heart*, than we.[16]

Several years later, in 1711, Benjamin Colman of Brattle Street Church echoed Mather's sentiments regarding feminine piety. "More and more of the Life and Power of religion is with you, than with us," he told an assembly of women, and "it may be partly owing to your Retiredness from the Cares and Snares of the World. . . . " The "*Curse pronounc'd upon our first Mother EVE*," he explained, has been "*turn'd into the greatest Blessing to Your Souls.*" He went on to say that "Your frequent Returns in Your *Apprehension towards the Gates of Death, by which We all receive our*

LIFE, suitably leads you to a returning serious Tho'tfulness for your Souls and of Your Spiritual State." To these and other ministers women were not by *nature* more religious than men; it would take a later generation to arrive at that conclusion. Rather, the private sphere in which women spent most of their lives seemed most conducive to devotion to Christ.[17]

The extent to which preachers pondered domestic themes in matters of practical piety is revealed in their treatises on the doctrine of regeneration, which frequently employed metaphors drawn from domestic experience to explain the process of conversion to the unregenerate. With the passing of the founding fathers of New England, the theme of a just and vengeful God threatening to invoke the terrors of the law on wayward and degenerate children gave way to that of a loving and merciful Christ extending gospel promises to the faithful, and in time pulpit literature took on a more domestic quality.[18] In the evangelical sermons of the late seventeenth and early eighteenth centuries, regeneration was compared with a holy espousal and marriage with Christ, a wedding contracted in heaven. Impenitent parishioners were exhorted to partake of a mystical marriage with their savior, to become brides of Christ. They were also urged to join "Mother Church" and to participate in the ordinances of the Lord's "House." In one sermon a minister came close to comparing the actions of the Holy Spirit with those of the pious mother with her children, extending them comfort and encouragement.[19] In a sense, the domestic experiences of the woman in particular became the model for the regenerate Christian, inasmuch as the faithful were supposed to submit to Christ and his church as wives were to subordinate themselves to their husbands. Given this stress on a feminine-like dependence and humility in conversion, it would seem easier for women than men to achieve piety, since women need not undergo any shift in culturally-prescribed roles before regeneration.[20] Moreover, it appears that women were less reluctant than men to submit to the authority of the pastor. In any case, by the time of the Great Awakening of the 1740s, when evangelical emphasis began to be placed on the religious affections, preachers started using homiletic metaphors that seem from a contemporary perspective characteristically feminine. The new religion of the heart

would eventually evolve into the ideal of the woman who possessed a natural instinct for piety and morality.

Early New England sermons on the themes of the virtuous
woman and domestic piety were made possible by and gained
sustenance from an important change in the composition of
church membership.[21] As Cotton Mather observed in 1692, "Indeed, there are more *Women* than *Men* in the Church; and the
more *virtuous* they prove, the more worthy will the church
be . . . ," and to the accuracy of this observation quantifiable admission records testify.[22] Extant New England Congregational
Church records show that by the time of the second generation,
when the pious woman and the mystical marriage were becoming a part of pulpit oratory, membership was in the process of
becoming feminized. During the lifetime of the founders, the
sex ratio of membership was in most cases either evenly balanced
or tipped in favor of males. During the 1640s in New Haven,
Connecticut 63% of the church's first admissions were men,
while during the 1630s in Boston 53% were. But beginning with
the 1660s women became preponderant at admission; during
this decade the ratio of women to men in communion increased
to an average of 65% and hovered around that figure for the
remaining decades of the seventeenth century and well into the
eighteenth. In any given decade churches often admitted as
many as two women for every one man, or more. Thus, during
the 1690s in Salem First Church 76% of the new members were
women, while at the same time in Boston First Church 75% of
incoming communicants were women. With the onset of the
revolution sex ratios became even more skewed, as churches
began admitting an average of 70% women. During the late
eighteenth century and beyond, Protestant communions experienced an intensification of the process of feminization, but not
feminization as such.[23]

As is to be expected, the sex ratio of church membership varied
from time to time and place to place, often considerably.
Throughout the early eighteenth century, churches in first-gen-
eration towns located on the eastern seaboard admitted between
75% and 80% women in any one decade, a figure that cannot
be explained solely by an imbalance of females in the population.
On the other hand, second- and third-generation communities

located in the interior of New England added at times between 50% and 55% women. But the ratio of women to men among new members rarely fell below 50% and, more importantly, ranged in most cases between 55% and 70% per decade. A heavy preponderance of females at admission was the rule, not the exception.[24]

To appreciate the numerical significance of feminization, it is necessary to point out that the process was linked closely to generational cycles in new membership, periodic upsurges in admission, and Puritan revivalism. If religious declension had taken hold of Puritan New England, as some historians say it did, then feminization would have had little numerical importance and would have constituted only a minor story in the grand epic of the descendants' Brownian descent from the exalted grace of the fathers. But, as recent studies have shown, New England churches admitted substantial numbers of people after the lifetime of the founders, with adult saints in many eighteenth-century communities making up 40% to 50% of the adult population.[25] With the generational repopulation of churches, frequent revivals in admissions, and finally and especially the Great Awakening, which some historians have interpreted wrongly as having had a particular appeal to men, large numbers of females were brought into Christian communion with women from prior generations.[26] Moreover, even though women were more likely than men to disappear from membership because of higher mortality and emigration rates, many churches still contained at any given moment a preponderance of females in membership. As a result, by the time of the third and fourth generations, women had acquired a striking visibility and presence in the New England Congregational Church, this at a time of perceived deterioration in religious orthodoxy.

It is one thing to establish the numerical importance of feminization, another to determine its cultural and social significance. What did the heavy population of churches by women mean to the clerical establishment? What importance did it hold for the participants? In the eyes of the spokesmen of the culture, the established ministry, feminine piety was sufficiently vigorous and visible to require recognition and explanation, perhaps

even cultivation. Women were welcomed warmly into communion by ministers who valued their contributions to the per-
petuation of orthodoxy, notwithstanding the apparent apathy
of men toward the church. For ministers such as Cotton Mather,
a female-dominated church, if coupled with a vigorous feminine
spirituality, could advance considerably the cause of the faith,
especially among the unchurched men of the community.

Through alliances with enchurched women Puritan preachers
could hope to convert the many unregenerate men whose firm
support was so crucial to a parish's fiscal and political well-being.
In addition, female communicants who had submitted themselves to the discipline of the church were considered important
cultural role models, exemplars of the behavior expected of all
Puritan women. At the same time, membership held certain
rewards for women, not only for the obvious religious reasons
but also for social and cultural ones. It gave them a certain status
in the community they would have lacked otherwise, signified
their importance as carriers of the culture, and provided them
with a support network of peers, who according to the ideals
of the covenant had responsibility for mutual fraternity, care,
love, and charity. That these ideals operated at the level of practice is suggested by marriage, birth, and death scenes of female
saints lending a comforting presence to their Christian sisters.[27]

Before we speculate even further on the cultural meaning of
church membership for women, we need to turn to local records
for what they tell us about the social circumstances of admission.
Who were these women who were choosing to enter the church
and by so doing were contributing substantially to the vitality
of institutional religion, making it a live and vigorous orthodoxy?
The answer to this question can be found in vital records and
admission lists. They tell us that in most parishes, at most times,
outside the period of the Great Awakening when teenagers and
young adults flocked into the church, female candidates for admission were usually in their middle or late twenties, thus about
three years younger than their male counterparts. They were
also mostly married and also frequently mothers, with an average of one to two children. Some were pregnant, often for the
first time, when they became communicants. In other words, at

the time of their admission they had attained that stage of life American Puritans considered consonant with adulthood and the attainment of social maturity.[28]

For both sexes, admission into the church intercepted the passage from youth to adulthood. Except for being younger, usually by three to five years, females shared with males the same circumstances at admission. At no time and in no place did these circumstances vary appreciably according to sex. Men and women alike chose to enter communion upon attainment of parenthood, when it came time to think of the spiritual welfare and religious nurture of children and when women in particular confronted the fear of dying in childbirth. In contemporary terms, the attainment of membership coincided with the generative stage of psycho-social development.[29]

In a good number of families, parents shouldered together the mutual responsibility for passing the benefits of membership on to children, especially baptism. In Colonial Connecticut, for example, 55% of households contained enchurched husbands and wives. Many householders also chose to exercise their mutual commitment to family orthodoxy by joining the church together, on the same day. This happened in 29% of Connecticut church families. But in many homes men deferred to women in the area of institutional religion, giving over to them the responsibility of working through the church for the spiritual well-being of offspring; 45% of the families had only one adult in communion, and in 76% of these the one adult was the wife.[30]

These women were intent on becoming communicants even if it meant passing through church candidacy alone, exposing their piety in public, without their spouses.[31] To be sure, female candidates did not always cut a solitary figure in the meetinghouse on admission day, for on numerous occasions they were admitted along with other men and women, usually close relatives such as siblings. Moreover, husbands and fathers could have been orchestrating the religious activities of their wives and daughters backstage, out of sight of the record takers. Indeed, women faced strong cultural pressures to fulfill their Christian duty as mothers, pressures that men could withstand or ignore more easily. At least for one seventeenth-century Puritan woman, Elizabeth White, paternal pressure to "receive the

Sacrament of the LORD's Supper" at the approach of marriage was so intense that she risked eating and drinking her "own Damnation" rather than suffer her father's displeasure.[32] Whatever the nature and strength of these cultural imperatives, as feminization took root and spread, women were often found professing alone their faith and doctrinal knowledge in public during sabbath assemblies.

Considering the Puritan's powerful commitment to household religiosity as a wellspring of adult piety and the cornerstone of orthodoxy, the significance of maternal piety for the church and culture was profound. In many families the woman was the only professor of religion and the church's sole link to the householder who had worked through the church to preserve and perpetuate the religious traditions of the line, and she was the only link in the chain connecting one generation of church members to another. In some exceptional cases, successive generations of women constituted an uninterrupted line in the historical continuum of family belief and practice. Some historians, such as Edmund S. Morgan, have detected in seventeenth-century New England a trend toward religious inbreeding, but this was tribalism of an ironic kind for a culture that placed so high a value on patriarchy.[33]

Women were obviously fulfilling important roles in areas where the family and church overlapped. But what of their functions within the household, out of public sight? In one important area of family life, the religious nurture and education of children, women began sharing responsibility with men or perhaps began shouldering it alone. This should come as no surprise, since if we take pastors at their word, that parents often taught children by example, then the mother by virtue of demonstrated orthodoxy was fulfilling that role in splendid fashion. But actual practice is more difficult to decipher; it must be teased out of the sources and examined closely over time.

As some historians have suggested, the spiritualization of the household in Reformation England increased the wife's dependence on the husband in all areas, including that of education. But in a recent study, Margo Todd argues convincingly that Puritans inherited from the humanists the ideal of mutual parental responsibility for the religious nurture of children; on occasion the task even fell directly onto the shoulders of mothers, especially in cases of paternal dereliction of duty. Thus, as Thomas Paget argued in *Demonstration of Family Duties*, "if the governor be remiss or indisposed hereunto, then his wife or some other ought to put the work forward."[34] In early New England the ideal of mutual parental responsibility for education persisted, but as Congregational churches took root and became firmly established, they began taking over the religious indoctrination of children under their jurisdiction. As Lawrence Cremin and James Axtell have shown, ministers began adopting an aggressive attitude as catechists during the 1660s and 1670s, and families gradually gave their education tasks over to the church. A number of parish records show pastors organizing communities into age groups and catechizing them in separate sessions on the sabbath or on lecture days.[35]

It seems, however, that ministers rarely bothered instructing children under the age of seven, deferring instead to parents when it came to providing infants and young children religious nurture. It is also apparent that pastors expected children coming under their care to have had some prior exposure to doctrine and even a reading knowledge of Scripture. While they considered regeneration in childhood a rare occurrence at best (although belief in baptismal regeneration increased in popularity over the course of the seventeenth century), ministers still expected parents to prepare their offspring for the event of conversion at a very early age, first through discipline and then through instruction.[36]

Did parents live up to clerical expectations? If so, in what ways did they actually prepare children for pastoral instruction and the new birth? And upon whose shoulders did the chore of inculcating grace in children fall? These are not easy questions to answer, since few records speak to the inner life of the family. But some diaries and relations of conversion offer tantalizing glimpses of mothers socializing children in religion and teaching them to read at very early ages.

Listen to what Increase Mather, a second-generation New Englander, has to say about the educative influence of his mother on his childhood.

My mother was a very holy and praying woman. She had a peculiar love for me, and her affection caused her to be the more earnest in prayer to God for me day and night. I remember she has sometimes said to me, when I was a child, that she prayed but for two things on my behalfe, first that God would give me grace, secondly that He would give me learning. . . . Moreover, when my mother lay on her death bed, she did with much affection exhort me to resolve . . . to serve God in the work of the ministry; and desired me to consider the Scripture Daniel 12.3 They that turn many righteous works shall shine as the stars forever. And these were the last words which my dear mother spoke to me, the remembrance of which had had no small impression on my spirit. I was then almost 16 years old.

I lived in my father's family for 12 years, and I learned to read of my mother. I learned to write of Father, who also instructed me in grammar learning, both in the Latin and Greeke Tongues.[37]

Richard Brown, a contemporary of Mather, had similar recollections of his mother's powerful influence on him:

[I was] educated under the wing [of] my parence, especially of my mother, who was a pious and prudent woman, and endeavored to instill into [me] the principals of Religion and holiness; . . . she was unwearied in her watchings, instructions, admonitions, warnings, reproofs & exhortations, that she might bring [me] up in the nurture and admonition of the Lord, and continued she to train me betimes, and when she had caused me to read well at home, she sent me to school. . . .[38]

Mather's and Brown's sentiments on pious motherhood are echoed by diarists of a later generation, including John Cleveland, Nathan Cole, Isaac Backus, and David Ferris—men who came to maturity during the 1720s and 1730s. Their personal papers testify to the indelible impression mothers could leave on sons, who remembered them for their piety and their devotion to their children. Such evidence fits the homiletic image of the mother reading daily to her children and praying dutifully for the redemption of their souls.

Perhaps the reading ability of Puritan women should surprise us, for we have learned to regard their skills in this area as lagging well behind that of men. In a recent study of mark-signatures in Colonial America, for example, Kenneth Lockridge finds that only 30% of seventeenth-century New England women could sign their names as contrasted to 60% of the men. By the end of the Colonial period, mark-signature rates for women, especially in the port areas, had risen but still remained well behind the men's (90% among males versus 50% among females).[39] While Lockridge argues that writing and reading skills approximate mark-signature rates, and thus as few New England women could read as could sign their names, recent findings suggest otherwise. In a study of popular religion in eighteenth-century Scotland, T.C. Smout concludes, on the basis of a minister's "examination" of his parishioners' literacy, that only one-tenth of the women could write, but all of them could read. "There proved to be little connection," he concludes, "between ability to read and ability to write."[40] Relations of conversion presented before Thomas Shepard's Cambridge, Massachusetts, church during the 1630s and 1640s testify strongly to the fact that the printed word, including the Bible, catechisms, sermon notes, devotional works, and religious narratives of one sort or another, served as popular sources of spiritual inspiration, sources upon which women drew for religious guidance and comfort. Thus in her relation of conversion Goodwife Jane Holmes describes how she "began to read the word and began to think it good to follow the Lord," and while "reading Psalms" she felt the comforting and nurturant presence of the Spirit. Similarly, Brother Crackbone's wife, after "reading out of Mr. Smith's book that [the] Lord require me the heart and if heart given then eye and foot never given," wished the Lord's forgiveness for sin. In the same vein, Barbara Cutter, "by certain [sermon] notes . . . found that the saints sometimes took Satan's part if some affection and at other times not."[41]

One hundred years later, during the period of the Great Awakening, another generation of women found similar spiritual succor in the reading of the Bible and devotional tracts. Separate confessions of faith delivered by women to the Freetown, Massachusetts, church between 1749 and 1760 reveal the profound importance of the written word in the gestation and growth of feminine piety. In her relation of regeneration, for example, Rebecca Dunfey recounts how "by frequent hearing the Word

preached, and Reading the Scriptures and other good Books . . .
I was brought to see my self in a most sinful miserable and
undone Estate and Condition," while in her account of conversion Irene Shaw tells how she "took down my Bible and read
the 15th of Luk[e] & as I was reading I felt a Hope of Mercy and
an Heart to turn to Christ and trust him for Salvation." In a
similar fashion Sarah Davis, after experiencing "a great Change
in the Temper of my Mind," started "to read & hear the Word
and pious Discourse with a new Delight . . . ," while Sarah West,
thinking there was "no mercy" for her, felt "if I read or prayd
i sind in it & this greatly distrest me. But upon the 11th of Luk[e]
I was encouraged to Continue Seeking Mercy, specially by Those
Words I say unto you Ask & yee Shall receive etc."[42] These and
other relations point to the diffusion of reading literacy among
Freetown's community of enchurched women.

Further investigation into the female world of print in Colonial
New England might reveal that the ability to read was fairly
common among Puritan women. But what of writing skills? This
is an area filled with profound historical importance, but as yet
it has received little scholarly attention. According to Lockridge,
female mark-signature rates were on the rise in the eighteenth
century, with regions, especially the Connecticut River Valley,
an area noted for religious orthodoxy, leading the way. As explanation, Lockridge points to the increase in population density
coupled with the growth of public schools.[43] A more recent study,
however, suggests that another force was working to drive up
female literacy rates.

In the Connecticut River Valley parish of East Windsor, female
mark-signature rates rose rapidly during the early eighteenth
century, due largely to the efforts of the minister, Timothy Edwards, who after his ordination in 1696, adopted an aggressive
posture toward the education of the community's daughters. In
1700 East Windsor became a separate parish, but unlike Windsor
Center or First Society, where the town meeting managed the
school, East Windsor turned the responsibility over to the ecclesiastical authorities, namely the church and its minister, Edwards. "The ecclesiastical authorities under the overarching
authority of the town meeting," says Linda Auwers, "presided
over the changes in education. The church assuming control of

education had a predominantly female membership."[44] Whether it was Edwards' female congregants who prodded him into changing the existing educational system is an unanswered question. Unquestionably, though, New England ministers had a hand in the expansion of female writing skills through local educational efforts as well as pastoral evangelism. Some preachers, for example, encouraged their female parishoners to record in writing their religious experiences and relations of conversion, as was the case in mid-century Freetown. These efforts, in addition to growing leisure time for middle-class women, prepared the way for a marked advance in female literacy during the second half of the eighteenth century.[45]

Advancing literacy for women gave more and more of them the chance to develop an identity distinct from men's. The same can be said for a concurrent development, the growth of separate religious sub-communities. In the "conventicles" or extraparochial gatherings of the English Puritans, women were "often extraordinarily influential" and at times were granted freedom to "try their gift" for prayer in public.[46] In early New England similar "private Meetings" of "private Christians" existed, but to what degree is unknown. From the 1680s onward, religious societies or voluntary gatherings of the laity appear more often in the historical record, especially in the extant works of Cotton Mather, which contain numerous references to religious meetings not only of ministers and young people but also of enchurched women. Mostly the creation of ministers, these religious collegia, as they were sometimes called, often operated independently of the clergy, bringing neighborhood women together on sabbath evenings for prayer and mutual confession of spiritual needs and feelings. While the history of such groups awaits comprehensive study, it is well known that they grew in number and influence during the 1730s and 1740s, the era of the Great Awakening. Evangelical ministers, such as Jonathan Edwards, encouraged their use as instruments of pastoral evangelism, much the way nineteenth-century preachers did, even while realizing their potential for subversion of sacerdotal authority. Originally under the purview of pastors, the societies, as the Awakening intensified, began to take on a life of their own, giving women and other lay groups segregated according to age and sex the opportunity to conduct their own religious exercises. Not only did they antedate and predict nineteenth-century voluntary societies, which recent historians consider powerful instruments of female identity and evangelism, but in a sense they surpassed them as an expression of local spiritual and social concern.[47]

Frequently, lay associations provided the springboard for Separatist activities, which characterized the period of the Awakening and in which women played a conspicuous role. Female Separatists helped organize new churches and often composed a majority of their membership. They were also vocal challengers of the existing system, criticizing established ministers for being unregenerate and running headlong into the system for failure to fulfill ecclesiastical duties, including payment of taxes. In addition, they exercised prophecy and organized meetings in private homes for group devotions, out of sight of the Establishment. Thus, in 1752 the mother of Isaac Backus, the famed Baptist historian, refusing to pay parish taxes, ended up in the Norwich, Connecticut, jail with several other tax resisters for many days. In another incident, in 1751 two women were instrumental in the gathering of a church around the charismatic Baptist preacher, Joshua Morse, while another woman, Zerviah Lamb, a vocal critic of the Establishment, precipitated a major separation from the Preston, Connecticut, Separate Church, when at a November 1752 church meeting she exclaimed publicly "that Infant Baptism or Sprinkling was nothing but a Tradition of Men and Came from the Whore of Babilon: and that our Pastor was Not Baptized: and that She Never would Commune with us any More." In a related case, in 1754 Samuel Clarke and his wife withdrew from communion with the Preston Separate Church, joining up in time with three "Baptist brethren" and five "sistors" [sic] to form a new religious community.[48]

The Great Awakening represented a turning point of sorts for New England women; both the Baptist and Quaker churches, which grew as a result of the revival, had traditionally allowed women more public visibility than the Congregational churches.[49] A greater appreciation of woman's religious instincts also came about as a result of the Awakening, as did the sources for the development of a distinct feminine identity.

Yet in the period before the Revolution, limits to feminine

piety remained, as one revealing source indicates. In a remarkable series of letters written to a close clerical friend, Joseph Fish, Sarah Osborn reveals her compatibility with colonial women and her marked contrast with those women of the Republic who would succeed her. A resident of Newport, Rhode Island, for much of her life, Osborn, like many other women, entered the Congregational Church soon after her marriage in 1737. Several years later, with the onset of the Awakening, she found herself the leader of a religious society. "A number of young women, who were awakened to a concern for their souls, came to me," she says, "and desired my advice and assistance, and proposed to join in a society; provided I would take care of them; To which, I trust with a sense of my own unworthiness, I joyfully consented. And much we enjoyed in these meetings."[50]

The Newport society met off and on until the eruption of another revival during the mid–1760s, when it became active again under the leadership of Osborn. In the meantime, Osborn had become a prominent religious teacher to a number of town groups which she entertained at home. There she met with them almost daily, discoursing on doctrine and piety and extending to them the benefits of her own apparently keen religious insight.[51]

But these activities were circumscribed by fixed and rigid cultural and social boundaries. While she carried on enlightened correspondence with Joseph Fish, she felt moved on frequent occasions to defer to his judgment, especially in spiritual matters. While she took an active part in religious instruction and was obviously skilled at it, she never attempted to edify adult males, for she was conscious of the prohibitions against doing so. Only children, women, and blacks fell under her purview as teacher. While she engaged freely in social discourse at home and even exercised lay prophecy, she dared not carry on such activities outside the home, in public. At the same time, she struggled courageously to carve out of a life of toil some private space for personal devotion, especially reading and writing religious literature. In a moving passage she describes the lengths to which she devoted herself to this task:

The dawning of the day mr. Osborn rises while it is yet dark, can Just see to dress etc. From which time I am alone as to any interruption, for driven by infirmity and want to conveniency, I was about a doz years ago constraind to Make my bed my closet, curtains drawd Except Just to Let in Light. I do not lie there but turn upon my knees my stomach soported with bolster and Pillows, and I am thus securd from the inclemency of all Seasons and from all inturruptions from family affairs. There I read and write almost Everything of a religious Nature. Thus I redeem an Hour or two for retirement without which I must starve and this priviledge blessed by God I Have been Enabled to Hold thro all my Seeans of business, sickness un family only Excepted.[52]

Although Sarah Osborn was a unique woman in many respects, her religious activities and experiences reveal, as do sermons, church records, and diaries, the distance women had travelled in religious areas from the time of the Great Migration; and yet they also bear striking testimony to how feminine piety was hedged about by Puritan mores, even amidst the lengthening shadow of a revolution that would alter considerably the lives of pious women.

NOTES

1. Mary Beth Norton, *Liberty's Daughters: The Revolutionary Experience of American Women* (Boston: Little, Brown, 1980); Linda Kerber, *Women of the Republic: Intellect and Ideology in Revolutionary America* (Chapel Hill: University of North Carolina Press, 1980); Nancy F. Cott, *The Bonds of Womanhood: "Woman's Sphere" in New England, 1780–1835* (New Haven: Yale University Press, 1977); Mary P. Ryan, *Cradle of the Middle Class: The Family in Oneida County, New York, 1790–1865* (Cambridge: Cambridge University Press, 1981); Carl N. Degler, *At Odds: Women and the Family in America: From the Revolution to the Present* (Oxford: Oxford University Press, 1980).

2. Norton, *Liberty's Daughters*, p. 298.

3. Leonard I. Sweet, *The Minister's Wife: Her Role in Nineteenth-Century American Evangelicalism* (Philadelphia: Temple University Press, 1983), p. 6.

4. Philip J. Greven, Jr., *Four Generations: Population, Land, and Family in Colonial Andover, Massachusetts* (Ithaca: Cornell University Press, 1970); Patricia Tracy, *Jonathan Edwards: Pastor* (New York: Hill and Wang, 1980); Lyle Koehler, *A Search for Power: The "Weaker Sex" in Seventeenth-Century New England* (Urbana: University of Illinois Press, 1980).

5. Cotton Mather, *El-Shaddi. A Brief Essay . . . Produced by the Death*

of . . . Mrs. *Katharin Willard* (Boston, 1725), p. 21; Cotton Mather, *Bethiah. The Glory Which Adorns the Daughters of God. And the Piety, Herewith Zion Wishes to See her Daughters Glorious* (Boston, 1722), pp. 34–35.

6. Cotton Mather, *Ornaments for the Daughters of Zion, or the Character and Happiness of a Vertuous Woman* (Cambridge, Mass., 1692), p. 48.

7. See, for example, Thomas Foxcroft, *Sermon Preach'd at Cambridge After the Funeral of Mrs. Elizabeth Foxcroft* (Boston, 1721); Thomas Reynolds, *Practical Religion Exemplify'd in the Lives of Mrs. Mary Terry . . . and Mrs. Clissould* (Boston, 1713); Jabez Fitch, *Discourse on Serious Piety. A Funeral Sermon . . . Upon the Death of Mrs. Mary Martyn* (Boston, 1725). A later expression of the same themes is Thomas Foxcroft, *A Sermon Preached the Lord's Day After the Funeral of Mrs. Anna Foxcroft* (Boston, 1749).

8. Charles Chauncy, *A Sermon on the Death of That Honorable & Vertuous Gentlewoman Mrs. Sarah Byfield* (Boston, 1731), pp. 34–37.

9. Mather, *Ornaments for the Daughters of Zion*, pp. 29–30.

10. John Demos, *Entertaining Satan: Witchcraft and the Culture of Early New England* (Oxford: Oxford University Press, 1982), p. 391.

11. John Demos, *A Little Commonwealth: Family Life in Plymouth Colony* (Oxford: Oxford University Press, 1970), pp. 82–83.

12. Mather, *Ornaments for the Daughters of Zion*, p. 52.

13. Cotton Mather, *Maternal Consolations* (Boston, 1714), pp. 43–44.

14. Mather, *Ornaments for the Daughters of Zion*, p. 96.

15. Thomas Prince, *A Sermon . . . Upon the Death of the Honourable Samuel Sewall, Esq.* (Boston, 1730), p. 32.

16. Mather, *Ornaments for the Daughters of Zion*, pp. 48–49.

17. Benjamin Colman, *The Duty and Honour of Aged Women, Deliver'd . . . After the Funeral of the Excellent Mrs. Abigail Foster* (Boston, 1711), pp. ii-iii.

18. Emory Elliott, *Power and the Pulpit in Puritan New England* (Princeton: Princeton University Press, 1975), pp. 13–15.

19. Mather, *Maternal Consolations*, pp. 25–26.

20. Gerald F. Moran, " 'Sisters' in Christ: Women and the Church in Seventeenth-Century New England," in *Women in American Religion*, ed. Janet Wilson James (Philadelphia: University of Pennsylvania Press, 1980), pp. 60–63. A similar argument regarding the natural affinity between the woman's secular position and Puritan piety is put forward in Amanda Porterfield, *Feminine Spirituality in America: From Sarah Edwards to Martha Graham* (Philadelphia: Temple University Press, 1980), pp. 27, 50. As Porterfield says, "A Christian wife might be a model Christian, but a Christian husband had to relinquish his authority in his relation with the heavenly husband." (p. 50)

21. Lonna M. Malmsheimer has argued that "initial revision of seventeenth-century attitudes seems to have been stimulated by the growing predominance of women on church membership roles." Lonna M. Malmsheimer, "Daughters of Zion: New England Roots of American Feminism," *New England Quarterly* 50 (Sept. 1977): 487.

22. Mather, *Ornaments for the Daughters of Zion*, p. 9.

23. Moran, " 'Sisters' in Christ," pp. 48–53; Richard D. Shiels, "The Feminization of American Congregationalism, 1730–1835," *American Quarterly* 33 (1981): 46–62.

24. Moran, " 'Sisters' in Christ," pp. 48–53; and Gerald F. Moran, "The Puritan Saint: Religious Experience, Church Membership, and Piety in Connecticut, 1636–1776" (Ph.D. diss., Rutgers University, 1974), chaps. 4, 7; Shiels, "Feminization of American Congregationalism," pp. 47–57.

25. In 1712, for example, 43% of the inhabitants of Milford, Conn., belonged to the church, and the ratio remained around that level for the next several decades. Gerald F. Moran, "Religious Renewal, Puritan Tribalism, and the Family in Seventeenth-Century Milford, Connecticut," *William and Mary Quarterly*, 3rd ser., 36 (1979): 246, n. 26. In many other Connecticut communities a similar ratio of church members to population prevailed; see Gerald F. Morgan *The Puritan Saint: Church Membership and Piety in Colonial Connecticut* (forthcoming).

26. Cedric Cowing, for one, argues that the Great Awakening had a particular appeal for males. But see Shiels, "Feminization of American Congregationalism," p. 53; and Gerald F. Moran, " 'Sinners are Turned into Saints in Numbers': The Social Demography and Geography of Revivalism in Eighteenth-Century Connecticut," *William and Mary Quarterly* (forthcoming).

27. For the many visitations to the widowed and ill on the part of one Christian woman, Esther Burr, the daughter of Jonathan Edwards, see Sweet, *Minister's Wife*, p. 25.

28. These observations are based on an analysis of the town and church records of a number of Connecticut communities, including Windsor, New London, Woodbury, Stonington, North Stonington, Milford, Canterbury, and Suffield, and on the following studies: J.M. Bumsted, "Religion, Finance, and Democracy in Massachusetts: The Town of Norton as a Case Study," *Journal of American History* 57 (1971): 817–31; Philip J. Greven, Jr., "Youth, Maturity, and Religious Conversion: A Note on the Ages of Converts in Andover, Massachusetts, 1711–1749," *Essex Institute Historical Collections* 108 (1972): 119–34; Tracy, *Jonathan Edwards, Pastor*, esp. chaps. 4–5; James Walsh, "The Great Awakening in the First Congregational Church of Woodbury, Connecticut,"

William and Mary Quarterly 28 (1971): 543–62; William F. Willingham, "Religious Conversion in the Second Society of Windham, Connecticut, 1723–1743: A Case Study," *Societas* 6 (1976): 109–19; and Gerald F. Moran, "Conditions of Religious Conversion in the First Society of Norwich, Connecticut, 1718–1744," *Journal of Social History* 5 (1972): 331–43.

29. On the concept of generativity, see Erik H. Erikson, *Childhood and Society* 2nd ed. (New York: Norton, 1963), and Erik H. Erikson, *Identity and the Life Cycle* (New York: International Universities Press, 1959).

30. Moran, "The Puritan Saint," p. 345.

31. This was the case especially after the passing of the founders, when joint church candidacies became less common and more and more women became communicants without their spouses. See Moran, "Religious Renewal, Puritan Tribalism, and the Family," p. 253; and Barbara Ellison Lacey, "Women and the Great Awakening in Connecticut" (Ph.D. diss., Clark University, 1982), Table 9.

32. Anon., *The Experiences of God's Gracious Dealings with Mrs. Elizabeth White. As They Were Written Under Her Own Hand, and Found in Her Closet After Her Decease, December 5, 1669* (Boston, 1741), p. 4.

33. Edmund S. Morgan, *The Puritan Family: Religion and Domestic Relations in Seventeenth-Century New England*, rev. ed. (New York: Harper and Row, 1966).

34. Quoted in R.C. Richardson, *Puritanism in North-west England: A Regional Study of the Diocese of Chester to 1642* (Manchester: University of Manchester Press, 1972), p. 106; Margo Todd, "Humanists, Puritans and the Spiritualized Household," *Church History* 49 (March 1980): 18–34.

35. James Axtell, *The School Upon a Hill: Education and Society in Colonial New England* (New Haven: Yale University Press, 1974), chap. 1; Lawrence A. Cremin, *American Education: The Colonial Experience, 1607–1783* (New York: Harper and Row, 1970), p. 156; Ross W. Beales, Jr., "In Search of the Historical Child: Miniature Adulthood and Youth in Colonial New England," *American Quarterly* 27 (Oct. 1975): 381–98.

36. Gerald F. Moran and Maris Vinovskis, " 'The Great Care of Godly Parents': Early Childhood in Puritan New England," in *Child Development in the Past and Present*, ed. John Hagen and Alice Smuts (forthcoming).

37. Increase Mather, "The Autobiography of Increase Mather," *Proceedings of the American Antiquarian Society* 71 (1961): 278.

38. Quoted in Axtell, *School Upon a Hill*, pp. 174–75.

39. Kenneth A. Lockridge, *Literacy in Colonial New England: An Enquiry into the Social Context of Literacy in the Early Modern West* (New York: Norton, 1974).

40. T.C. Smout, "Born Again at Cambuslang: New Evidence on Popular Religion in Eighteenth-Century Scotland," *Past and Present* 97 (Nov. 1982): 121.

41. Bruce Chapman Woolley, "Reverend Thomas Shepard's Cambridge Church Members 1636–1649: A Socio-Economic Analysis" (Ph.D. diss., University of Rochester, 1973), pp. 116, 119, 128, 164.

42. J.M. Bumsted, "Emotion in Colonial America: Some Relations of Conversion Experience in Freetown, Massachusetts, 1749–1770," *New England Quarterly* 49 (March 1976): 100, 102–3, 105.

43. Lockridge, *Literacy in Colonial New England*, pp. 57–71.

44. Linda Auwers, "Reading the Marks of the Past: Exploring Female Literacy in Colonial Windsor, Connecticut," *Historical Methods* 13 (Fall 1980): 212.

45. Cotton Mather, for one, encouraged his female parishioners to record their religious experiences in writing. Sweet, *Minister's Wife*, p. 25.

46. Patrick Collinson, "Towards a Broader Understanding of the Early Dissenting Tradition," in *The Dissenting Tradition*, ed. C. Robert Cole and Michael E. Moody (Athens: Ohio University Press, 1975), p. 13.

47. For an insightful treatment of the New England societies, see Richard F. Lovelace, *The American Pietism of Cotton Mather: Origins of American Evangelicalism* (Grand Rapids: Eerdmans, 1979), pp. 215–24.

48. C.C. Goen, *Revivalism and Separatism in New England, 1740–1800: Strict Congregationalists and Separate Baptists in the Great Awakening* (New Haven: Yale University Press, 1962), pp. 195, 227, 235.

49. Mary Maples Dunn, "Saints and Sisters: Congregational and Quaker Women in the Early Colonial Period," *American Quarterly* 30 (1978): 582–601; Mary Maples Dunn, "The Role of Women in 18th Century Virginia Baptist Life," *Baptist History and Heritage* 8 (1973): 158–67.

50. Mary Beth Norton, ed., " 'My Resting Reaping Times': Sarah Osborn's Defense of Her 'Unfeminine' Activities, 1767," *Signs* 2 (1976): 517.

51. Ibid.

52. Ibid., p. 527.

6

Expanding Horizons:
Women in the Methodist Movement

Frederick A. Norwood

From ancient times women have been the mainstay of the church. From ancient times women have been denied access to governing power in the church. These two opposite and apparently contradictory themes dominate any discussion of the role of women in church history, including the history of Methodism. This family of denominations illustrates the way in which the tensions were being resolved, until by the later part of the twentieth century women had entered every part of the structure of authority and decision.

THE WESLEYAN TRADITION

The English setting was determined by the position of Methodism as a movement within the Church of England, in which both the Wesleys, John and Charles, were ordained ministers. The first consideration, therefore, is that the role of women found expression in and developed from their role in the Anglicanism of the eighteenth century. John Wesley clearly and firmly held the prevailing views against women in positions of visible authority. Paul's injunctions were taken seriously with little interpretive modification. As leader of the Methodist movement, however, Wesley learned how to interpret and adapt.

There were three powerful factors at work to modify the founder's views. In the first place Methodism was understood not to be a church but to be a movement within the church. Hence, what might not be formally admitted in the ecclesiastical structure could be accepted informally among the "people called Methodists." Equally important was a second factor, that of the "extraordinary call." This refers in the first instance to Wesley's own special mission as leader of the Methodists. This would eventually justify his ordination of preachers and his participation in the formation of the Methodist Episcopal Church. He was compelled to recognize an extraordinary call at another point, the admission of lay preachers. At first he was startled at the thought that an unordained layman might engage in leadership of a congregation to whom he preached. Wesley squirmed and hedged, allowing witnessing in informal groups but not preaching (that is, from a text). Yet he soon discovered that his lay "helpers" or "assistants" were good preachers, though not ordained. Hence the distinction between "preacher" (Methodism) and "priest" (Church of England).[1] One more step naturally led to the recognition of women as lay preachers. Although Wesley resisted the evidence for a long time, he finally admitted that women too could have an extraordinary call to do that which was traditionally prohibited, to speak in meeting, to testify in faith, to instruct—yes, finally, to preach (but still without a text).[2]

A third factor overcame any lingering resistance. Yes, he said, we are doing this only in our movement, and we have acknowledged an extraordinary call. But in addition there exists a present need, based on pragmatic considerations. Because the circuits needed pastors and leaders, he urged the appointment of lay preachers to serve them in itinerant ministry. The Methodists in the former Colonies needed the sacraments, hence preachers were ordained in order that they be served. Acknowledging that certain women, through the grace of God, had been called to the work of pastor and preacher, he encouraged them, for they were needed in class meetings and the societies. In all this Wesley clung to distinctions that were always melting away: societies rather than churches, testifying rather than preaching, or maybe preaching without taking a text.[3]

Wesley never had doubts about the general ministry of women as part of "the priesthood of all believers." They could and should minister to the sick and troubled,[4] and like all Christians they should minister to one another. Beyond this there lay an uncertain area in which women should tread cautiously. Wesley's advice to Sarah Crosby, whose success in itinerant ministry surprised and almost alarmed both of them, is a daintily balanced exercise in equivocation.[5] One may also mention Mary Bosanquet Fletcher, Hester Ann Roe Rogers, and Mary Barritt Taft.[6]

Susannah Annesley Wesley, mother of John and Charles, might be included at the head of the list, except for the fact that she always tried to keep the same distinctions of ministry which her son fought a losing battle to preserve. She never formally broke from the traditional place defined for her as wife of an Anglican rector. Yet her husband's extended absences afforded her considerable pastoral opportunity. Her role as mother of the family extended to that of spiritual guide, which stretched to include numbers of neighbors. Prayers and Bible study extended to formal worship and finally reached the liturgy of evening prayer—but in the rectory, not the church.[7]

More visible in terms of leadership was Selina Shirley Hastings, countess of Huntingdon, called by some with little exaggeration Methodism's first woman bishop. Malicious critics dubbed her "Pope Joan." She indeed administered the Whitefield branch of Methodism like an episcopal overseer. Of course she came to her position of influence and authority with the accoutrements of aristocracy, no small advantage in the eighteenth century.[8]

EARLY AMERICAN METHODISM

Aristocratic title, of course, played no part in the development of Methodism in America. Barbara Ruckle Heck was about as far from the social position of Countess Selina as it was possible to get. Yet she has been called, again without too much exaggeration, "the mother of Methodism in the New World." She grew up as a Methodist in Ireland and in 1760 married Paul Heck, who migrated to New York the same year. There she exercised that form of ministry best described as a burr under the saddle, urging Philip Embury to form a Methodist class meeting and thereafter to make himself useful in religious leadership. The Hecks continued to organize Methodist classes in the Champlain area and, after 1778, in Upper Canada in the St. Lawrence River valley. Heck had no pretensions to ministry or preaching, but her unflagging energy in fostering the societies long before formation of the Methodist Episcopal (M.E.) Church in 1784 has made her something of a "mother."

For almost a century the women of Methodism filled the traditional niches of local church worker, amateur deaconess, and minister's wife. Francis Asbury, heir to Wesley's disciplined view of the itinerant minister, was reluctant even to sanction the last-named role. He preferred his preachers to remain single, thus more freely appointable. The frontier did not lend itself to settled family life. Rare indeed was the woman able to surmount the multiple obstacles of tradition, male prejudice, lack of education, and the barbaric frontier.

Among the surviving names, that of Catherine Livingston Garrettson is outstanding. Daughter of a judge, descendant of a former governor of Delaware, and sister of Robert Livingston, one of the framers of the Declaration of Independence, she had many advantages. Subsequent to her conversion and membership in the Methodist Church, she met and married one of the outstanding itinerant preachers, Freeborn Garrettson, in 1793. Thereafter she provided a sort of headquarters for itinerants in the Hudson valley, used her effective influence for the spread of the movement, and kept a notable spiritual diary that survives (at Drew University). She outlived her husband by twenty-two years. A more average depiction of the life of a minister's wife in the mid-nineteenth century may be found in H. Eaton, *The Itinerant Wife: Her Qualifications, Duties and Rewards* (1851). This and other sources of the time gave little promise for women in the ministry.[9]

Here is another definition of ministry, that of hostess to itinerants and fosterer of faith, a role not limited to women of the parsonage. Prudence Ridgely Gough, wife of the owner of Perry

Hall, Henry Gough, provided a comfortable hostel for travelling preachers in the Baltimore area. In this mansion, plans were laid in December 1784 for the famous Christmas Conference, where the Methodist Episcopal Church was formed. But most resting points for the pioneer preachers were not mansions or stately houses along the Hudson but rustic log cabins or at best small dwellings in frontier villages. Who has preserved the names of those countless women who helped the preachers on their way, gathered class meetings in the wilderness, and in their lives gave priceless testimony?

There were occasional women remembered for services in Sunday Schools or local mission projects. Before mid-century, however, the few women who achieved some particular form of ministry were limited to groups other than Methodist Episcopal.[10] Jarena Lee, who died in the 1840s, was an early black woman preacher in the African Methodist Episcopal (A.M.E.) Church, as was Rebecca Gould Steward. Hannah Pearce Reeves preached among the Methodist Protestants, while Lydia Sexton received a license to preach among the United Brethren. Only after the Civil War did women in considerable numbers stand forth publicly in vigorous and effective, though still controversial, forms of service in the churches.[11]

INSTITUTIONALIZATION OF WOMEN'S WORK

Only four years after the cessation of the Civil War, the Woman's Foreign Missionary Society (W.F.M.S.) of the M.E. Church was formed. The next two decades saw similar developments by and for women in the separate strands of American Methodism. These were either missionary or educational in purpose. Each denomination presently had womens' foreign and home societies which grew out of scattered local groups with limited and specific purposes. One major concern of the women in all of these activities was to preside over an organization of their own. Repeatedly they were rebuffed by male leaders already established in their bureaucracies, who sought either to thwart separate organizations or to dominate them. Their favored form was the "auxiliary."

A desire for independent action was one of the motives in the formation of the M.E. Woman's Foreign Missionary Society in the Tremont Street church in Boston in 1869. One of the founders was Clementina Rowe Butler, wife of William Butler, missionary to India. Their daughter, also named Clementina, was executive secretary of the society from 1889 to 1933. From the beginning such women were able to retain full control of their organization and its finances. This is still evident in the Women's Division of the United Methodist Board of Global Ministries. The storm that assailed Boston that March evening in 1869 is symbolic of the struggles for autonomy. The women certainly did not stagnate once they organized. Within two months a new magazine appeared, *The Heathen Woman's Friend,* and before the end of the year the first two missionaries supported by the Society, Isabella Thoburn and Dr. Clara Swain, sailed for India.[12]

In spite of opposition within the church, by 1912 the W.F.M.S. enjoyed a large and wide-spread membership and contributed 35% of the entire budget for foreign missions. It was the largest of the women's denominational missionary societies and the largest of the women's organizations and clubs. Their reluctance to expand into home missions and social service is partly explained by the original understanding that foreign missions offered a special calling for women to deal with women. Also many middle-class women were threatened by radical feminism and social liberalism close to home. But individual leaders in this and other missionary societies were actively concerned about women's rights and social justice. The W.F.M.S. was not a refuge for tradition-bound conservatives.

The decision to restrict work to foreign areas left a gaping hole in the broader involvement of women, especially with freedmen in the South and with Indians and needy people anywhere. Among the local projects that appeared was social and educational work among women in New Orleans by Jennie Culver Hartzell, wife of a Methodist Episcopal minister appointed to that city. When the General Conference of 1880 failed to make any provision, a group of women met in Cincinnati and responded to a call by Hartzell for a home mission organization. The result was the Woman's Home Missionary Society, designed especially for work with women and children of all races anywhere in the United States. Under the prestigious leadership of Lucy Webb Hayes, wife of the recent president of the United States, the society coordinated and expanded existing welfare and educational projects and quickly added more. After a flurry of interference by the general Missionary Society which paralleled its attempts to control the foreign group, this new women's organization maintained its autonomy and provided another field for women's activities and careers.

Parallel organizations appeared a little later in the M.E. Church, South. The Helm sisters were among active participants in the organization of both foreign and home societies.[13] Lucinda Helm was secretary of the Woman's Department of Church Extension, organized in 1886, while Mary Helm was assistant secretary of the Woman's Foreign Missionary Society, organized in 1878. The former led to the establishment of the Woman's Parsonage and Home Mission Society (W.H.M.S) by the General Conference of 1890. Although the Board of Church Extension retained control of the "parsonage" aspect of the work, the women were relatively autonomous in their enlarged sphere of home missions. Both Sue and Belle Bennett were active participants.

Unfortunately the southern women were less successful in maintaining autonomy and control. Against strong opposition from the women's groups, the male power center in the General Conferences of 1906 and 1910 pushed through a reorganization in which the two societies were merged and placed under a central Board of Missions. There the women had only one-third of the members and their work was under a unified Woman's Missionary Council. Although influential and articulate Belle Bennett, president of the W.H.M.S., yielded at this time, she made her position clear on the rights of women in governing their own affairs. The southern women were less successful in retaining control of their own finances. When *Our Homes*, published by the W.H.M.S., was merged into the male-oriented *Missionary Voice*, Mary Helm, editor of the former, resigned. In this she was more rebellious than moderate Belle Bennett, who believed she could keep an effective voice for women in the church. The General Conference of 1910 recognized this, however reluctantly, by inviting her to address the Conference. She did so, making a strong plea for women's rights, especially as lay leaders in the church. The struggle continued until the lay rights of women were finally recognized in 1918.[14]

What women were up against in the South is illustrated by an article in the southern *Methodist Quarterly Review* in 1896 by Bishop R.K. Hargrove. He averred that

man and woman are each preeminent in their respective positions assigned them, while either would be inferior in that of the other. . . . There is nowhere in the Old Testament nor in the New an indication that God intended woman for priestly or ministerial functions . . . [though he listed services of hospitality, devotions, Sunday School, etc.]. Thus womanhood in these organizations sustains its proper relation to the ordained ministers of the word, not as invaders and usurpers of their peculiar functions, but, as God ordained, are *"helpers* meet". . . . [15]

The same process took place in the Methodist Protestant Church earlier and more rapidly. Although this denomination, founded in 1830 as a democratic movement, began with fine ideals of equality, women after a while had virtually no voice of their own. Between 1878 and 1892 this changed notably. The women had both foreign and home societies, with autonomy and control of their own funds. Women were elected as lay delegates to both General and Annual Conferences. They also began to enter the ordained ministry, although their status was uncertain.[16]

In the United Brethren and Evangelical Association the definition of women's roles was defined both positively and negatively between 1870 and 1910.[17] Both developed missionary societies. But from the start these organizations sailed in quite different ecclesiastical seas. Among the United Brethren the reception was relatively friendly, and the women acted with freedom. In the Evangelical Association, where a conservative German-speaking faction was still strong, the seas were stormy and threatening. The male Board of Missions controlled almost everything. The situation was complicated by the destructive effects of the schism in the church in the 1890s.

In one other area women entered positions of responsibility: education. Part of the story involves the opening of schools to women and the opportunities given for higher education. The record of Methodism here is an honorable one. The story also includes the entry of women into positions of educational leadership. That record can be neatly bracketed by the experience of two women in Evanston, Illinois, Lucy Rider Meyer and Georgia Harkness.[18] The former led the way in organizing schools specifically designed to train women for service in the church and thus to create new career opportunities. She opened the Chicago Training School in 1885 with minimal resources. For decades the school graduated young women trained in the basics of religion and the Bible to become deaconesses, missionaries, teachers, social workers, evangelists, musicians, and, yes, ministers' wives. The second institution was the New England Deaconess Home and Training School, begun in Boston in 1889. It had a strongly practical program but gradually developed an organized curriculum.

Belle Bennett was one person deeply influenced by Meyer. Encouraged by the promise of the Chicago Training School, she promoted a similar institution in southern Methodism. The result was the Scarritt Bible and Training School, founded in 1892 in Kansas City, Missouri, and later moved to Nashville. It was at first closely related to the W.F.M.S., but later expanded work in home missions. When the southern church provided for deaconesses in 1902, many were trained at Scarritt. Religious education was another of the school's special fields.

These institutions served an important function until well into the twentieth century and opened many doors for women to enter specific careers in the church. Educational developments and the Great Depression conspired to do them in. They finally merged with nearby educational institutions, except for Scarritt, which struggled on independently. The original purpose of these schools was the training of lay women for service as other than ordained clergy. Pressure for ordination of women, in fact, was one cause of their decline.

An instructive contrast is provided by the career of another famous Methodist, Mary McLeod Bethune.[19] Daughter of a devout Methodist couple, both of whom had been slaves, she dreamed of founding a school for black girls. With encouragement from Dwight L. Moody and Booker T. Washington, in 1904 she formed the Daytona Normal and Industrial School for Negro

Girls. In 1923 it became, under Methodist auspices, Bethune-Cookman Institute. Although she was an early black woman lay delegate to the General Conference and a member of the church's Board of Education, much of her work was outside ecclesiastical circles. Notable was the National Council of Negro Women. Tremendously influential, she lived until 1955.

In black Methodist churches the role of women was different. At no time during the nineteenth century and well into the twentieth were the traditional positions of authority in the African Methodist Episcopal, African Methodist Episcopal Zion, and Christian Methodist Episcopal Churches open to women. They were male-dominated groups, in spite of the heavy preponderance of female members. There were differences between the denominations as well as individual exceptions, but the power structure was composed of men.

In the A.M.E. Church, under pressure, special positions and activities were designed for women: stewardess, deaconess, and, with restrictions, preaching evangelist and missionary.[20] The General Conference of 1868 provided for the position of stewardess. Rather than opening new doors, however, the action confirmed women's subordinate position. It gave them neither wider role nor power. They were "assistants" who had "no legislative or judicial discretion," though it offered them a certain status. In the General Conference of 1900 another step was taken with the establishment of the office of deaconess. Although men were ordained deacons, deaconesses were not ordained. The new position gave no more authority in leadership than had that of stewardess.

Nevertheless, black women *did* enter visible and influential preaching ministries, but without official recognition and sometimes against opposition. Jarena Lee was the first known black woman evangelist. She asked Richard Allen for approval even before organization of the denomination in 1816, but he refused. Not until 1884 did the A.M.E. Church allow the licensing of women to preach. In the meantime they went ahead anyway. The most famous was Amanda Berry Smith, who was known throughout the country in the latter half of the nineteenth century. But the effort of Bishop Henry McNeal Turner to ordain one woman as deacon was rebuffed. The action of the General

Conference of 1884 in licensing women was strictly limited four years later to prohibit ordination. The creation of the position of deaconess in 1900 did not alter the situation as far as governing power was concerned.

Women were also involved in the development of other black Methodist groups. They were always active in the A.M.E. Zion Church, but not in positions of visible leadership. This church, however, nourished one of the most famous black women, Harriet Tubman, courageous in the anti-slavery campaign and the underground railroad. Women were also active in the Christian M.E. Church, which began in 1870 as the Colored M.E. Church. The same may be said of the "Spencer churches," so named after their founder Peter Spencer, the African Union Methodist Protestant Church (A.U.M.P.) and the Union American Methodist Episcopal Church (U.A.M.E.). Several women earned unofficial recognition as "Mother," but they occupied traditional female roles in the church. A significant development, however, which distinguishes the Spencer churches, was the approval before the Civil War of the licensing of women to preach. In 1852 the Discipline of the Union Church of Africans (predecessor of A.U.M.P. and U.A.M.E.) stated with approval the Quaker practice of permitting women to preach. Although apparently few women rose to the opportunity, the way was open to them in principle.[21] By the end of the century a number of women had been licensed and were active. Probably the best known was Lydia Archie.

No wonder that Theressa Hoover, speaking of black women generally but especially of those within the church, concludes that they operated under a "triple jeopardy": race, sex, and church.[22] The black woman "has given the most and, in my opinion, has gotten the least."

CAN WOMEN BE LAYMEN?

Some aspects of the role of women in positions of leadership have already been noted. A crucial issue, especially in Episcopal Methodism, was the place, if any, of women as lay representatives in the conferences of the church. This issue did not come alive until the admission of lay men as delegates after the Civil

War. Some of the smaller groups, especially the Methodist Protestants and the United Brethren, had made early advances. But
the classic struggle took place in the M.E. Church in the last
two decades of the nineteenth century and in southern Methodism a little later. The smaller denominations had a more open
view of lay participation generally and a more informal ordering
of the ministry. If lay men were to have a voice, could women
be far behind?

In the Methodist Episcopal tradition, still rooted strongly in
the Wesleyan (i.e., Anglican) understanding of ministry and lay
participation, the barriers were more formal and the mood for
change less lively. The effects of frontier life were felt locally but
not in the upper levels of organization. The dual struggles by
women and their supporters for lay rights on the one hand and
admission to clerical orders on the other went on at the same
time but were only indirectly related to each other. They were
long, frustrating, sometimes discouraging, and occasionally dramatic. Lay rights for women did not come into effect until early
in the twentieth century, first in the North, then in the South.
Ordination for women was not approved until 1956.

A preliminary skirmish occurred at the General Conference
of 1880 (M.E.), when Frances Willard was invited to speak on
temperance. She was already nationally famous as a leader of
the Woman's Christian Temperance Union (W.C.T.U.), in which
she had served as the influential corresponding secretary for six
years. Now in 1879 she was president of the national union, a
position she held until her death. She was active in the M.E.
Church in various capacities, including that of corresponding
secretary of the American Methodist Ladies Centenary Association for the centennial observances of 1865–66, that of President
of the Evanston College for Ladies, and subsequently that of
Dean of the Female College of Northwestern University. In the
W.C.T.U. she asserted a very broad sphere for activity including
many areas of social service and even political involvement.
When she arrived at the General Conference to speak, a lengthy
debate ensued, strongly influenced by James M. Buckley, the
redoubtable and conservative editor of the New York *Christian
Advocate*, over the propriety of allowing her ten minutes. Although the vote finally confirmed the invitation, Willard refused

to appear under these circumstances. She was appalled and disgusted by the obstinacy of the men.

Eight years later she was one of the five women elected by the Annual Conferences as lay delegates to the General Conference. The bishops set the tone in their episcopal address, which stated that the issue of seating the "elect ladies" must be made on the basis of the law of the church in the Discipline—which spoke only of laymen. Buckley made sure everyone understood what that term meant: it meant just what it said—the women were not seated. The furor continued through the next General Conference, where the dispute got bogged down in constitutional matters. Four women were elected delegates for 1896, but they withdrew at the outset for the same reason that Willard had refused to speak in 1880. Finally, when a new constitution was voted in 1900, "equal laity rights" were accorded to women members. The first women delegates were seated at the next quadrennial meeting.

A similar process went on in the M.E. Church, South, only later.[23] Reference has already been made to the roles of women like Belle Bennett in the work of the missionary societies. Many of them were also deeply involved in the struggle for women's lay rights. They faced resistance not only from traditional southern culture but also from an episcopal authority more strongly expressed than in the North. They carried on the struggle in the societies themselves and also at the level of lay delegation to the General Conference. A memorial prepared by the Woman's Home Missionary Society precipitated an immense debate both before and after, as well as inside and outside the General Conference in 1910. This was the occasion for the dramatic and effective address given by Belle Bennett—the first time in southern Methodism that a woman spoke in the conference. Although the memorial, which had requested full lay rights for women, was duly and expectedly defeated, the stage was set for the next effort. The slow culmination of the campaign came in the General Conference of 1918, which acted favorably on women's rights after only a half hour's discussion. The main question now was how to implement this decision. Even here the bishops tried to stop the action by declaring the vote of the conference unconstitutional. The delegates replied to this ploy with a roll-call vote of 270 to 50 against the bishops. The necessary approval by the Annual Conferences came through strongly. The struggle in this church, as in all the others, for full realization of the promise of the equality went on through the twentieth century.

ORDINATION

On the issue of ordination the pattern was more complex, because the various denominations responded in different ways. Again the major notes were struck in the Methodist Episcopal Church. The southern church heard about the idea of ordaining women but did nothing. The Evangelical Association did not even hear about it. The United Brethren and the Methodist Protestants are special cases.

The former group was well ahead of the rest in accepting and ordaining women as preachers. Although there is some vagueness about the action, the White River Conference gave to Charity Opheral in 1847 what amounts to a license to preach.[24] From 1851 on Lydia Sexton had a quarterly conference license but was denied one from the Annual Conference by General Conference action in 1857. The big change came with the new constitution (accompanied by schism) in 1889. This major shift included a provision on women as ministers: "She may be licensed to do so [preach] and . . . may be ordained after the usual probation." Within a year or two several women, notably Ella Niswonger and Maggie Thompson Elliott, were ordained. Sarah Dickey was ordained in 1894. Unfortunately, at the time of merger with the Evangelical Church in 1946, clergy rights for women were given up in the midst of embarrassing silence on the subject.

Much ambiguity surrounds the ordination of women among the Methodist Protestants. Central to the theme is the experience of Anna Howard Shaw, well known as a proponent of women's suffrage and other causes, both in and out of church.[25] A native of Michigan, she received a local preacher's license there in 1873. Five years later, she graduated from the Boston University School of Theology. With support from the school and the New England Annual Conference, she and Anna Oliver petitioned the General Conference of 1880 to authorize the ordination of women. When both were rebuffed, Shaw left the M.E. Church to seek ordination in the Methodist Protestant (M.P.) Church. That was done by the New York Conference in 1880, but not without difficulty. She was also unsuccessful in receiving regular appointments through the years, but she remained in good standing. Nevertheless, the General Conference of the M.P. Church did not support the action of the Annual Conference, hence the ambiguity. Shaw's comments on her experience confirm the uncertainties and reveal that she and Anna Oliver did not get along well. The latter remained in the M.E. Church and continued, unsuccessfully, to seek ordination.[26] Ambitious and energetic, Oliver pressed her case before the General Conference by all possible means. When she died in 1892, Shaw delivered a moving tribute.

Frances Willard joined the struggle in 1888 with a documentary book, *Woman in the Pulpit*. Had she not been otherwise occupied, she herself might have been interested in being ordained. In fact some of the most active and successful women were themselves not ordained; and some, such as Lucy Rider Meyer, Maggie Van Cott, Belle Bennett, and, later, Winifred Chappell, did not even seek ordination. The struggle for the ordination of women in Episcopal Methodism stretched down to the middle of the twentieth century, after three denominations (M.E.; M.E., S.; M.P.) had been merged to form the Methodist Church. The General Conference of 1956 finally removed all impediments. There remained only the task of putting the new opportunities into effect. This was almost 200 years after Barbara Heck prodded Philip Embury into action in New York. Is it any wonder that some women became impatient?

WOMEN ON THE "FRONTIERS"

Most of the women active in Methodism, whether lay or clergy, moved in the mainstream of church life. But in the later nineteenth century certain individuals stood on the "edges," right or left. On the conservative side were women who belonged to the holiness movement, which affected many denominations but was largely of Methodist origins and leadership and proceeded both inside and outside of the main groups.[27] Some of them were lay evangelists, some fully ordained.

At the center was Phoebe Palmer, lay woman in New York, editor of the *Guide to Holiness*, famous for her fine preaching at her "Tuesday Meeting" in which she promoted the doctrine of holiness or Christian perfection or perfect love. This work began in 1829. Thirty years later she wrote *The Promise of the Father*, which defended the right of women to preach in public. Here the doctrine of the Holy Spirit was important because it emphasized the direct individual call to the ministry apart from any ecclesiastical restriction. Palmer was undeniably successful. Here again was a special form of Wesley's affirmation of an "extraordinary call" which bypasses prejudice and ecclesiastical tradition. Characteristically, however, Phoebe Palmer never urged ordination for women. A call to preach through the work of the Holy Spirit was deemed more important than ecclesiastical procedures to confirm that call.

In the same category as Palmer was Martha Foster Inskip, wife of the well-known leader of the holiness movement, John S. Inskip. Even before the landmark National Camp Meeting at Vineland, New Jersey, in 1867, the couple worked together as a team. This continued till John's death in 1884. Thereafter Martha continued to be active in the movement as preacher and leader, but like Palmer she never sought a license to preach. The comment of a friend, "she never pretends to preach," must be understood in the context of Methodist preaching of the times. She used her numerous talents in gospel singing and work with children, thousands of whom were converted under her influence. A recently discovered diary, which covers the painful time of her husband's death, amplifies her significance and explains the degree to which she took up the work of her husband. The judgment of one scholar is that "John and Mary Inskip may be seen as forerunners of the modern concept of ministry—both of them as clergy couple, and she alone as woman in ministry."[28]

Probably the best-known woman evangelist was Maggie Van Cott, the first woman formally licensed to preach in the M.E. Church.[29] Born Margaret Newton, she came from an Episcopalian family. Converted under Methodist influence, she grew in faith. After her husband's death she joined the M.E. Church and began with singing, Sunday School, and prayer meetings. After 1868 she did evangelistic work full time, and in 1869 she was given a license to preach. Her successful work received a mixed reception in the Methodist press and church. She was seen as a threat to the traditional male pulpit. Hence the General Conference of 1880, which had denied ordination to Oliver and Shaw, also decreed against licensing women as local preachers. She herself, like many of the evangelists of the day, did not actively seek ordination.

Amanda Berry Smith, already mentioned, was a black woman evangelist. Under the influence of Phoebe Palmer and the Inskips, she embarked on a remarkable preaching career which extended to India and West Africa.

Among the smaller holiness churches which have Methodist roots, an early surge of feminism pervaded their development. Most of them arose in connection with issues of slavery and the Civil War. The biblical arguments against slavery carried over to arguments for women's rights. Not only were women active as lay leaders, evangelists, and lay preachers, but they also moved successfully into the ordained ministry.

Of particular interest are the Wesleyan Methodists and the Free Methodists. The Women's Rights Convention of 1848, held at Seneca Falls, New York, took place under the hospitality of the Wesleyan Methodist church. Luther Lee, a Wesleyan Methodist minister, was vigorous in defense of women's rights. When a woman was ordained an elder in the Illinois Conference in 1864, the General Conference refused to forbid it. Except for a brief prohibition in 1887, this was the stance of the denomination.

At the foundation of the Free Methodist Church in 1860, the right of women to preach was affirmed, but there was hesitation about ordination. Although B.T. Roberts advocated ordination without regard to sex, the denomination only came to that position in 1907, with the provision that the order of deacon was appropriate for women but not that of elder. This restriction remained until 1974. Roberts continued firm on full equality for women, writing a forthright book, *Ordaining Women*, in 1891.

The Church of the Nazarene, founded in 1894, gave women the right to preach as a matter of course. Many of them were ordained. One conference for a time had only women ministers. In 1905 Fannie McDowell edited a book in which they defended their role.

Many factors explain the openness to ministerial roles for women in these small groups. One was their tiny size, which encouraged informality and utilization of available resources. Another was the influential ministry of Phoebe Palmer in the larger M.E. Church. Her views and activities, tied to the doctrine of holiness, suggested that God called persons to leadership regardless of sex. The parallel between anti-slavery arguments and pro-women arguments carried great weight in the early years. Ultimately more important was the understanding that Pentecostal experience opens ways unknown in traditional circles.

In the twentieth century this eager affirmation of the ministry of women in the church was blunted. The early reformist spirit associated with the fight against slavery declined. The development of strong fundamentalist attitudes went counter to the views of women such as Roberts, nor did biblical literalism work to the benefit of women as leaders and ministers. Inevitably long-term cultural accommodation set in. As a result the number of women ministers declined noticeably. The holiness groups recently have had to rediscover their early openness to women.

On the other "frontier" were women who embraced the new liberal views. They tended to react against some aspects of the holiness movement, although some, such as Frances Willard, bridged the gap. They certainly opposed the tides of rigid biblical fundamentalism, joining with men as participants in the social gospel. One of the earliest and most important was Frances Willard, already mentioned as a feminist. As an influential leader of the Woman's Christian Temperance Union she adroitly moved the women to a more visible and active position on issues which went far beyond that of alcoholic drinks. Using terms that bridged the gap between traditional passivity and social action, such as "gospel politics" and "home protection," she effectively mounted a "Do Everything Policy."[30] This included investigation of the social roots of alcoholism, problems of labor and race relations, as well as the status of women. She was personally acquainted with labor leaders and supported the right to negotiate, including strikes, although she cringed at the thought of violence. "Home protection," for all its innocent sound, really meant the entry of women into politics.

The main impact of the social gospel, however, came in the

next century, especially in the Methodist Federation for Social Service. In that organization, the most effective participant, after Harry F. Ward and Bishop Francis J. McConnell, was Winifred Chappell, who served on the staff as research secretary and co-editor of the *Social Service Bulletin* from 1922 to 1936. After graduating from Northwestern University and the Chicago Training School she served on the faculty of the latter institution for fifteen years before going into partnership with Ward in New York. The *Bulletin* shows her mark year after year. In addition she investigated and reported on specific problems, such as political prisoners and strikes. A particularly poignant experience and report came from her involvement in the textile strike in New Jersey in 1926. She clearly sympathized with left-wing labor leadership. During the depression she supported many radical social causes.

A much less radical expression of social conscience may be seen in the careers of three Methodist women of the M.E. Church, South, all leaders in the Commission on Interracial Cooperation from 1920 to 1970.[31] They were Carrie Parks Johnson, Jessie Daniel Ames, and Dorothy Rogers Tilly. Moving into positions of responsibility for women's work in that interdenominational organization, they exemplified a growing awareness of social issues in the southern church. They were active in both the women's organizations of their church and in programs designed to deal especially with race relations, such as the Association of Southern Women for the Prevention of Lynching and the Fellowship of the Concerned.

In the mid-twentieth century probably the best known woman in the field of social ethics (as well as theology) was Georgia Harkness, professor of Applied Theology for many years at Garrett Theological Seminary and the Pacific School of Religion. Her first concern, which lasted throughout her life, was world peace: her pacifist stance was unwavering. She dealt forthrightly with problems of economic justice and race relations from the standpoint of Christian ethics. In the Methodist Church probably her finest hour was the recognition by the General Conference in 1956 of her part in winning full clergy rights for women, which was approved at that time.

The Wesleyan movement began in England and carried on in

America with a powerful force for the recognition of women in
the church as leaders and ministers: that extraordinary call which
gave John Wesley his authority to exercise leadership of the
People Called Methodists and his justification for ordination of
certain persons to provide sacramental ministry in the former
colonies. It also gave to his lay preachers the power of proclaiming saving grace and to women the right of participating along
with men. Moreover, in every step the need was clear. Finally,
the programs worked. All these factors gave promise that women,
long limited by ecclesiastical views largely inherited from the
Anglican tradition, would ultimately win equal recognition.

NOTES

1. A full discussion of this theme may be found in Frank Baker,
John Wesley and the Church of England (Nashville and New York: Abingdon Press, 1970).
2. John Wesley, *The Letters of the Rev. John Wesley*, 8 vols. (London:
Epworth Press, 1931), 5: 131.
3. For both English and American aspects a full bibliography is
available in, Kenneth E. Rowe ed., *Methodist Women: A Guide to the
Literature*, United Methodist Bibliography Series No. 2, (Lake Junaluska,
N.C.: General Commission on Archives and History, 1980).
4. See Wesley's note on Rom. 16:1 in *Explanatory Notes upon the New
Testament* (London: Epworth Press, 1952).
5. See Frank Baker, "John Wesley and Sarah Crosby," *Wesley Historical Society Proceedings* 27 (Decemler 1949): 76–82. Especially important
is her letter to Wesley printed as "The Grace of God Manifested in an
Account of Mrs. Crosby of Leeds," *Arminian Magazine* 29 (September
1806): 418–23, 465–73, 516–21, 563–68, 610–17; and Wesley, *Letters*, 4:
132–33; 5: 131.
6. An excellent recent study is Earl Kent Brown, "Women of the
Word: Selected Leadership Roles of Women in Mr. Wesley's Methodism," in *Women in New Worlds*, ed. Hilah F. Thomas and Rosemary
Skinner Keller, 2 vols. (Nashville: Abingdon Press, 1981–82), 1: 69–87.
These volumes are a landmark in research on women in Methodism,
especially its American side.
7. Frank Baker, "Susanna Wesley: Puritan, Parent, Pastor, Protag-
onist, Pattern," in *Women in New Worlds*, 2: 112–31, esp. pp. 119–27.
8. Mollie C. Davis, "The Countess of Huntingdon: A Leader in

Missions for Social and Religious Reform," in *Women in New Worlds*, 2: 162–75.

9. See Julie Roy Jeffrey, "Ministry through Marriage: Methodist Clergy Wives on the Trans-Mississippi Frontier," in *Women in New Worlds*, 1: 143–60.

10. For Jarena Lee and other women of the African Methodist Episcopal Church see Jualynne Dodson, "Nineteenth-Century A.M.E. Preaching Women: Cutting Edge of Women's Inclusion in Church Polity," in *Women in New Worlds*, 1: 276–92.

11. The even more restricted role of Methodists of Hispanic background is told in Clotilde Falcón Nañez, "Hispanic Clergy Wives," in *Women in New Worlds*, 1: 161–77.

12. Wade Crawford Barclay, *History of Methodist Missions* (New York: Board of Missions, 1957), 3: 139–48; Patricia R. Hill, "Heathen Women's Friends: The Role of Methodist Episcopal Women in the Women's Foreign Mission Movement, 1869–1915," *Methodist History* 19 (April 1981): 146–54; Norma Taylor Mitchell, "From Social to Radical Feminism: A Survey of Emerging Diversity in Methodist Women's Organizations, 1869–1974," *Methodist History* 13 (April 1975): 21–44; Theodore L. Agnew, "Reflections on the Women's Foreign Missionary Movement in Late 19th Century American Methodism," *Methodist History* 6 (January 1968): 3–16.

13. See Arabel Wilbur Alexander, *The Life and Work of Lucinda B. Helm, Founder of the Woman's Parsonage and Home Missionary Society of the M.E. Church, South* (Nashville: Publishing House of the M.E. Church, South, 1898).

14. Virginia Shadron, "The Laity Rights Movement, 1906–1918: Woman's Suffrage in the Methodist Episcopal Church, South," in *Women in New Worlds*, 1: 261–75.

15. R.K. Hargrove, "Woman's Work in the Church," *Methodist Quarterly Review* (South) 43 (1896): 3–14.

16. William T. Noll, "Laity Rights and Leadership: Winning Them for Women in the Methodist Protestant Church, 1860–1900," in *Women in New Worlds*, 1: 219–32.

17. Donald K. Gorrell, " 'A New Impulse': Progress in Lay Leadership and Service by Women of the United Brethren in Christ and the Evangelical Association," in *Women in New Worlds*, 1: 233–45.

18. Martha L. Scott, "Georgia Harkness: Social Activist and/or Mystic," in *Women in New Worlds*, 1: 117–42; Virginia Lieson Brereton, "Preparing Women for the Lord's Work: The Story of Three Methodist Training Schools, 1880–1940," in *Women in New Worlds* 1: 178–99; Joan Chamberlain Engelsman, "The Legacy of Georgia Harkness," in *Women*

in New Worlds 2: 338–58; Isabel Horton, *High Adventure: Life of Lucy Rider Meyer* (New York: Methodist Book Concern, 1928).

19. Clarence G. Newsome, "Mary McLeod Bethune as Religionist," in *Women in New Worlds*, 1: 102–16.

20. Dodson, "Nineteenth-Century A.M.E. Preaching Women," pp. 276–89.

21. Lewis V. Baldwin, "Black Women and African Union Methodism," *Methodist History* 21 (July 1983): 225–37.

22. Theressa Hoover in *Response* 5 (May 1973): 17–21.

23. Shadron, "The Laity Rights Movement." For the general process of change in Southern Methodism see Robert Watson Sledge, *Hands on the Ark* (Lake Junaluska, N.C.: Commission on Archives and History, 1975).

24. James E. Will, "Ordination of Women," in *Women in New Worlds*, 2: 290–99, gives an overview for the United Brethren. Cf. Donald K. Gorrell, "Ordination of Women by the United Brethren in Christ, 1889," *Methodist History* 18 (January 1980): 136–43.

25. In addition to her autobiography see Ralph W. Spencer, "Anna Howard Shaw," *Methodist History* 13 (January 1975): 33–51; Anna Howard Shaw, "My Ordination: Anna Howard Shaw," ed. Nancy N. Bahmueller, *Methodist History* 14 (January 1976): 125–31.

26. Kenneth E. Rowe, ed., "Discovery," *Methodist History* 12 (April 1974): 60–72.

27. Among recent research: Ernest Wall, "I Commend unto You Phoebe," *Religion in Life* 26 (1957): 396–408; Lawrence E. Breeze, "The Inskips: Union in Holiness," *Methodist History* 13 (July 1975): 25–45; Lucille Sider Dayton and Donald W. Dayton, " 'Your Daughters Shall Prophesy': Feminism in the Holiness Movement," *Methodist History* 14 (January 1976): 67–92; Nancy Hardesty, Lucille Sider Dayton, and Donald W. Dayton, "Women in the Holiness Movement: Feminism in the Evangelical Tradition," *Women of Spirit*, eds. Rosemary Ruether and Eleanor McLoughlin (New York: Simon and Schuster, 1979), pp. 225–54; Kenneth O. Brown, " 'The World-Wide Evangelist'—The Life and Work of Martha Inskip," *Methodist History* 21 (July 1983): 179–91.

28. Brown, " 'The World-Wide Evangelist'," p. 190.

29. See Dayton, " 'Your Daughters Shall Prophesy'," especially pp. 84 ff.

30. Carolyn DeSwarte Gifford, "For God and Home and Native Land: The W.C.T.U.'s Image of Woman in the Late Nineteenth Century," in *Women in New Worlds*, 1: 310–27.

31. Arnold M. Shankman, "Civil Rights, 1920–1970: Three Southern Methodist Women," in *Women in New Worlds*, 2: 211–33.

7

To Make the World Better: Protestant Women in the Abolitionist Movement

Blanche Glassman Hersh

Abolitionism in the 1830s began as a direct extension of evangelical Protestantism. Abolitionists were deeply religious people who viewed slavery as a sin against God and man. Conversion to the goal of immediate emancipation was the duty of all Christians and the only path to the redemption of mankind. Anti-slavery was a divine cause which they pursued with the fervor and zeal of true missionaries.

While men and women both participated in the anti-slavery movement, the experience of the male leaders in the movement was different from that of women leaders in a number of important ways. While the men were to be found in all of the Protestant denominations, women activists, regardless of their religious origins, were clustered in the liberal and radical sects. Male leaders were divided between the radical followers of William Lloyd Garrison and the moderate faction which, after the split in 1840, took the route of political anti-slavery work; women leaders remained entirely with the Garrisonians regardless of their views on the use of political means. The explanation for both these differences is the same: it was only in the liberal Protestant sects—and only in the Garrisonian wing—that women were permitted to move out of the traditional female sphere into the "male" roles of anti-slavery agents, lecturers, editors, and writers. Women who chose to stay with the more conservative abolitionists in the predominantly orthodox denominations remained in traditional subservient roles.

The Garrisonian women, forced to defend their right as women to speak out against slavery, became the leaders of the earliest movement for women's rights.[1] Because the attacks on them came principally from clergymen and because they themselves were deeply pious and felt a special moral obligation as women to combat evil, the feminist ideology they developed relied to a large extent on Scriptural sources.

Even the left-wing Protestant denominations, notably the Quakers and Unitarians, were often inhospitable homes for the early anti-slavery women and men whose views and practices were held to be obnoxious. Many therefore left the institutional church to practice a purer, more radical form of religion, rejecting the form but retaining the spirit of Christian perfectionism. To these reformers, efforts to cleanse their society of sin became, in effect, their religion. Here was the supreme irony: in order to work for their holy cause, they were forced to sever their formal religious affiliations.

One notable aspect of the Garrisonian crusade was the emphasis on the sin of racial prejudice in the North as well as slavery in the South. Though their goal of abolishing discrimination against the free black population was never achieved, they did provide in their own lives models of interracial friendships and associations which were at least as daring for the time as their defense of women.

It is these themes—the movement of radical abolitionist women away from orthodox denominations and ultimately away from the institutional church entirely, the development of the first feminist ideology in response to clerical challenges, the crusade against racial prejudice as well as slavery—that will be discussed in this essay. The first section will describe the involvement of the women in the anti-slavery movement; the second part will discuss the historical consequences of their actions both for reform and religion.

WOMEN IN THE ANTI-SLAVERY MOVEMENT

The campaign for immediate and unconditional emancipation began with William Lloyd Garrison, a Boston printer and journalist, in the first issues of his *Liberator* in 1831. Here he established the themes that would mark his controversial efforts and attract the small band of followers who would form the nucleus of his radical crusade. With fiery Calvinist righteousness, he denounced as blighted by racial prejudice the gradualist efforts of those who had supported colonization as a solution to the problem of slavery; only a commitment to immediate emancipation recognized the equality of blacks under God. Moral suasion was to be the prime instrument to bring about the conversion of northerners as well as southerners, since both were guilty of the sin of denying blacks their humanity. Garrison launched a particularly fervent attack on the churches for their hypocritical complicity with slavery and with the slaveholding mentality that permeated and debased the nation. In short, he issued a call to battle with evil as uncompromising as that of the most zealous evangelical.

Garrison made a special effort to appeal to women and to arouse their indignation and sympathy for the cause. His early issues contained a "Ladies Department" headed by a picture of a kneeling slave woman in chains and captioned with the entreaty "Am I Not A Woman And A Sister?" He implored his female readers to take note of the one million enslaved women "exposed to all the violence of lust and passion—and treated with more indelicacy and cruelty than cattle," and he urged them to work for immediate emancipation. He continued to pound away at this theme week after week in articles, speeches, and letters: "Women of New England . . . if my heart bleeds over the degraded and insufferable condition of a large portion of your sex, how ought you, whose sensibility is more susceptible than the windharp, to weep, and speak, and act, in their behalf?"[2]

The majority of New England women, like their male counterparts, were indifferent or hostile to Garrison's appeal. A few unusual Boston women, however, responded enthusiastically and became his staunch supporters. The abolitionist cause changed their lives drastically, moving them from positions of status and respectability to places among the outcasts and the martyrs of their society. They, in turn, transformed the traditional auxiliary role of women in anti-slavery into a more active, independent force in the next decade. Two of these women were Maria Weston Chapman and Lydia Maria Child.

Maria Weston Chapman was one of the first to respond to Garrison's appeal and became a leader in his campaign. A strong-minded and elegant young matron from one of the first families of Boston, she and her merchant husband were members of William Ellery Channing's Unitarian Church, but she brought a flaming Calvinist spirit to the struggle against those who lagged in their Christian duty. Her grandson, the critic and writer John Jay Chapman, described her as a heroic and noble type who looked like a cameo but was a "doughty swordswoman" in conversation. She always "flashed the sword of Gideon," he recalled, whenever the Garrisonians were attacked, and was "more religious than the Pope himself" in her single-minded devotion to the cause."[3]

In 1832 Chapman and three of her sisters led in organizing the Boston Female Anti-Slavery Society, which would become one of the two major centers of radical female abolitionism in the 1830s. Like its parent group, the male New England Anti-Slavery Society, it was racially integrated from its founding.[4]

Lydia Maria Child was a talented writer who had achieved some degree of fame as the author of several romantic novels and a popular cookbook. She was also the editor of the first American periodical for children, *Juvenile Miscellany*. The descendant of an early Puritan family, she converted to Unitarianism under the influence of her brother, a minister in that faith. Through her husband, she met Garrison who "got hold of the strings of my conscience and pulled me into reforms. . . . Old dreams vanished, old associates departed, and all things became new."[5]

Child antagonized Boston literary circles and jeopardized her career when, in 1833, she wrote *An Appeal on Behalf of That Class of Americans Called Africans*, the first anti-slavery work to be published in book form in this country. This work, which had a strong impact on Channing and other distinguished Bostonians, was notable for its condemnation of racial prejudice in the North. Child documented her attack by compiling facts on the treatment of free blacks in the schools, churches, and public accommodations, as well as on the illegality of interracial marriages. She concluded with the prediction that "public opinion is on the verge of a great change." She felt that anti-slavery reformers would be successful because "God and truth is on their side."[6]

The other nucleus of female activism was in Philadelphia, where Lucretia Coffin Mott presided as the moving force. Tiny but with a commanding presence, she was a minister in the Society of Friends who, with her husband James, had been involved with anti-slavery since the 1820s. Their home was a focal point of the underground railroad which helped fugitive slaves, and it became the Philadelphia outpost of Garrisonian abolitionism.

Following the example of the Boston women, Lucretia Mott and sister Friends organized the Philadelphia Female Anti-Slavery Society in 1833, immediately after the first convention there of the American Anti-Slavery Society. Like the Boston group, the Philadelphia female society was a biracial group whose founding members included four Afro-American women. Sarah Mapps Douglass was a teacher who came from a prominent free black Philadelphia Quaker family. The three Forten sisters— Sarah, Margaretta, and Harriet—were the daughters of wealthy black shipbuilder James Forten, Sr., a principal financial supporter of Garrison. Harriet was married to Robert Purvis, also a Garrisonian abolitionist and a leader in the effort to aid fugitive slaves. Three generations of the Forten-Purvis family were active in anti-slavery as well as women's rights and other reforms.[7]

The Boston and Philadelphia female anti-slavery societies, led by women who disputed traditional social roles and customs as well as orthodox religious beliefs, were to perform a vital function in the next decade. They raised funds and provided much of the financial support for the movement. They organized new groups and played an important role in the effort to transform public opinion on the slavery issue. They were also crucial in the political campaign to circulate petitions to Congress, a significant extension of woman's role into the public sphere. Hundreds of thousands of signatures were gathered, usually by the painstaking and often traumatic method of going door-to-door, facing the rejection and opprobrium of friends and neighbors.[8]

A third important locus of anti-slavery work was New York City, but here the male leaders were orthodox evangelicals, including a group who had been converted by Charles Grandison Finney. Though devoted in their abolitionism, they were conservative in their views on woman's proper sphere and opposed efforts to expand women's role in anti-slavery. Following the dictates of their husbands and fathers, the Ladies' New York City Anti-Slavery Society, unlike their sisters in Boston and Philadelphia, remained in a traditionally subordinate role. Also unlike their radical sisters, they were organized in separate white and "colored" societies.[9]

An unlikely addition to the radical abolitionist women in the 1830s were Sarah and Angelina Grimké, extraordinary emigrants from an aristocratic slaveholding family in Charleston, South Carolina. They became, for a brief time, the center of attention in anti-slavery and were influential in shaping the future of the movement. They would follow the somewhat unusual religious route of conversion from Episcopalians to Presbyterians to Quakers, and, finally, to a radical, highly devout form of non-church-going private faith.

The experience of Sarah and Angelina Grimké, though atypical in other ways, does illustrate all the themes of this essay and therefore merits detailed attention. In 1836, when they became actively involved in anti-slavery, they were ages forty-four and thirty-one. Sarah, the elder, had been frustrated in her childhood by the lack of opportunity for women to pursue a useful calling as well as by the injustice of the slave system. Deeply religious, she sought an activity that would give her life meaning. Accompanying her sick father to Philadelphia in 1818 for medical consultation and then remaining alone with him for many months until his death was a cataclysmic experience for her. The trip also brought her first contact with the Society of Friends. Three years later, after much reading and tormented soul-searching, she announced to her family that she had been called to go north and become a Quaker. Once there, she faced further frustration in her efforts to be designated a Quaker minister, having inadvertently become involved in the political rift within the Friends which finally ended, in 1828, in an open split into Orthodox and Hicksite factions.[10]

Angelina Grimké, more self-assured than her older sister, was spared the trauma of self-doubt. From her early years she exhibited a sense of divine mission which guided her in unorthodox pursuits. At thirteen, she firmly refused to go through with the confirmation ceremony because she did not agree with the pledge required in the Episcopal faith. After she converted to Presbyterianism, she threw herself into church work with great zest. Among other activities, she established the unheard-of practice of monthly female interfaith meetings among Baptists, Methodists, Congregationalists, and Presbyterians. Supremely confident in her own rightness, she appeared at a meeting of the elders of her church to try to persuade them to speak out against slavery. Her uncompromising moral positions ultimately led to her expulsion, a situation that would become common among radical abolitionists. In 1828, preparing to leave South Carolina to join Sarah in Philadelphia, she wrote in her diary: "I feel that I am called with a high and holy calling, and that I ought to be peculiar, and cannot be too zealous." Here was an expression of the quintessential spirit of the true crusader.[11]

Angelina Grimké gravitated naturally to the anti-slavery work of the Garrisonian group in Philadelphia. Inspired by a speech by visiting British abolitionist George Thompson in 1835 and appalled by the anti-abolitionist violence that followed him and other radical anti-slavery men as they lectured in the North, she wrote an eloquent personal letter to Garrison, which he promptly published in the *Liberator*. In it she praised him for holding to his principles: "The ground upon which you stand is holy ground: never—never surrender it. . . . If persecution is the means which God has ordained for the accomplishment of this great end, EMANCIPATION; then . . . I feel as if I could say, LET IT COME; for it is my deep, solemn deliberate conviction, that it is a cause worth dying for. . . ."[12]

Angelina's letter, which brought upon her opprobium from diverse groups, including her fellow Quakers, was the beginning of the involvement of the two sisters (Sarah at first cautious and reluctant) in a brief but remarkable episode in the history of anti-slavery. In 1836 Angelina wrote *An Appeal to the Christian Women of the South* in which she urged her southern sisters to influence husbands and brothers to act against slavery. In explaining her bold action she wrote: "God has shown me what I can do ... to speak to them in such tones that they *must* hear me, and through me, the voice of justice and humanity."[13] Her pamphlet was published by the American Anti-Slavery Society and circulated widely in the North. In the South it coincided with a swell of anti-abolitionist activity and was publicly burned by the postmaster in Charleston, making its author an outlaw in her home state.

In 1837 the three major female anti-slavery societies joined in New York City for the first Anti-Slavery Convention of American Women. Angelina Grimké again held center stage with her eloquent address challenging the "Women of the Nominally Free States" to break their own bonds to aid those of their sex who were in slavery. She also emphasized the need to abolish racial prejudice in the North. Published as a seventy-page pamphlet by the convention, the address served to enhance the reputation of both sisters among the abolitionists.

Following this convention, the Grimké sisters were invited by Maria Weston Chapman to address the Boston Female Anti-Slavery Society. They were especially desirable as speakers because of their unique experience with slavery. They went on from Boston to speak to other women's groups in the area. Prim and plain in their Quaker bonnets, they impressed their audience with their intense devotion to the cause. In addition, Angelina was becoming widely known for her oratorical powers. For all of these reasons, churches and meeting halls were filled to overflowing when the Grimkés lectured. They found themselves addressing audiences of both men and women, a situation which abolitionist women had not faced before. Even staunch anti-slavery people doubted the wisdom of defying convention to this extent. The Unitarian minister Samuel J. May, for example, was hesitant about allowing Angelina to speak from his pulpit before a mixed congregation, but he was won over completely by the force of her address and became her ardent supporter.

The Grimkés' speaking tour lasted about six months and included over sixty New England towns. Though they successfully gained attention for their cause, they also brought down upon themselves the wrath of the orthodox clergy of Massachusetts. This body was already hostile to the Garrisonians, who constantly attacked the church for its complicity with slavery. The action of the Grimkés in defying much-hallowed custom in addition to preaching radical abolitionism was more than the clerics could tolerate. The General Association of Congregationalist Ministers issued an edict to all its member churches, in effect condemning the Grimkés (without specifically mentioning them) for the unfeminine act of addressing "promiscuous" or mixed audiences.

The pastoral letter attacking the Grimkés triggered the first extended public controversy over women's rights because it spoke directly to the question of woman's proper sphere, an issue that would dominate the nineteenth-century women's movement. Its language clearly revealed the boundaries of acceptable female behavior in 1837. Citing the New Testament as its authority, the letter emphasized that woman's power lay in her dependence. Likening her to a vine "whose strength and beauty is to lean upon the trellis-work," it warned that the vine which "thinks to assume the independence and the overshadowing nature of the elm" not only would cease to bear fruit but also would "fall in shame and dishonor into the dust." The character of the woman who "assumes that place and tone of man as a public reformer . . . becomes unnatural."[14]

This was a harsh public attack on the Grimkés, which served also as a warning to other women who might dare to venture outside their prescribed sphere. To withstand such an assault the sisters could rely on their own piety, an important weapon in the battle as well as a source of strength for them personally. Their state of mind is revealed in the large correspondence they carried on during the ensuing controversy. To Henry C. Wright, their most loyal supporter, Sarah wrote that Angelina was troubled about the clerical uproar, "but the Lord knows that we did not come to forward our own interests but in simple obedience to his commands." In another letter she reiterated their determination to resist intimidation: "If in calling us thus publicly to advocate the cause of the downtrodden slave, God has unexpectedly placed us in the forefront of the battle which is to be waged against the rights and duties and responsibilities of woman, it would ill become us to shrink from such a contest."[15]

Though their critics initiated the controversy, the abolitionist women were not entirely unprepared for it. At the start of their New England tour, the Grimkés had spent a social evening at the Chapman home and discussed their situation. Angelina's comments, written in a letter to a friend, are significant:

> I had a long talk with the brethren on the rights of women, and found a very general sentiment prevailing that it is time our fetters were broken. L.M. Child and Maria Chapman strongly supported this view; indeed, very many seem to think a new order of things is very desirable in this respect. . . . I feel it is not only the cause of the slave we plead but the cause of woman as a moral, responsible being. . . . [16]

The most immediate issue for the women was the right to continue their public anti-slavery work. The question of women's equal participation in the work of the American Anti-Slavery Society was not made explicit at this point but emerged naturally from the initial debate. Other basic grievances were also brought to mind by the controversy: the denial of legal rights to married women, the lack of opportunity for higher education and dignified employment, and a host of other inequalities and indignities. The cause of the slave opened a Pandora's box of grievances and demands on behalf of women.

Many abolitionist women were not ready for the Grimkés' "new order of things." Instead, they felt comfortable in their separate female auxiliaries and useful in their work of gathering petitions and holding fund-raising affairs. Sharing the prevailing view of woman's sphere, they were content to allow their men to represent them in public and make the decisions for the national organization. Although radical in their defense of the slave, they had not made the connection, as the Grimkés had, between the rights of slaves and the rights of women. The controversy over the sisters' public speaking forced them to become involved in this "woman question."

Anne Warren Weston, sister of Maria Weston Chapman, was one of those who attempted to gain support for the Grimkés' right to speak. Addressing the Boston Female Anti-Slavery Society, she used many of what would become the principal arguments of the feminist-abolitionist cause. The very theologians who had used the Scriptures to justify slavery were now "perverting the same sainted oracles" to sanction woman's inferiority and subordination. "Will you," she demanded, "allow those men who have been for years unmindful of their own most solemn duties to prescribe yours?" Those who considered women as goods and chattels were not fit judges of the sphere woman should occupy; they had not objected that the slave woman in the rice fields was "out of her sphere." Weston concluded that the Grimkés, working for the slave, were "in the very sphere to which God has appointed every Christian."[17]

The Grimkés stood firm in their own defense, claiming that men and women had the same moral right and duty to oppose slavery. They were clearly sensitive to the broader implications of the controversy and made a conscious decision to speak for all women, calling on the broad doctrine of human rights rather than merely claiming rights for themselves. At stake was the right of women not merely to an equal role in anti-slavery but to an equal position in all areas of society. The sisters were defending not only their right to speak publicly but also the rights of all women to be as free as men to develop their talents and to enjoy lives of usefulness, respect, and independence.

Because Angelina was more in demand as a speaker, Sarah took on the job of publicly defending their position in a series of "Letters on the Province of Woman," which ran in the *New England Spectator* beginning in July 1837. The publication of these letters caused the sisters difficulty with friends who had not opposed their speaking but who feared that a public defense would stir unnecessary controversy and injure the anti-slavery cause. Theodore Weld, their close co-worker who later became Angelina's husband, took their cause seriously and, in fact, was a solid "woman's rights man." But even he, for purely tactical reasons, opposed "agitating the question" and advised them to go on with their lecturing "without making any ado about 'attacks' and 'invasions' and 'oppositions' "; their example alone would be the most convincing argument for women's rights and duties.[18]

The sisters did not agree. As Angelina explained in a letter, *"We must establish this right* for if we do not, it will be impossible for *us* to *go on with the work of Emancipation*. . . . Can you not see that woman *could* do, and *would* do a hundred times more for the slave if she were not fettered?" Responding to the charge that the time was not right, she wrote to Weld: "I think this must be the Lord's time and therefore the best time, for it seems to have been brought about by a concatenation of circumstances over which we had no control." After much debate, a compromise was effected: Sarah's letters would continue, but the subject was not discussed in their talks, and Angelina gave up her idea of a series of lectures on women's rights.[19]

Sarah's letters, published in 1838 as *Letters on the Equality of the Sexes, and the Condition of Woman*, constituted the first serious discussion of women's rights by an American woman. In them, she made an important contribution to the development of a nineteenth-century feminist ideology by basing her defense on the Scriptures, thus challenging her critics on their own ground. She argued that the Bible, properly translated and interpreted, taught that men and women had been created in perfect equality and should be granted the same rights, duties, and privileges. Adam and Eve fell from innocence, but not from equality, since their guilt was shared. Conventional interpretations, based on false translations by men, incorporated male prejudice. For example, God's pronouncement upon woman, "Thy desire shall be to thy husband and he shall rule over thee," was meant as a simple prophecy rather than a command—a prediction of the consequences of sin rather than a divine endorsement of male superiority. The statement had been incorrectly translated from the Hebrew, she argued, by men who substituted "will" for the original "shall" because they were accustomed to exercising authority over their wives. This feminist exegesis created a precedent to be followed by others throughout the century who reinterpreted passages from the New Testament as well as the Old.[20]

More significant even than the pastoral letter was the condemnation of "women out of their sphere" by clergymen *within* the anti-slavery movement. What began in 1837 as a confrontation with forces which were anti-abolitionist as well as antifeminist became an internecine conflict which lasted from 1838 to 1840 and eventually contributed to the division of the entire abolitionist movement. The focal point of this controversy was the right of women to vote and participate in the business of the "male" anti-slavery societies. The final division in the movement came in 1840, when Abby Kelley, an intense young Quaker who was among the most radical and uncompromising Garrisonians, was appointed to a committee of the American Anti-Slavery Society. Garrison and his followers supported Kelley's appointment, while their opponents demanded her resignation. Kelley refused to resign and, like the Grimkés, defended her position on the ground that men and women had the same moral rights and duties. The impasse over her appointment split the national society. The group of New York abolitionists who opposed her seceded to form a second organization.

Abby Kelley was the appropriate person to stand firmly at the center of the explosion over the woman question. While the Grimkés' role in the limelight was brief, Abby Kelley's public stand in 1840 was only the beginning of her long and arduous service in defense of the rights of slaves and women. When the sisters retired to the sidelines after Angelina's marriage to Theodore Weld in 1838, the role they had created as female anti-slavery lecturers was taken over by the younger Abby Kelley.

Like the Grimkés, Kelley was driven by a desire to rid the world of evil, a religious perfectionism that was shared by all the Garrisonians. As a young teacher in a Friends' school in Lynn, Massachusetts, she had circulated petitions and solicited funds for her local anti-slavery society. She saw her father's death in 1836 as a sign of God's will and threw herself even further into reform work, contributing her small inheritance to the cause and selling some of her clothing to obtain additional funds. A family letter written the following year reveals her ingenuous optimism: "'Tis a great joy to see the world grow better in anything—Indeed I think endeavors to improve mankind is the only object worth living for."[21]

Kelley gave her first speech at the second Anti-Slavery Convention of American Women in May 1838 in Philadelphia, a meeting which coincided with the Weld-Grimke wedding. This convention was a traumatic one for all concerned and a dramatic beginning to Kelley's career. The abolitionists were attacked by a stone-throwing pro-slavery mob on the first day and saw their newly built Pennsylvania Hall burned to the ground on the second. Maria Weston Chapman became so distraught that she suffered a temporary mental breakdown.

In spite of the threatening crowd outside, Abby Kelley's speech had been so eloquent that Theodore Weld assured her that God meant her to take up the anti-slavery mission: "Abby, if you don't, God will smite you." She spent the next year in intense soul-searching, confessing in a letter to the Weld-Grimke family that she was praying most earnestly "that this cup might pass from me." They responded that the Lord was trying her faith and advised her "to wait for *him* to make a way where there seems now to be no way." In 1839 she decided to go ahead, after seeing divine confirmation for her call in this Scriptural passage: "But God hath chosen the foolish things of the world to confound the wise. . . . " She gave up her teaching job to become an anti-slavery agent. A year later she was at the center of the culminating controversy over women in the movement.[22]

The "woman question" was the more explosive of the two issues dividing abolitionists in 1840. The other conflict, more tactical and less ideological, was over the value of political action. The radical Boston group, which defended women's equal participation, chose to continue using moral suasion as their chief anti-slavery tactic. These Garrisonians were "come-outers" who opposed any association with institutions tainted by slavery, which included the government as well as the established churches. The New York group, called "New Organization" men by the Garrisonians, was led by Lewis Tappan, James G. Birney, Henry B. Stanton, and others and favored broadening the base of the movement by political activity and coalition tactics; many of them went on to form the Liberty Party. They accused the Garrisonians of dragging in "extraneous questions" like the women's rights issue, which they feared would antagonize possible supporters and hurt the anti-slavery cause. They sensed that women's rights was an even more controversial issue than abolition.

While some New Organization men wished to suppress the women's rights issue purely for tactical reasons, their leaders included a core of conservative evangelical clergymen who, like their pro-slavery counterparts, saw the "woman question" as a social threat. One of this group expressed "grief and astonishment" that this issue was forced upon the anti-slavery cause. Women's rights principles, if carried out, "would strike a death blow at the purest and *loveliest* social condition of man" and tear up the "foundations of human virtue and *happiness*." The group was already antagonistic to Garrison because of his head-on assault on the churches, as well as his espousal of nonresistance and other "ultraist" causes. The Garrisonians' defense of women's rights was the final insult.[23]

Regardless of their stand on political action, virtually all of the anti-slavery women who were feminists remained with the Garrisonians: only there were they accepted on an equal basis with men. Many women were not sympathetic to the feminist cause, however, and chose to maintain their traditional role in male-dominated organizations. One of Maria Chapman's associates described a New Organization meeting where the women dutifully left when the men got down to business. She deeply regretted "that they can find any 'sisters' who will allow themselves to be dismissed for I feel that if Woman would not consent to her own degradation her Emancipation would be sure."[24]

Following the fight over the woman question in this country, the Garrisonians shortly faced a similar challenge in Britain at the World's Anti-Slavery Convention, held in London in 1840. Lucretia Mott and the other women delegates from the United States faced intense opposition to their request to be seated. (Though the Motts' liberal Quaker views were also anathema to the orthodox Friends who organized the convention, it was Mrs. Mott's sex that was crucial; James Mott had no difficulty being seated.) In a heated debate reminiscent of the exchange between the Grimkés and the Massachusetts clergy, members of the English clergy cited the Scriptures as the authority for relegating women to their "God-ordained" sphere. To give the vote to females, they argued, was to act in opposition to the Word of God. They also called upon the powerful source of custom which prevented them from subjecting the "shrinking nature of woman" to the indelicacies involved in a discussion of slavery.[25]

The ultimate decision was to adhere to custom. The women

were compelled to listen to the proceedings from a screened-off area; they were supported by Garrison and several other male sympathizers. Among these women was Elizabeth Cady Stanton, then a young bride who had chosen to accompany her husband to this meeting as a honeymoon trip. The rejection of the women delegates was an important feminist experience for Stanton, and her long talks with Lucretia Mott made an even more lasting impression on her. Out of the meeting of these two came the idea to organize women to take action in their own defense. The Seneca Falls meeting in 1848 was the logical fruition of the "woman question" controversy.

In the period following the split in the movement and the London meeting, the Garrisonian women merged their societies with the male groups which remained in the American Anti-Slavery Society. They were now able to work with greater freedom and to expand their activities. Child, Chapman, and Mott served on the executive committee of the national society; Child became editor of their newspaper, the *National Anti-Slavery Standard*; Abby Kelley lectured and organized in the West. Maria Chapman insisted that they were stronger for the defection because women "who were not easily discouraged" were more valuable to the cause than men "whose dignity forbade them to be fellow-laborers with women."[26] This rhetoric notwithstanding, the movement as a whole was weakened by the division and never again achieved the strength and unity which it possessed in the 1830s.

HISTORICAL CONSEQUENCES

The women who were abolitionist leaders in the 1830s have a historical significance that extends beyond their direct contributions to the anti-slavery movement. Their efforts in three interrelated areas (corresponding to the themes delineated in the introduction) are particularly noteworthy in the context of this essay: because of their rebellion against doctrinal restrictions on them as women as well as the rejection of them by their churches, they separated themselves from institutionalized religion and made reform work their religion; because they belonged to the first generation of female reformers, their influence on younger women who would become future leaders was enormous, especially in providing the foundation for a scripturally based feminist ideology and helping them to free themselves from the repressive bonds of religion; because they were intensely aware of the harmful effects of racial prejudice, they attacked this evil wherever it was to be found—in themselves, in their movement, in their churches, and in their society.

The early religious backgrounds of the feminist-abolitionist women had a significant influence on their development as reformers. It is not coincidental that a disproportionate number came from Quaker homes. Quakers were taught that, spiritually at least, women and men were equals. They were provided from birth with role models generally denied other women: Quaker women by custom spoke in meeting on an equal basis with men and played a more prominent role in family decisions as well; Quaker women were designated as ministers and permitted to travel about the country without their husbands, an unusual display of female independence in a society in which married women were permitted few freedoms and particularly suffered the humiliation of being nonpersons under the law. In addition, they benefitted from the Quaker commitment to educating their daughters as well as their sons and to preparing both for lives of usefulness. This, too, was in sharp contrast to the more common custom in the nineteenth century, even among middle- and upper-class families, of expecting women to be only wives and mothers and permitting them only minimal education.

Quakerism was an important training ground for reformers in still another way: it provided the experience from early years of being part of an unconventional and unpopular minority. Because of the external pressures on them, Quakers raised their children with a firm sense of their own identity as well as a strong community and group consciousness—no small help in facing a hostile world as reformers. Finally, the Quaker emphasis on fidelity to conscience above external authority encouraged women to be self-reliant and "strong-minded" individuals.

Lucretia Coffin Mott was the quintessential example of this influence. Raised on Nantucket by a Quaker fisherman's wife who managed both family and business during her husband's extended absences, she attributed her lifelong feminism to this double heritage of self-reliance: "I grew up so thoroughly imbued with women's rights," she said many times, "that it was the most important question of my life from a very early day." She did not limit her world view to the confines of her religious theology, however. Her special brand of intellectual liberalism was built upon Quaker beliefs but extended beyond them. Extraordinarily open and tolerant of nonconforming ideas, she carried on a lifetime crusade for freedom of religion and liked to say of this effort, "Call me a radical of the radicals." She prided herself on always placing fidelity to conscience above external strictures and relied on her favorite motto in speeches and sermons: "Truth for authority, not authority for truth." The superiority of practical Christianity over ceremonial religion was a favorite theme, and she was a steadfast critic of narrow dogmatism and petty sectarianism.[27]

An important part of Mott's enormous influence among the feminist-abolitionists was her effectiveness in helping them to liberate themselves from orthodox religious dogma. Garrison described her influence precisely when he wrote that he felt indebted to her (and her husband) for helping his mind to burst the bonds of theological dogma and to interpret the Scriptures so that, instead of being "killed by the letter," he had been "made alive by the spirit."[28]

Unitarianism was viewed approvingly by Lucretia Mott, and she liked to quote this passage by William Ellery Channing, which expressed her own view as well as his:

There is one principle of the soul which makes all men essentially equal. I refer to the *sense of duty*, to the power of discerning and doing right, to the moral and religious principle, to the inward monitor which speaks in the name of God. This is the great gift of God,—we can conceive no greater.[29]

This creed enabled her to endure a lifetime of battling a variety of evils with a calmness and grace that was the envy of her younger comrades.

Lucretia Mott, along with her husband, was active in the political controversy among the Quakers in the 1820s, joining the progressive Hicksite faction which actively supported anti-slavery against the resistance of the conservative Orthodox wing. Even among these "Unitarian Quakers," she was a constant irritant, although she was never expelled and, unlike other abolitionist women, she chose not to resign. Her personal emancipation from religious dogma was best expressed in an address she gave at the founding in 1867 of the Free Religious Association, an organization formed after the premature death of Boston reformer and Unitarian minister Theodore Parker, hero of the feminist-abolitionists for his progressive views on women as well as religion. In this speech, Lucretia Mott exhorted her listeners to preach the truth and predicted that in time all religions would be one, "and there will come to be such faith and such liberty as shall redeem the world."[30]

Those women raised in orthodox Protestant homes, as most Americans born in the early nineteenth century were, had to endure a greater struggle before they could be free to work for reform. Not only was Calvinist determinism and the concept of original sin personally oppressive to them and totally incompatible with their optimistic notions of the world, but they also had to confront the traditional Scriptural view of women. Better educated and more intelligent and strong willed than average, they painfully but with great determination subjected these beliefs to intense scrutiny and repeated reexamination. As a result of this process, they left the churches of their childhood and moved to more comfortable religious homes.

Often, while becoming Unitarians or Universalists in practice, they retained much of the old Calvinist spirit. Lydia Maria Child, who spent much of her adult life looking for a faith she was truly comfortable with and left a bequest in her will to the Free Religious Association, was a good example of this spiritual bifurcation. Having herself converted to Unitarianism, she complained regularly about orthodox beliefs: "Calvinism grates and creaks harsher and harsher discord in the ears of my soul. If it were the Lord's will, I would I might be out of the hearing of it." At the same time, she retained a decidedly Calvinist view of the world, as expressed in her published letters: "Whoso does not see that genuine life is a battle and a march, has poorly read his origin and his destiny. . . . "[31]

The feminist-abolitionist women, regardless of their religious origins, were all influenced by the spirit of the widespread evangelical revivalism of the 1820s and 1830s, though they rejected the institutional forms and much of the religious content. They were drawn to the missionary drive of the movement's leaders in denouncing sin and evil as well as their optimistic emphasis on the possibility of individual salvation. They also shared the "come-outer" spirit insofar as it involved the duty of the individual to secede from sinful institutions, although ironically their actions in carrying out this duty often brought them into conflict with their evangelical brethren.[32]

Abby Kelley, who in 1841 was disowned by the Society of Friends for her abolitionist activity and promptly resigned to protest their equivocal position on slavery, personified the evangelical spirit of the Garrisonians. She also exemplified the adoption by the abolitionists of the "Methodist circuit rider" means of communication.[33] Because of her eloquent and forceful style of oration in her years of travelling to proselytize for anti-slavery, she left in her wake a string of converts and female anti-slavery societies. An indication of her powerful evangelical style is this letter to the editor of the Ohio-based *Anti-Slavery Bugle*: "When Abby was here, I felt convinced that God was in his providence sending her through the country to proclaim the truths of his word, against the sin of slavery, and I said, don't let us oppose her lest we be found opposing God."[34]

The Grimké sisters offer the best illustration of religious unorthodoxy. In 1837, when they were still members of the Society of Friends, Angelina typically referred to moral reformations as "parts only of our glorious whole and that whole is Christianity, pure *practical* Christianity." Firm in her belief that she was acting as a good Christian, she steadfastly held her ground when she was disowned by the Quakers for marrying Theodore Weld, a Presbyterian minister. Sarah, too, had no regrets when she also was disowned for attending Angelina's wedding. By this time, she had become so disillusioned by the actions of the Friends that, as she wrote to a friend, "the discipline which cuts us off from membership for an act so strikingly in conformity with the will of God . . . must be anti-Christian, and I am thankful for the opportunity to testify against it."[35]

A year earlier, Sarah Grimké had already been expressing her intense frustration at the treatment she was receiving from male brethren who had denied her the role of minister and were repeatedly shutting her up in meeting. To Weld she described her "spiritual bondage" and acknowledged that she would "almost rejoice in the prospect of release from the *duty* of attending public worship, for truly it has been a weariness to my soul." In another letter, from Brookline, Massachusetts, where the sisters were lecturing, Sarah wrote that she had given up going to any place of worship because they were all alike, "places of spiritual famine." The more she examined the Bible, she said, the more persuaded she was that religious meetings were never instituted by God "either under the Jewish and Christian dispensation anything like the present system of ministry or worship."[36]

After the Grimké-Weld marriage, the sisters settled into a plain, spartan life, leaving the public sphere. Seeing themselves as serving the Lord in a different capacity, they busied themselves with domestic chores, rearing the Weld children and helping Theodore with his abolitionist writings. Weld, too, formerly a principal evangelical anti-slavery orator, withdrew to a more quiet life and even severed all formal religious affiliations.

The period of public activity of the Grimkés was brief, but it had a huge impact on future reform leaders. The controversy that followed the pastoral letter denouncing them had not only heightened abolitionist women's awareness of the obstacles they faced because of their sex but also served to intensify the feminist sensitivities of some not yet in the movement.

Lucy Stone, who became a major leader of the postwar suffrage movement, heard the pastoral letter read in the Congregational Church in North Brookfield, Massachusetts, where she was teaching. Only nineteen years old, she was already sensitive to her inferior position as a woman. Her church had refused to permit her to vote or join in its discussions, and her father adamantly rejected her plea to follow her brothers to college. The low pay she received as a teacher, compared with male salaries, undoubtedly added to her mortification. All these resentments were intensified as she heard the condemnation of the Grimkés. She later described her feeling of rebelliousness: "If I had felt bound to silence before by interpretation of Scriptures, or believed that equal rights did not belong to woman, that 'pastoral letter' broke my bonds."[37]

Sarah Grimké's *Letters on the Equality of the Sexes* also left an indelible impression on younger feminist-abolitionists because it not only articulated all the major themes of the antebellum women's movement but also provided a Scriptural basis for countering the arguments of their chief opponents, the clergy. Lucy Stone had written to her brother in 1838 that the *Letters* were "first rate" and "only help to confirm the resolution I had made before, to call no man my master."[38] In the 1840s she began to speak as an agent of the American Anti-Slavery Society, stressing the same Garrisonian themes that the Grimkés had voiced in their path-breaking lectures in the previous decade. As she felt the increasing need to devote some of her speeches solely to women's rights (and became in 1848 the first abolitionist to do so, on her own time), she drew on the central argument elaborated on by Sarah Grimké in her *Letters* ten years earlier: as moral and responsible beings, women had the same God-given sphere of action as men, and the same duties and responsibilities devolved on both.

While Sarah's letters provided the basis for a feminist ideology, Angelina's public actions also furnished inspiration to future leaders. In 1838 she triumphantly capped her brief public career by appearing before a committee of the Massachusetts legislature to present anti-slavery petitions on behalf of 20,000 women of the state. Supported by the presence of her new friends from Boston and surrounding cities, she delivered a powerful and impassioned address on behalf of women as well as slaves. Mary Livermore, a leading reformer and lecturer of the postwar era, played hooky from school for the day to hear Angelina speak. She later recalled that the experience forever fixed in her mind the conviction that women ought to be free to do whatever their powers enabled them to do well.[39]

Lucretia Mott, even more than the Grimkés, was an influential role model and advisor for younger women. Her most distinguished protégé was Elizabeth Cady Stanton, the boldest thinker and chief propagandist of the nineteenth-century women's movement. Especially crucial in Stanton's development was Mott's aid in releasing her from the burden of the stern brand of Calvinism that had weighed heavily on her all through childhood and tormented her with the specter of eternal damnation. The fire of Stanton's feminism was fueled by her religious experience. The 1837 pastoral letter denouncing the Grimkés was an outrage for which she never forgave the orthodox clergy. When she met Lucretia Mott at the World's Anti-Slavery Convention in London in 1840, she was more than ready to be liberated. Hearing Mott deliver a sermon in a Unitarian Church was to her "like the realization of an oft-repeated happy dream."[40]

In the long discussions that Elizabeth Stanton and Lucretia Mott had in London and in the active correspondence that followed their return home, they dwelled on the subject of religion as well as the position of women. The older woman encouraged the younger to divest herself of the "creeds and dogmas of sects" that were encumbrances on "the simple and benign religion of Jesus" and share her own goal of "obedience to manifested duty—leading to practical righteousness, as the Christian standard. . . . " Stanton more than followed the advice—she carried on a lifelong crusade against the church as "a terrible engine of oppression, especially as it concerns women."[41] She would produce, in the 1890s, her *Woman's Bible*, a feminist commentary on those portions of the Bible dealing with women, a fitting summation to a long and controversial career.

Elizabeth Stanton's longtime co-worker, Susan B. Anthony, probably is the best-known disciple of the Garrisonians. Brought up in a liberal Quaker anti-slavery home in western New York, she began attending the Unitarian Church with her family in the 1840s after her father was disowned for his unorthodox beliefs and practices. Anthony was encouraged by Abby Kelley and others to join in lecturing on anti-slavery, but she stood in awe of the Garrisonians whom she felt had received "that higher, holier light." Finally, in 1856 she became the chief agent of the American Anti-Slavery Society in western New York. More than any of her feminist-abolitionist co-workers, reform became her religion. Single-mindedly devoted to making the world better, she told an interviewer in her later years that work and worship had been one with her—she prayed every second of her life, she said, but with her work rather than on her knees.[42]

Perhaps the least known of the efforts of the radical abolitionists was their battle with racial prejudice, which they presciently viewed as an even more pervasive evil than slavery, which was only its current manifestation. In this most difficult of struggles they made use of a variety of weapons. Rhetorically, they appealed to women to join them by comparing the effects of prejudice on both women and slaves. In organizing their societies, they pointedly welcomed women of color. In Massachusetts, considered the most progressive state, they publicly protested the law barring racial intermarriage. In all of these endeavors, they found resistance within the anti-slavery movement and open hostility outside. The sight of black and white women walking arm in arm was undoubtedly the final outrage for those Philadelphia citizens who set fire to Pennsylvania Hall during the second Anti-Slavery Convention of American Women in 1838.

Their successes were, at best, small ones. They are to be found in the special friendships that developed between black and white women working for the same cause. Such a relationship was the lifelong association between Sarah and Angelina Grimké and Sarah Mapps Douglass, co-workers in the Philadelphia Female Anti-Slavery Society. Sarah Douglass corresponded with Sarah Grimké until the latter's death, after which she continued to communicate with Angelina and her family. Their extant letters are a reminder of the possibilities that exist when prejudice is truly overcome.

The Grimkés met Sarah Mapps Douglass and her mother at the Arch Street Meeting in Philadelphia. Douglass at the time was teaching at a school she founded for black girls, an endeavor that was financially supported by the Female Anti-Slavery Society for several years. In 1853 she became head of the girls' preparatory department at the Institute for Colored Youth—newly established under Quaker auspices—a position she held until her retirement in 1877.[43]

The Grimkés, perhaps even more than other Garrisonians because of their direct experience with slavery, were extremely sensitive to the effects of racial prejudice and included in all their anti-slavery talks a discussion of the character of free people of color and the cruelty they suffered at the hands of white northerners, in addition to the usual appeals to end slavery. They were outraged, therefore, when they found that the Quaker meeting house had segregated people of color on a back bench. They protested this by sitting with their black friends. They also requested of Sarah Douglass that she furnish them with detailed information about the treatment she and her mother had received at the hands of Friends, hoping to publicize it: When they failed to find a publisher in the United States, they transmitted the material to Quaker friends in Britain, who published it in pamphlet form.[44]

Sarah Mapps Douglass was acutely aware that hostility toward people of color did not diminish when the latter were educated and respectable, and she noted the "noble few" among the Friends who "have cleansed their garments from the foul stain of prejudice." If all Friends felt as her "beloved sisters" Sarah and Angelina Grimké did, prejudice would "be driven from the bosom of the professed followers of Christ." Lucretia Mott and Abby Kelley were also cited by her as Friends who had turned their back on prejudice.[45]

The Weld-Grimké wedding was a small but successful effort to translate principle into practice. The guests were racially mixed and included two former slaves of the Grimké family. Prayers were said by a black minister as well as a white one. The groom took the opportunity to abjure all authority over his bride, and the ceremony was carried out in the traditional Quaker manner, by the participants themselves. The recent description of this wedding by an historian of abolitionism as an appropriate symbol of the quest for personal liberation from repressive institutions seems totally accurate.[46]

Perhaps even more controversial than their private friendships with people of color, the feminist-abolitionists encouraged black men and women to represent their anti-slavery societies as agents, often meeting opposition from others in the anti-slavery movement. Several black women who became important reformers began their careers as anti-slavery lecturers supported by the Garrisonians. Sarah Parker Remond, active in the Salem Female Anti-Slavery Society, joined her brother Charles Lenox Remond in meetings in New York and Ohio in the 1850s as an agent of the American Anti-Slavery Society. Frances Ellen Watkins Harper, a notable lecturer, author, and reformer well into the twentieth century, was raised by an abolitionist uncle in Baltimore. As a young woman in the 1850s, she lectured widely under the auspices of the Garrisonians. She also contributed poems, stories, and essays to the *Liberator*. Sojourner Truth, probably the best known of the black feminist-abolitionists, was recruited to the anti-slavery movement by Garrison's brother-in-law and worked enthusiastically in the 1850s, making the offices of the *Anti-Slavery Bugle* her headquarters.[47]

To sum up, the radical abolitionist women in the 1830s were indeed driven by religious impulse, but they expressed it for the most part outside of religious institutions. Because clergymen were the chief challengers of their right as women to speak and act publicly, they were compelled to reexamine their religious beliefs and as a result developed the first feminist ideology. Because their reform efforts came before all else in their lives, they were compelled to leave the confines of the institutional church and shape their own brand of practical Christianity based on moral principles and on their faith that men and women by their own efforts could indeed make the world better. While they firmly rejected orthodox Calvinism as incompatible with their world view, they drew from diverse other Protestant strains—Evangelical, Unitarian, Quaker—to create an eclectic, working religion of reform.

In disputing even the more liberal Protestant sects, the abolitionist women raised important questions that are still relevant and still largely unresolved today—questions about the role of women in the church and the attitude of male clerics toward women, questions about the racial prejudice that still permeates the churches as well as the rest of society. They provided answers insofar as they created models of what could exist in a world without bias toward those deemed inferior, whether women or racial minorities.

Less interested in theological subtleties than in basic ethical truths, the abolitionist women expressed their beliefs in their daily lives. Serving God meant living lives of usefulness. The circumstances of religious reformers making a religion out of reform was best expressed in a typical anti-slavery appeal to other women: "We are born into the world for a purpose. . . .

We are here to do good as we have the opportunity. . . . This is our religion, and it is all the religion we have."[48]

NOTES

1. Blanche Glassman Hersh, *The Slavery of Sex: Feminist-Abolitionists in America* (Urbana: University of Illinois Press, 1978). I use "feminist-abolitionists" to refer to those anti-slavery people, men and women, who supported women's rights and the expansion of woman's sphere.

2. *Liberator* 2 (Boston), 7 Jan. 1832; Walter M. Merrill ed., *Letters of William Lloyd Garrison; Vol. 1: I Will Be Heard, 1822–1835* (Cambridge: Belknap Press of Harvard University Press, 1971), p. 209.

3. John Jay Chapman, *Memories and Milestones* (New York: Moffat, Yard, 1915; reprinted, Freeport, N.Y.: Books for Libraries Press, 1971), pp. 209–22.

4. Sharon Harley and Rosalyn Terborg-Penn, eds., *The Afro-American Woman: Struggles and Images*, (Port Washington, N.Y.: Kennikat Press, 1978), p. 18. Susan Paul is cited here among the black founders.

5. Lydia Maria Child, *Letters of Lydia Maria Child* (Boston: Houghton Mifflin, 1883), p. 255.

6. Lydia Maria Child, *An Appeal on Behalf of That Class of Americans Called Africans* (New York: John S. Taylor, 1836), p. 146.

7. For Sarah Mapps Douglass, see Anna Bustill Smith, "The Bustill Family," *Journal of Negro History* 10 (October 1925): 638–47; Janice Sumler-Lewis, "The Forten-Purvis Women of Philadelphia and the American Antislavery Crusade," *Journal of Negro History* 66 (Winter 1981–82): 281–88.

8. See "Political Activities of Anti-Slavery Women" in Gerda Lerner, *The Majority Finds Its Past*, (New York: Oxford University Press, 1979), chap. 8. Petitions dealt with three major issues on which Congress had the authority to act: the abolition of slavery in the District of Columbia and other territories, the opposition to the annexation of Texas, and the outlawing of the internal slave trade.

9. Amy Swerdlow, "Abolition's Conservative Sisters: The Ladies' New York City Anti-Slavery Societies, 1834–1840" (paper given at Third Berkshire Conference on the History of Women, 9–11 June 1976). Among other comparisons, Swerdlow contrasts the religious composition of the female groups in New York (mostly Presbyterians plus a smaller number of Methodists), Boston (Quakers, Unitarians, and Episcopalians were included along with Presbyterians, Methodists, and Congregationalists), and Philadelphia (virtually all Quakers).

10. Gerda Lerner, *The Grimké Sisters from South Carolina* (Boston: Houghton Mifflin, 1967; New York: Schocken Books, 1971).

11. Ibid., p. 74.

12. Ibid., pp. 123–24.

13. Catherine H. Birney, *The Grimké Sisters, Sarah and Angelina Grimké* (Boston: Lee & Shepard, 1885; reprinted, Westport, Conn.: Greenwood Press, 1969), p. 138.

14. Maria Weston Chapman, *Right and Wrong in Boston* (Boston: Annual Report of Boston Female Anti-Slavery Society, 1837), pp. 46–47.

15. S. Grimké to H.C. Wright, 27 Aug. 1837, Garrison Papers, Boston Public Library.

16. Birney, *Grimké Sisters*, p. 178.

17. Anne Warren Weston, Address to Boston Female Anti-Slavery Society, 21 Aug. 1837, Weston Family Papers, Boston Public Library.

18. Theodore Dwight Weld et al., *Letters of Theodore Dwight Weld, Angelina Grimké Weld and Sarah Grimké, 1822–1844*, ed. Gilbert H. Barnes and Dwight L. Dumond (New York: D. Appleton-Century for the American Historical Association, 1934), 1: 433; hereafter cited as *Weld-Grimké Letters*.

19. Ibid., pp. 415, 429.

20. Sarah Grimké, *Letters on the Equality of the Sexes, and the Condition of Woman* (Boston: Isaac Knapp, 1838; reprinted, New York: Source Book Press, 1970). See also Hersh, *Slavery of Sex*, chap. 6.

21. Abby Kelley to Olive and Newbury Darling, 10 Dec. 1837, Kelley-Foster Papers, Worcester (Mass.) Historical Society.

22. W.P. and F.J. Garrison, *William Lloyd Garrison 1805–1879, the Story of His Life Told by His Children* (Boston: Houghton Mifflin, 1894), 2: 216; Weld, *Weld-Grimké Letters*, 2:747; Angelina and Theodore Weld to Abby Kelley, 24 Feb. 1839, Kelley-Foster Papers, Worcester Historical Society; Abby Kelley Foster's Reminiscences, Worcester Historical Society.

23. Rufus A. Putnam to Amos A. Phelps and Orange Scott, 27 March 1839, Amos Phelps Papers, Boston Public Library.

24. Charlotte Austin to M.W. Chapman, Oct. 1839, Weston Family Papers, Boston Public Library.

25. Elizabeth Cady Stanton, Susan B. Anthony, Matilda Joslyn Gage, eds., *History of Woman Suffrage*, 6 vols., vols. 1–3 (New York: Fowler & Wells, 1881–87), 1: 58–59, 60.

26. Maria Weston Chapman, *Right and Wrong in Massachusetts* (Boston: Dow & Jackson's Anti-Slavery Press, 1839; reprinted, New York: Negro Universities Press, 1969), p. 12.

27. Otelia Cromwell, *Lucretia Mott* (Cambridge: Harvard University Press, 1958), p. 125; Anna Davis Hallowell, ed., *James and Lucretia Mott: Life and Letters*, (Boston: Houghton Mifflin, 1884), p. 470.

28. Hallowell, *Mott*, pp. 296–97.

29. Ibid., p. 109.

30. Cromwell, *Mott*, p. 207.

31. Lydia Maria Child to Caroline Weston, 7 March 1839, Lydia Maria Child Papers, Boston Public Library; quotation from 1852 edition of her *Letters From New York*, cited in Gail Parker, ed., *The Oven Birds: American Women on Womanhood, 1820–1920*, (New York: Doubleday & Co., 1972; Anchor Books, 1972), p. 24.

32. See Lewis Perry, *Radical Abolitionism: Anarchy and the Government of God in Antislavery Thought* (Ithaca: Cornell University Press, 1973).

33. See Leonard L. Richards, "The Jacksonians and Slavery," in *Antislavery Reconsidered*, ed. Lewis Perry and Michael Fellman (Baton Rouge: Louisiana State University Press, 1979).

34. Letter from "Friend of the Cause," *Anti-Slavery Bugle*, 5 Dec. 1845.

35. Weld, *Weld-Grimké Letters*, 1: 431; 2: 678.

36. Ibid., 1: 373, 402, 498. The Grimkés became associated with the orthodox faction of the Friends when they moved to Philadelphia, which undoubtedly exacerbated Sarah's trials.

37. Address by Lucy Stone, "Workers for the Cause," ca. 1888, Blackwell Family Papers, Library of Congress.

38. Lucy Stone to Francis Stone, 31 Aug. 1838, Blackwell Family Papers, Library of Congress.

39. *Woman's Journal*, 23 July 1870.

40. Hallowell, *Mott*, p. 187.

41. Lucretia Mott to Elizabeth Cady Stanton, 23 March 1841, Elizabeth Cady Stanton Papers, Library of Congress; Elizabeth Cady Stanton, *Eighty Years and More: Reminiscences 1815–1897* (European Publishing, 1898; reprinted, with new introduction by Gail Parker, New York: Schocken Books, 1971), p. 44.

42. Ida Husted Harper, *Life and Work of Susan B. Anthony*, 3 vols. (Indianapolis: Bowen-Merrill, 1898–1908), 1: 133; 2: 859.

43. Dorothy Sterling, *We Are Your Sisters: Black Women in the Nineteenth Century* (New York: W.W. Norton & Co., 1984).

44. Lerner, *Majority Finds Its Past*, p. 99.

45. Weld, *Weld-Grimké Letters*, 2: 829–31; Sterling, *We Are Your Sisters*, p. 130.

46. Weld, *Weld-Grimké Letters*, 2: 678; description is by Perry, *Radical Abolitionism*, p. 106. The Grimké sisters, true to their beliefs, later publicly acknowledged their brother's two black sons as their nephews and supported their education; see Lerner, *Grimké Sisters*.

47. For Remond, Harper, and Truth, see Edward T. James, Janet

Wilson James, and Paul S. Boyer, eds., *Notable American Women, 1607–1950: A Biographical Dictionary*, 3 vols. (Cambridge: Belknap Press of Harvard University Press, 1971), 2: 137–39, 479–81; 3: 136–37.

48. *Anti-Slavery Bugle*, 28 Nov. 1845.

8

Questions of Power and Status: American Presbyterian Women, 1870–1980

Lois A. Boyd and R. Douglas Brackenridge

Prior to 1870, the place of women in the Presbyterian Church, U.S.A., was clearly defined: she should be subordinate to the male, submissive to his decisions and policies, and silent in the church.[1] Such a definition pertained to the limitation of her right to speak and pray before parish and juridical mixed assemblies as well as the denial of ordination as deacon, elder, and minister. Although women constituted a majority in many nineteenth-century congregations and were said by clergy and social commentators to be "inclined toward religion," they had neither voice nor vote in Presbyterian church councils. The most accorded them was a somewhat ambiguous and certainly tenuous "influence" that they might use on the male and the right to organize in segregated female humanitarian, benevolent, and prayer groups.

Although restricted in participation in the governing bodies of the church, females tended to vest considerable time and energy in their societies. After the Civil War, however, there was a marked change in the nature of these groups. Instead of the scattered local associations, churchwomen developed larger regional or national boards in order to centralize activities, resources, and programs for the benefit of home and foreign missions. Interdenominational in character initially, participants began to break away in the 1870s and organize separate boards within their own denominational structures. Presbyterian women followed this pattern, establishing within the decade a national board for home missions and seven regional boards for foreign missions.[2]

As these boards grew in size, influence, and budget, a recognizable and substantive issue emerged concerning women's power and status in the church. This essay will study the interrelatedness of the growth of the organizations with the growing unrest among women with church policies on ordination. It will examine the events of the 1920s in particular, when, in formally addressing the role of women, men and women discovered that "power" and "status" were issues that needed attention but that one did not necessarily connote the other. It will conclude with a discussion of the events leading toward women's receiving full ordination rights and the beginnings of total equality in the church.

As we attempt here to recount institutional actions and public utterances that represented the "norm" as evidenced by policies of the church, we fully realize that one cannot generalize attitudes. Further, one cannot separate women's history from the broader view of Presbyterian, ecumenical, and secular history. Similar to other Protestant denominations, the Presbyterian Church in the U.S.A. has been and continues to be influenced by social, political, ecclesiastical, and economic trends of American life. In terms of the role of females in the church, the rise of women's missionary organizations parallels the emergence of the other religious and secular voluntary organizations in the nineteenth century. Interest in the issue of equality and granting women ordination and policy-making rights was stimulated in part by the suffrage movement of the late nineteenth and early twentieth centuries. The sudden flurry of concern for the implementation of legislation and programs to insure women more than a *de jure* equality in the church received an impact from the feminist uprising in the 1960s. It is not within the scope of this essay to describe these relationships in detail, but our description of events recognizes such a context.

GROWING ORGANIZATIONS AND THE "WOMAN QUESTION"

Presbyterian Church Fathers in the nineteenth century based their view of women's place in the church on an interpretation of Scripture that posited female subordination and male supremacy and forbade women to "teach and exhort, or to lead in prayer, in public and promiscuous assemblies."[3] This view, prevalent in other Protestant denominations as well, was undergirded in Presbyterianism by an interpretation of John Calvin's understanding regarding women in church and society and was reinforced by generations of theologians, preachers, and leaders.[4] It was buttressed by cultural and social mores that assigned women a separate sphere and relegated them to a powerless position in political, economic, professional, and ecclesiastical realms.[5]

Signs of change began to surface in the mid-nineteenth century. In 1848 the first public discussion of "the social, civil, and religious condition and rights of woman" came out of the well-known meeting at Seneca Falls, New York, which led to the suffrage movement.[6] The opportunity for higher education for women arose, particularly after the advent of Vassar College in 1865, which portended women's entrance into a variety of professional positions.[7] Especially notable just after the Civil War was the propensity of females to organize into large industrial, domestic, educational, charitable, and religious groups.[8] Along this line, denominational activity toward associations that supported missionary enterprises proliferated.

With such a new climate came considerable debate in Presbyterian courts and pulpits on the so-called "woman question" in which men argued the biblical as well as the practical aspects of her role. The issue became particularly volatile in the wake of highly publicized incidents of females speaking from the pulpits of some major Presbyterian churches in the East.[9] In 1876 one such occasion in which two women representing the temperance movement spoke at the regular Sunday worship services of the Wickliffe Presbyterian Church in Newark, New Jersey, led to an ecclesiastical trial that involved three governing bodies of the Presbyterian Church, U.S.A. and received national attention from newspapers, magazines, church leaders, and the leaders of the women's rights movement.[10] The Presbytery of Newark sustained the charge that the minister, Isaac See, disobeyed a Scriptural ordinance, although it declined to condemn him of "conscious and willful disobedience." It stated:

> We hold that the passages of Scripture referred to in the charge do prohibit the fulfilling by women of the offices of public preachers in the regular assemblies of the Church. And, while we admit that a different interpretation of them may be honestly held, we think that the action of Brother See in inviting women to preach in his pulpit at the regular public services on the Sabbath Day was irregular and unwise, and contrary to the views of the Scriptures and of Church order derived from them. . . . We affectionately counsel and admonish Brother See to abstain from it in the future.[11]

The judgment was upheld on appeal by the Synod of New Jersey and the General Assembly.

Presbyterian women generally acceded to such a church policy, some openly arguing for the impropriety of women's assuming male prerogatives.[12] By the same token, these same women often were active in church affairs that fell within their "sphere" and were especially committed to their female societies. Consequently, indirectly and probably inadvertently, they had a role in challenging church policy on women's speaking in the church as their participation in the benevolent, humanitarian, missionary, and praying associations led to increasing occasions when women needed to give public reports, lecture on mission needs, and pray publicly for the missionaries.[13] When the local organizations coalesced into large regional or national boards and as these boards became more autonomous and sophisticated in their operations, women in fact grew to have considerable impact on church policies in financial and programmatic areas.

Although the female leaders of the boards and their constituents saw themselves as auxiliary and loyal to the male boards,[14] they soon realized that their coalition gave them a considerable power base. Beginning with staffs of volunteer officers who provided travel and supply expenses out of their own pockets, the boards evolved into professionalized units that built schools,

hospitals, and churches, developed huge distribution and publishing programs, recruited missionaries, helped educate and
support women physicians, teachers, and church workers, lob-
bied for social reform, published their own widely read missionary magazines, and instituted policy for their many
responsibilities in the United States and abroad.[15] Women also
were teaching in Sunday Schools at local levels, but the leaders
of the boards moved among the highest ranks of the denominational bureaucracy.[16] As their influence increased, so did tensions between the female and male boards. Charges that women
were establishing a separate church and diverting contributions
from the regular budget came from one side; anger, though
rarely publicly expressed, at unilateral decisions that excluded
the women's input came from the other.[17]

The tension itself indicated an obvious change in women's
roles in church affairs. Nevertheless, church fathers steadfastly
maintained the traditional interpretation of Scripture and doctrine, although attitudes wavered on the degree of restrictions.
The debate over the "woman question" erupted more frequently
as practice overtook policy, but the discussion turned from the
earlier theological generalities without particular pressure to specific issues raised within a context of new patterns of behavior.
The influence represented by the women's boards could not be
ignored. Neither could their impact on the widening professionalization of women in the church: the boards recruited large
numbers of single female missionaries, doctors, and teachers to
serve alongside the missionary wives; their mission schools
turned out young women who became "Christian workers,"
especially in the American South and West; the boards themselves were developing professional staff persons in the boards'
offices.[18] Because of the nudging by such cultural, social, and
economic forces, churchwomen began to question whether the
church was sensitive to the changing styles.[19] Like other mainline Protestant denominations, the Presbyterian Church itself
had to recognize changes and modify its policies, but it did so
only gradually.

In terms of pronouncements, since 1811 the General Assembly
had been commending "pious females" for their evangelical and
benevolent interests throughout the nineteenth century, specif-

ically indicating its recognition of the importance of their financial contributions to the denomination through their organizations. Various overtures and directives spoke to details of the women's organizations but the first formal acknowledgment by the General Assembly of changing attitudes toward women's status did not come until 1891. At that time it envisaged neither ordination nor full equality for women, but it recognized a need for adjustment in the definition of "women's sphere." A committee reporting on deaconesses reported that "a majority in the church are in favor of securing in some orderly way the services of godly women to assist in religious work, and are desirous of clothing them with some measure of authority."[20]

The rising support of diaconal service by women was aided in the latter part of the nineteenth century by the introduction of a new biblical hermeneutic that gave intellectual respectability to a sociological and historical interpretation of the Bible. This gave proponents of sexual equality some ground on which to argue publicly against the traditional Scriptural definitions concerning women.[21] In 1892 the church approved providing sessional appointment of "godly and competent women . . . for the care of the poor and sick, and especially of poor widows and orphans."[22] Very few women entered the deaconess movement, for it did not seem to have strong appeal for Presbyterians.

As the nineteenth turned to the twentieth century, the highly visible officers of the women's boards maintained positions of high prestige and influence among denominational leaders. On the foreign mission field, women missionaries, although charged to minister only to women and children, out of expediency found themselves teaching, preaching, and providing medical services to men also in the various stations. Women served in some of the smaller congregations as lay evangelists, and documentation exists that women actually served without ordination as deacons, elders, and ministers in churches where there were not enough men to fill the positions.[23] Women taught in the church schools, worked among immigrants in the cities and among blacks and mountain people in the South, yet the denomination withheld the status of ordination as elder and minister.

Despite the lack of status, what the women had gained through their organizations was a great deal of power in terms of jurisdiction, control over decisions, influence, and authority. Not the least of importance was the economic impact of the consistently generous contributions toward missions. For example, the Woman's Board of Home Missions passed the half-million dollar mark in gifts after only twenty-eight years and held property worth hundreds of thousands of dollars within the first two decades of its existence. The Woman's Board of Foreign Missions at its Golden Jubilee celebration noted more than $13 million donated in fifty years. Consequently, Presbyterian women entered the 1920s assuming they would continue much as before.

THE 1920s: QUESTIONS OF POWER AND STATUS

As the decade began, however, it began to appear that there was a changing attitude among some churchwomen toward the traditional women's organizations in particular and toward the role of women in the church in general. Although not prominently discussed, two issues seemed clear: first, a general decline in interest in missions, and second, dissatisfaction with restrictions imposed on women by the church. The first argument called for more diverse organizations that included interests in educational and social problems as well as missions; the second felt that the church omitted women from too many areas in terms of service and status. One woman claimed, "The Presbyterian Church does little less than insult the intelligence of its womanhood. . . . "[24] Such outspoken criticism was rare, however, and those who objected apparently chose instead to pursue careers or engage in activities outside the church.

Nevertheless, many churchwomen continued to work in a volunteer capacity through the local and national mission boards. Their power base appeared solid in the light of their fiscal and programmatic responsibilities.[25] These women also recognized the implications of the successful national suffrage campaign and were optimistic that times were favorable for a change in their subordinate position within the church. In fact, in 1919 several presbyteries had developed and sent overtures to the General Assembly, asking it to reconsider the status of women in the church and open the offices of deacon, elder, and minister to female constituents.[26]

In response, the General Assembly appointed a select committee to study the question and to report the following year. Although the committee concluded that the Bible did not forbid ordination to women, it was not united in recommending full ordination rights immediately. Instead, it proposed giving presbyteries the opportunity to vote separately on two offices: elder and deacon. Ultimately the overture on ordination as elder was defeated by a narrow margin, but diaconal ordination received overwhelming approval.[27] To be eligible to serve as deacon definitely upgraded women's status, but it awarded them no voting privileges in the denomination since governing bodies were composed only of elders and ministers. Nevertheless, the large number of presbyteries voting for ordination encouraged women to anticipate reconsideration of the office of elder in the near future.

Church leaders heralded another decision three years later as being a further step in giving women official status in denominational structures. In 1920 the General Assembly had appointed a committee to consider ways in which twenty boards and agencies and a number of permanent committees of the church could be consolidated. The committee recommended a sweeping reorganization that would combine existing groups into four major boards—National Missions, Foreign Missions, Christian Education, and Ministerial Relief and Sustentation. When approved in 1923, this plan dissolved the Woman's Boards and subsumed their work under the Boards of National and Foreign Missions.[28]

At the time, both male and female church leaders stressed the elevation of status that reorganization provided for women. Previously their missionary boards, although powerful in their own right, were in fact auxiliary entities whose decisions were subject to final review and approval by the Boards of Home and Foreign Missions, composed entirely of males. Now women were represented by a fixed numerical formula on each of the four new boards, thus allowing them to participate and to vote directly on a wider range of church policies. Moreover, in the reorganization women were assigned some leadership roles parallel to those of men, and each missionary board retained specific committees and divisions to preserve and incorporate the specially designated "women's work" of the old boards. In addition, women had representatives on the General Council, the executive committee of the General Assembly, perhaps the single most powerful group in the entire denomination. Based on these factors, women seemed to have significantly improved their ability to influence the denomination's decision-making processes.[29]

Despite the positive public stance regarding their elevated status, more personal evidence reveals that women recognized the potential threat that reorganization posed to their established power base. Furthermore, private correspondence shows that the reorganization committee had a hidden agenda in its decisions affecting the future of women's work in the church. For example, if the committee had pressed for its original proposal for the disposition of women's work, the results would have been even more dramatic. From records of the committee's deliberations, some letters and memos indicate that a majority of the committee favored disbanding women's local and regional organizations as well as the national boards. The committee apparently pulled back in the face of an outcry from women leaders who warned that such action would have an immediate effect on the financial support from churchwomen. As one minister observed, "We men better let alone the goose that lays the golden egg."[30]

Some committee members also felt that women's organizations in fact constituted a "church within the church" and that their continued existence ultimately threatened denominational unity. From the late nineteenth century on, many Presbyterian men believed that the increasing financial contributions of women to their missionary projects would result in reductions of gifts to the church-at-large. Even Robert E. Speer, head of the Foreign Board and an outspoken advocate for female equality, questioned the existence of separate organizations for women. "If we have in our churches women's organizations, what have we got? Haven't we got two churches?" Pointing out the overlap of the social, educational, and religious programs, he said, "We do not want to divide what is spoken of as 'the church' and 'the women.' "[31]

Churchwomen were aware of such attitudes but did not agree that there was any conflict. They resented having their loyalty questioned and, in particular, resented the unilateral action of the General Assembly in abolishing the women's boards. As they always had, however, they vented their anger privately, especially to Katharine Bennett and Margaret Hodge, who had been presidents of the two women's boards for home and foreign missions respectively and were now vice presidents in the new organizational structure. A woman from Indiana queried: "Why should the women of the church who are the loyal faithful supporters of our Woman's Work have this taken from our hands, and given to the management of men who can't begin to do it well?"[32] Another complained of the "high-handed measures" and "ruthless actions" of insensitive General Assembly commissioners.[33] Initially, Bennett and Hodge, certainly the leading spokespersons for Presbyterian women, suppressed their personal feeling and articulated a "positive good" theory that the reorganization process actually would give women more power than they had previously enjoyed.[34]

Despite these public assurances from respected women leaders, the seemingly elevated position of women turned out to be more cosmetic than concrete. The General Assembly allotted women fifteen seats out of forty on the Boards of National and Foreign Missions, twelve out of thirty-six on Christian Education, and three out of fifteen on the Board of Ministerial Relief and Sustentation. Women had two representatives on the General Council, which functioned as an executive committee of the General Assembly, but both were ex-officio with a voice but no vote. As one female board member observed caustically in private correspondence, " 'God bless the efforts of these good women' can be uttered with fervor, since in a ratio of one to three their opinion can never change anything."[35]

In addition to the problems of representation, women also lost their power to nominate and elect their own national officers. Instead, board representatives were selected by the General Assembly, which was all male. Furthermore, women lost much of their visibility within the denomination. Concurrently, the demise of the boards broke up a carefully cultivated communications network among women from the local to the national levels. This damaged the overall program and resulted, at least temporarily, in reduced contributions.[36]

Women also discovered that the dynamics of working with men was quite different from their experience of functioning only among women. Already outvoted, females were not skilled in the techniques of confrontation and negotiation that were a part of long-established male patterns. Women expressed themselves less frequently in public and as a rule deferred to the male majority. One woman reflected,

The result of the integration of men and women has not been happy for women, nor has it contributed to the success of women's work. Doubtless the men have been irritated also, but as their will almost invariably prevails, they are better able to bear it with fortitude. I do not believe that the attitude of men is hostile or antagonistic to women's service. Rather, it is an unconscious tolerant amusement over women's efforts when cooperation cannot be avoided.[37]

In the area of finances women discovered that with no national organization individual ministers and judicatories more easily could divert women's resources to local projects. Letters from presbyterial and synodical officers reported specific examples of financial tampering, such as when a missionary society, "under pressure," gave $1,500 for a church organ and therefore could not reach its missionary pledge.[38] Bennett and Hodge had known of similar incidents for some time.[39]

As they became increasingly aware of the effects of reorganization, leading churchwomen worked through official channels and behind the scenes in an attempt to ameliorate the situation. Since they saw their power to reside in the autonomous organizations, the spokeswomen continued to put most of their emphasis there. Both Bennett and Hodge first pressed the General Council to solve the organizational problem before it raised the issue of status (i.e., ordination). The women recognized the relatedness of status and power and agreed that both goals needed implementation. The first priority, however, at least in Bennett's and Hodge's minds, was to convince the General Council of the need for a national women's organization of a more inclusive nature than the old missionary boards. Then they would seek official status as elders and ministers. Without enfranchisement, they knew that women would always be second-class members on the periphery of decision making. But status, they believed, would not ensure immediate influence on the councils of the church proportionate to women's numbers on the membership rolls or to their interest in missions and education. They also feared that if the emphasis were put on status, and some gain indeed were made, the male leaders might completely lose interest in the issue of women's organizations.[40]

Between 1925 and 1930 Bennett and Hodge played key roles in keeping the issue before the denomination through their personal influence, their positions as vice presidents in the new structure, their continuing communication with the women in the church, and by publication in 1927 of a carefully documented study entitled "Causes of Unrest Among Women of the Church," the first such critical analysis written by women rather than men.[41] Based on data obtained from Presbyterian women throughout the country, this candid report reflected the dissatisfaction of a small "but intellectually keen" group of women with their position in the church in terms of status, particularly with the loss of their national organizations. Recognizing that few women "as yet" had any interest in preaching, the authors identified lack of representation on denominational councils even without the formalities of ordination as a pressing problem.[42] They concluded that "most ask for no one thing, only that artificial inhibitions that savor of another century having been removed, they may take their place wherever and however their abilities and need of the church may call."[43]

This document prompted the General Council to hold a conference with churchwomen. This meeting—at which women amplified the issues of their unrest—was the first such occasion when men and women met specifically to discuss questions relating to sexual equality in the church. As a result, a committee was charged to bring back recommendations concerning the role of women in the church for eventual submission to the General Assembly in 1929. Robert E. Speer was chairman, and the other members were Hodge, Bennett, and Stated Clerk of the General Assembly Lewis Mudge.[44]

In the course of working out a specific proposal, the four corresponded frequently. Although space does not permit describing the details of this correspondence, its general content and thrust can be summarized.[45] The two men from the beginning focused their attention on the question of status. The two women repeatedly reminded the men that they saw the issue of reinstating women's organizations to have priority, based on their understanding of churchwomen's attitudes. Indeed, both Bennett and Hodge were willing to lay aside the question of status altogether until the question of women's organizations could be definitively settled. Under pressure from Speer and Mudge, however, they agreed to address the issue of official status through ordination, with the assurance that it would not mean ignoring the future of women's organizations. What transpired though was that the final committee report recommended a series of overtures proposing various levels of ordination for women, which addressed the question of status, but touched on women's organizations only to the extent of suggesting that another conference be held to discuss women's organizational concerns.[46]

Although they did not say it publicly, both Speer and Mudge tolerated the existence of women's groups only because they did not want to see a collapse in mission interest and contributions, but they visualized the day when, as part of the evolutionary process of male-female integration in the church, women's groups would cease to exist. Status, they reasoned, would bring women into the mainstream of church life, would give them the equality they desired, and would result ultimately in the exercise of influence and power.[47]

Bennett and Hodge, on the other hand, acknowledged the desirability of a truly unified program in which men and women functioned as equals, but they and other leaders did not share the men's confidence that official status would produce such results. Instead, they reasoned that the power base supplied by a woman's organization would lead to increased influence and eventually status and equality in church courts. As women noted at a Conference on Women's Status and Service in the Church held in 1929,

the ideal is that we are working toward a time when the Church shall *in reality* be an institution where it will be possible for all members of the Church to find their place of service without other discrimination than ability and capacity. When that ideal shall be realized, there *may* be no further need to separate women's organizations.[48]

The theory expressed by the various participants in the conference supported Bennett and Hodge's position:

Power → Equality → Status.

TOWARD EQUALITY

Subsequent events confirmed the women's views about the resolution of their roles in the church. Given an option of overtures on ordination, presbyteries voted to approve only ordination as elders. Ministerial ordination was deferred and not approved for another quarter of a century. Moreover, the future of women's organizations remained unresolved. Despite repeated pleas by churchwomen to rethink the reorganization decisions of 1923, the General Council maintained the status quo. Efforts by the Board of Christian Education to tap the financial resources of the women's missionary societies in the early 1930s precipitated a series of confrontations between churchwomen and the General Council which made male leaders even less inclined to reconsider the status of women's organizations in the total life of the church.[49]

Denominational leaders hailed the appearance of five women elders as commissioners to the General Assembly in 1931 as the beginning of a new era of female participation in church life. Some optimistically predicted that women would soon be a majority in the General Assembly and that through their influence ministerial ordination for women would readily be approved. Their optimism proved unfounded. Women did not enter the eldership in any significant numbers either because their congregations did not choose to elect them or because they themselves thought it improper to serve.[50] Moreover, hit hard by the economic impact of the Great Depression, the Presbyterian Church did not give priority to women's issues which were so prominent in the 1920s. With hundreds of ministers unemployed, the denomination displayed no interest in the subject of ministerial ordination for women. Denominational judicatories and newspapers made no mention of the issue of sexual equality, and the hierarchy of the church continued to be predominantly male.

The General Assembly relieved some of the necessity for female ordination by upgrading and expanding the office of deaconess into the more prestigious position of Director of Christian Education. In the 1920s, curriculum reform and teacher training programs to improve the quality of church schools prompted the appearance of a new type of educator, one not formally ordained but who by special training in religious education supplanted the traditional Sunday School teacher. The Presbyterian Church opened training schools in Baltimore, Philadelphia, and Chicago to prepare lay workers for a variety of parish responsibilities. Although the schools enrolled both sexes, the student body was predominantly female. The denomination formalized the status of Christian educators by creating the office of Commissioned Church Worker (C.C.W.) in an overture approved by the General Assembly in 1938. The basic requirements for a C.C.W. included a high school diploma plus four years of study in approved schools (two years of which were to be in religious training schools), a personal appearance before a presbytery, and an annual examination while under the care of a presbytery.[51]

During the 1920s, changes relating to the professionalization of missionaries were also affecting women. Efforts to reexamine mission concepts and personnel, especially in the foreign field, led to the demand for more specialized training, including a college degree, courses in missionary schools, knowledge of history, sociology, and comparative religious beliefs, and systematic Bible study. In terms of status, although earlier women in individual mission stations might have been allowed to vote in local mission councils, after 1920 the Board of Foreign Missions *Manual* was amended to give women and men equal rights with regard to the transaction of the business of the mission.[52]

Such developments did not change attitudes that ministerial ordination appeared to be a dead issue at least for the time being. Thus, churchwomen persisted in efforts to reconstitute their national organization. At a series of conferences held in the 1930s, leaders in presbyterial and synodical missionary societies discussed ways in which a new organization could be constituted which would have a much more inclusive and appealing program than the former missionary boards. With the support of William Barrow Pugh, who replaced Lewis S. Mudge as stated clerk in 1938, women decided at a conference in 1942 to petition the General Council to recommend to the General Assembly that a new Presbyterian Women's Organization (P.W.O.) be created. The Council agreed in 1943 only after several extended discussions, during which some members again expressed the oft-repeated concern that this might be the beginning of a "woman's church."[53] In presenting the report to the General Assembly, council member Helen Weber raised again the issues of power and status that had surfaced twenty years earlier. She chided her audience that of the 464 commissioners that year only eight were women but nevertheless assured them, "Do not be anxious, the women have no desire to separate from you, taking their contributions with them.... You know that the women have never failed in loyalty and service."[54]

The creation of the P.W.O. in 1943 led indirectly to another emergence of the question of whether organizations, powerful as they might be, were enough without full status for women. The executive committee of the P.W.O. invited Tamaki Uemura, an ordained minister of the Church of Christ of Japan, to officiate at a communion service during a P.W.O. national meeting in May 1946. Because the P.W.O. was not a church court, it could not hold a communion service without the approval of the General Council. When it sought that approval, Stated Clerk Pugh and Moderator William Lampe took the position that since women could not be ordained in the Presbyterian Church they could not administer the sacraments at a service under denominational sponsorship. Although a majority of the General Council concurred with this interpretation, they realized that the time had come to remove such sexist prohibitions from the *Form of Government*. With Pugh's concurrence, the General Council proposed an overture to the presbyteries that "the office of minister may be either men or women."[55] When the overture was sent down for presbyterial consideration, it lost by a margin of 128 to 100 with eight no-action votes. The measure generated virtually no national debate in the denomination and surprisingly did not receive any organized support from the P.W.O. other than to notify women in its monthly magazine that the question of ordination was being considered by the local presbyteries.[56]

Despite the conservative stance of the Presbyterian Church in this rejection, there were signs that the status quo would not long be maintained. Social conditions in America and indeed throughout the world continued to change rapidly. During the war women assumed leadership roles in both secular and ecclesiastical spheres. With the postwar population boom and expanding church programs, the demand for trained workers increased dramatically. Arguments that women would be competing with men for limited positions no longer had relevance. Moreover, organizations such as the newly formed World Council of Churches and the National Council of Churches gave prominent consideration to the expanding role of women in church life and called for a reexamination of the theological and practical arguments for sexual equality. In particular, the publication in 1952 of a study commissioned by the World Council of Churches, *The Service and Status of Women in the Church*, evoked a wide-ranging, positive response in the United States. In the same year, the United Church Women initiated a study of the status of women in denominations associated with the National Council of Churches. The Presbyterian Church participated in the study. Its report indicated that there was considerable sentiment among a new generation of denominational leaders, the most prominent of whom was the newly elected Stated Clerk, Eugene Carson Blake, to reconsider the ordination issue in the near future.[57]

More quickly than anyone anticipated, Presbyterians had an opportunity to express their views on ministerial ordination for women. The impetus did not come directly from the ecumenical studies and denominational committees, however, but from the indignation of one Presbyterian woman, Lilian Hurt (Alexander), a ruling elder in the Third Presbyterian Church in Rochester, New York. Although an active church member, Hurt was unaware that Presbyterian Church policy officially barred women from the pulpit. She learned of this only when a friend described how her daughter had graduated from seminary but could not be accepted as a ministerial candidate simply because she was female. Angered at this blatant discrimination, Hurt drew up a petition requesting the local session to recommend that the Presbytery of Rochester ask the General Assembly in 1953 "to initiate such actions as may be necessary to permit the ordination of women to the ministry of Jesus Christ"[58] and sent it on to the General Assembly for action.

This time around churchwomen threw their support behind the movement to ordain women. The P.W.O. published a number of articles in its monthly magazine commending the overture and organized women in presbyteries and synods to encourage commissioners to vote favorably on it. Even before the overture was formally considered by the General Assembly in 1955, sixty-five presbyteries had publicly indicated their endorsement.[59] Although leaders proceeded cautiously because of delicate reunion negotiations with other Presbyterian denominations that did not ordain women, the right of ordination of women became church law in 1956. The overture added a brief sentence to the *Form of Government* in the section headed "Bishops and Pastors, and Associate Pastors." The sentence read: "Both men and women may be called to this office."[60]

On the eve of its 250th anniversary, the Presbyterian Church in the U.S.A. had at last granted women full ecclesiastical parity with men. The ordination of Margaret Towner, a graduate of Union Theological Seminary in New York, on 24 October 1956, marked the first time that a woman officially assumed the mantle of ministerial authority.[61] Nevertheless, granting women *de jure* equality did not result in a flood of women into seminaries or pulpits. As had been true when they received approval to become elders in 1931, women appeared reluctant to push forward into an all-male establishment. Most of the early candidates for ordination did not contemplate being pastors but utilized it as a way of giving more status to their role of a Christian educator. Fifteen years after ordination for women had been approved, there were only sixty-seven ordained women in the denomination representing a meagre 0.518% of the denomination's ministers.[62]

The culturally ingrained reluctance of women to enter the ministry was reinforced by the attitude of male leaders in the

Presbyterian hierarchy. On the one hand, they were committed to the principle of equality, which they saw emanating from basic theological convictions. On the other hand, they assumed little or no responsibility for breaking down the *de facto* inequality that persisted in most aspects of church life. Executive positions continued to be held almost exclusively by men, and male commissioners dominated the proceedings of the General Assembly. Seminaries, for the most part, remained insensitive to problems encountered by female students studying for ordination in a predominantly male faculty and student body.[63]

In the decade following the granting of ministerial ordination for women, the denomination turned its attention to a series of crucial social and theological issues ranging from school integration and civil rights to the ethical implications of the widening conflict in Vietnam. The General Assembly also adopted a controversial new *Book of Confessions*, joined in the formation of the Consultation on Church Union (C.O.C.U.), and contemplated a major restructuring of boards and agencies, the first since 1923. Although a few voices expressed dismay that *de jure* equality for women had led to little advancement in the participation of women in the decision-making processes of the church, they seemed to have little impact on denominational policy. Most active churchwomen continued to support their powerful national organization, now called United Presbyterian Women (U.P.W.), which raised large sums of money for a variety of missionary, educational, and social projects and trained women for leadership roles in local societies.[64]

Despite an outward serenity, a new generation of churchwomen was dealing with the same issues of an earlier decade: that status does not automatically lead to power and equality and that power, to be effective, must be utilized in ways other than through traditional women's organizations. Encouraged by the rapid growth and visibility of the feminist movement in secular society, a small group of Presbyterian women, both lay and clergy, decided to confront the denomination publicly with its inherent sexism and to rally support for some radical changes in its policies and practices. The women caucused to develop a strategy of presenting their grievances; and through the assist-

ance of Stated Clerk Eugene Carson Blake, they were referred
to the Office of Church and Society as a channel of communication with the church at large.[65]

Based on a recommendation from the Office of Church and
Society, the General Assembly in 1967 appointed a committee
to study the role of women in society and church. Two years
later the committee issued a report which candidly described
the extent of sexual discrimination in ecclesiastical life and called
for the creation of a Task Force on Women as an advocacy group
for women's concerns. The Task Force on Women assumed permanent form in reorganization as the Council on Women and
the Church (C.O.W.A.C.). With financial support from the denomination and assistance from U.P.W., C.O.W.A.C. developed programs to assist both professional and lay churchwomen.
C.O.W.A.C. also closely monitored General Assembly policies
and programs and sponsored specific legislation designed to
remove sexism from church life.[66] In response to these efforts,
the General Assembly between 1970 and 1980 approved the creation of a new women's support group, initiated a series of
overtures to guarantee women equal opportunity of service,
sponsored workshops and study sessions for intensive examination of problems facing women in the 1970s, wrestled with
the presence of sexist language in theology and liturgy, took
stands on controversial issues such as E.R.A. and abortion, and
opened executive positions and committee assignments previously reserved exclusively for males.[67]

Despite the obvious gains made by Presbyterian women in
the century 1870–1980, few observers believed that the struggle
for genuine equality was over. Conservative reaction to some of
the changes resulted in the defection of congregations from the
denomination and the formation of groups opposed to further
legislation. Many women themselves demonstrated the traditional ambivalence about their proper place in church life, even
refusing to accept church offices. Others lamented that the denomination was moving too slowly and feared that the momentum achieved in the early 1970s was dissipating. One of the most
perceptive appraisals was made by Patricia Doyle in an address
to the General Assembly in 1970."The equality of women is
related to every other search for freedom. It will be the single

most difficult item to achieve on the agenda of the church and the world. As such, it will need years of strong effort on the part of the Church."[68]

NOTES

1. The research on which this essay is based comes in large part from materials in the Presbyterian Historical Society (P.H.S.), Philadelphia, Pa., and is used with its permission. An expanded discussion of the role of women in the Presbyterian Church appears in Lois A. Boyd and R. Douglas Brackenridge, *Presbyterian Women in America: Two Centuries of a Quest for Status* (Westport, Conn.: Greenwood Press, 1983). The treatment here deals only with the Presbyterian Church in the U.S.A. The church was known between 1958 and 1983 as the United Presbyterian Church in the United States of America (U.P.U.S.A.). In 1983 it united with the Presbyterian Church in the United States to become the Presbyterian Church (U.S.A.). The smaller denominations (United Presbyterian Church in the U.S.A., Cumberland Presbyterian Church, and Presbyterian Church in the U.S.) had histories parallel to that described but within different time frames.

2. See Boyd and Brackenridge, *Presbyterian Women in America*, for a detailed description of the organization of Presbyterian women. The Women's Executive Committee of Home Missions was organized in 1878. The seven regional boards for foreign missions were centered in New York, Philadelphia, Chicago, Albany, St. Louis, Portland, and San Francisco. The Albany and New York boards merged in 1908. These regional boards joined in a Central Coordinating Committee, but each handled its funds and programs separately. They merged into one Woman's Board of Foreign Missions in 1920.

3. Presbyterian Church in the U.S.A., *General Assembly Minutes*, (Philadelphia, 1832), p. 378. Hereafter cited as *G.A.M.*

4. John Calvin, *Commentaries on the First Book of Moses Called Genesis*, 1 (Grand Rapids: Wm. B. Eerdmans, 1948): 129–30; John Calvin, *The First Epistle of Paul the Apostle to the Corinthians* (Grand Rapids: Wm. B. Eerdmans, 1960), p. 233; Albert Barnes, *Notes, Explanatory and Practical, on the First Epistle of Paul to the Corinthians* (New York: Harper and Brothers, 1837); and Jonathan F. Stearns, *Female Influence, and the True Christian Mode of Its Exercise* (Newburyport, Mass., John G. Tilton, 1837) provide an example of the type of literature and sermons that prevailed.

5. Among the many studies in this area are: Nancy F. Cott, *The Bonds of Womanhood: "Woman's Sphere" in New England, 1780–1835* (New Haven: Yale University Press, 1977); Ann Douglas, *The Feminization of*

American Culture (New York: Knopf, 1977); Eleanor Flexner, *Century of Struggle: The Woman's Rights Movement in the United States*, rev. ed. (Cambridge: Harvard University Press, Belknap Press, 1975); Ann Firor Scott, *The Southern Lady: From Pedestal to Politics 1830–1930* (Chicago: University of Chicago Press, 1970); Alice Felt Tyler, *Freedom's Ferment: Phases of American Social History from the Colonial Period to the Outbreak of the Civil War* (New York: Harper Torchbooks, 1962). See also Elizabeth Cady Stanton, Susan B. Anthony, and Matilda Joslyn Gage, eds., *History of Woman Suffrage*, (New York: Arno and the New York *Times*, 1969, facsimile; originally published New York: Fowler and Wells, 1881).

6. Stanton, Anthony, Gage, *History of Woman Suffrage*, 1: 67.

7. *The Critic* 9 (4 December 1886): 273. See also Frances A. Wood, *Earliest Years at Vassar: Personal Recollections* (Poughkeepsie: Vassar College Press, 1909).

8. These categories are defined in Kate Gannett Wells, "Women's Organizations," *Atlantic Monthly* 46 (September 1880): 360–69.

9. Theodore L. Cuyler, prominent Presbyterian clergyman and author, invited a Quaker woman to preach from the pulpit of the 1,400–member Lafayette Presbyterian Church in Brooklyn in 1872 and again in 1874. The same woman, Sarah Smiley, was invited to preach at Second Church in Geneva, N.Y., in the same year. "A Woman in the Pulpit," *Harper's Weekly* (2 March 1871), p. 1; *The Presbyterian* (6 July 1872), p. 4; "Minutes of the Presbytery of Brooklyn," 12 January 1874, and 26 January 1874, Presbyterian Historical Society, hereafter P.H.S.

10. The specifics of the trial can be found in "Minutes of the Presbytery of Newark" for the period of the proceedings, and from the General Assembly Study Document entitled *The Case of the Rev. E.R. Craven against the Rev. I.M. See, in the Presbytery of Newark and the Synod of New Jersey*, P.H.S. hereafter cited as *Case*. A full account of the trial is in Lois A. Boyd, "Shall Women Speak? Confrontation in the Church, 1876," *Journal of Presbyterian History* 56 (Winter 1978): 281–94.

11. *Case*, p. 1.

12. "Feminine Oratory," *The Presbyterian* (6 January 1872), p. 8; "The Woman Question," *The Presbyterian* (24 June 1876), p. 14; *Congregational Quarterly* (16 April 1874), p. 279. According to *The Presbyterian* (6 July 1872), when Sarah Smiley preached at Second Church, Geneva, N.Y., the opposition came "chiefly from the ladies of the church" (p. 4).

13. "Women's Prayer," *Woman's Work for Woman* 13 (January 1883): 91–92; "Encouragement to Christian Women," *The Presbyterian* (2 March 1872), p. 1; *Herald and Presbyter* (4 March 1874), p. 4; Boyd and Brackenridge, *Presbyterian Women In America*, p. 108.

14. In an "Appreciation" to the Board of Home Missions on 11 May

1915 (Record Group 105, P.H.S), the officers of the Woman's Board of Home Missions claimed that "Mrs. James [the president from 1886–1909] brought us up with deference and obedience to the Assembly's Board. 'Loyalty to the Board' was one of her re-iterated maxims, and when her mantle fell upon her associate Mrs. Bennett, the same policy was pursued."

15. For details, see "Woman's Boards: A Vital Asset in Nation-Building, 1878–1923," in Boyd and Brackenridge, *Presbyterian Women in America*, pp. 35–57.

16. Emeline G. Pierson to Mrs. T.C. Hamlin, 10 April 1900, Record Group 51–4–17, P.H.S.

17. Boyd and Brackenridge, *Presbyterian Women in America*, p. 53.

18. Ibid., pp. 38, 49–50, 164–65. See also "Colored Women as Christian Workers," *Home Mission Monthly* 17 (April 1903): 131–37. The author noted that the black women who wished to enter foreign missions could not be commissioned by the Presbyterian Church in the U.S.A. "Our own church does not commission colored misionaries, only educates for other Boards" (p. 137).

19. This did not become an openly expressed issue until the 1920s. See Boyd and Brackenridge, *Presbyterian Women in America*, pp. 124, 125, 128–29.

20. G.A.M. 1789–1820, 1811: 310; 1817: 26; 1891: 139.

21. Boyd and Brackenridge, *Presbyterian Women in America*, p. 108. Especially important was a book by George P. Hays, *May Women Speak?* (Evanston, IL: WCTU, 1898). Hays, a distinguished minister and theologian, was a former moderator of the General Assembly and former college president.

22. G.A.M. 1892: 170.

23. Boyd and Brackenridge, *Presbyterian Women in America*, pp. 101, 166, 170–71. Notices of such occurrences can be picked up in church newspapers and magazines. One example came from a letter to the editor in *Presbyterian Life* (September 1951) in which a daughter wrote that her mother, widow of a Presbyterian clergyman, had been ordained as minister in the Congregational Church in 1930 but had always filled Presbyterian pulpits in Kansas and Missouri. Her mother was a pastor of a Presbyterian church when the letter was written. The daughter added, "Isn't it a shame that the Presbyterian Church, which prides itself on being progressive, is so slow to recognize legally the excellent work of so many highly educated and deeply consecrated women?" (p. 3). We found several other instances in which the wife assumed a pulpit after a husband's death or filled one pulpit while he was filling a second in a multiple-church parish. A wife stepping into her deceased spouse's position on the mission field was not uncommon.

24. Boyd and Brackenridge, *Presbyterian Women in America*, p. 124.

25. The network of women's missionary societies by this time encompassed some 6,000 local societies which raised about $3 million dollars annually for missionary endeavors. See Boyd and Brackenridge, *Presbyterian Women in America*, pp. 59–60.

26. *G.A.M.* (U.S.A.) 1919, I:267; and "Minutes of the Presbytery of Dallas" (U.S.A.), 12 April 1919, P.H.S.

27. *G.A.M.* (U.S.A.) 1920, I: 126; 1921, I: 20, 44.

28. *G.A.M.* (U.S.A.) 1923, I: 111–45. Much of the material in this section is from R. Douglas Brackenridge and Lois A. Boyd, "Questions of Status and Power: A Case Study of Presbyterian Women in the 1920s" (Paper presented at the American Society of Church History, San Francisco, 29 December 1983).

29. *G.A.M.* (U.S.A.) 1923, I: 111–45.

30. "Comments Received During the Syllabus Controversy," 1931, Record Group 81–41–19, P.H.S., p.6. See also Stone correspondence in Record Group 81.

31. "Conference of the General Council with Fifteen Representative Women," 22 November 1928, Record Group 105, P.H.S., p. 2.

32. In Record Group 121–27, P.H.S.

33. Ibid. There are many other letters of a similar nature in this Record Group.

34. See, for example, Margaret Hodge, "Votes for Women," *Women's Work for Missions* (January 1923), pp. 89–90.

35. Ellen Lauderbaugh to Robert E. Speer, 23 January 1929, P.H.S.

36. Katharine Bennett and Margaret Hodge, *Causes of Unrest Among Women of the Church* (Philadelphia: General Council, 1927), p. 18.

37. Ellen Lauderbaugh to Robert E. Speer, 23 January 1929, Record Group 105, P.H.S.

38. Margaret Hodge to Robert E. Speer, 23 January 1929, Record Group 105, P.H.S.

39. Katharine Bennett to Margaret Hodge, 28 February 1925.

40. Margaret Hodge to Robert E. Speer, 28 January 1929, and Katharine Bennett to Robert E. Speer, 5 February 1929, Record Group 105, P.H.S. Earlier Bennett had proposed the creation of a third class of representation in addition to ministers and elders specifically for women. Katharine Bennett to Lewis S. Mudge, 7 February 1928. Mudge opposed the idea because he thought it would ultimately work against full equality for women.

41. "Minutes of the General Council of the Presbyterian Church in the United States of America," 30 November 1927, p. 26, Record Groups 81–99, P.H.S., hereafter referred to as General Council Minutes. See also *G.A.M.* (U.S.A.) 1929, I: 186.

42. Bennett and Hodge, *Causes of Unrest Among Women of the Church*, p. 25.

43. Ibid., p. 27.

44. General Council Minutes, 28 November 1928, p. 17.

45. For details, see R. Douglas Brackenridge, "Equality for Women? A Case Study in Presbyterian Policy 1926–1930," *Journal of Presbyterian History* 58 (Summer 1980): 142–65.

46. *G.A.M.* (U.S.A.) 1929, I: 189.

47. Lewis S. Mudge to Robert E. Speer, 9 February 1929, P.H.S.

48. *Findings of the Conference of Women's Status and Service in the Church* (Philadelphia: Office of the General Assembly, 1929), pp. 3–4.

49. For details of this controversy, see Boyd and Brackenridge, *Presbyterian Women in America*, pp. 69–75.

50. For a survey of attitudes in the denomination, see Information Service, "Women's Status in Protestant Churches," *Federal Council of Churches Bulletin* (16 November 1940), pp. 4–8.

51. *G.A.M.* (U.S.A.) 1938, I: 71–75. By 1956, when ministerial ordination for women was approved, of 237 registered C.C.W.'s only sixteen were men. Subsequently, interest in the C.C.W. movement declined, and the position was eliminated in 1976.

52. Boyd and Brackenridge, *Presbyterian Women in America*, pp. 166–67, 170–73.

53. General Council Minutes, 2 March and 26 May 1943.

54. *Women and Missions* (July-August 1943), pp. 17–18.

55. General Council Minutes, 21 May 1946.

56. *G.A.M.* (U.S.A.) 1947, I: 129.

57. Mossie A. Wyker, "Church Women in the Scheme of Things," *Outreach* (February 1954), p. 35; and Mossie A. Wyker, "Statement Regarding the Position of Women in the Presbyterian Church, U.S.A.," typescript, n.d., pp. 5–6.

58. "Minutes of the Session of Third Presbyterian Church, Rochester, New York," 13 January 1953, P.H.S.

59. *Presbyterian Life Magazine* (17 March 1956), p. 16.

60. Ibid. (9 June 1956), pp. 29–30.

61. Ibid. (27 October 1956), p. 18.

62. *G.A.M.* (U.P.U.S.A.) 1969, I: 319.

63. Mary Ann Gehres, "Women's Place in the Pulpit," *Presbyterian Life* (15 September 1959), pp. 12–14; Elisa Des Portes Wheeler, *Women in Ministry: The Case of Anne Montgomery* (Hartford: Research Report of the Hartford Seminary Foundation, (1975), pp. 3–5.

64. Boyd and Brackenridge, *Presbyterian Women in America*, pp. 83–87.

65. Wilmina Rowland Smith, interview by R.D. Brackenridge and Lois A. Boyd, 5–6 May 1977; *Presbyterian Life* (15 June 1967), p. 42.

66. *G.A.M.* (U.P.U.S.A.) 1972, I: 252–53.

67. A summary of these actions can be found in R.D. Brackenridge and Lois A. Boyd, "United Presbyterian Policy on Women and the Church—An Historical Overview," *Journal of Presbyterian History* 59 (Fall 1981): 400–406.

68. *Presbyterian Life* (15 June 1970), p. 27.

9

Participation of Women in the Public Life of the Anglican Communion

V. Nelle Bellamy

The Anglican Communion is a worldwide fellowship of dioceses or regional churches in communion with the See of Canterbury. The churches have inherited a sacramental Catholic tradition with its doctrine of the ordained ministry, and they have also been informed by the tenets of the Reformation on the Continent. The participation of women in the public life of the churches, that is in the ministry and government, raises, therefore, special issues in the Anglican Communion not germane to those faced by women in other non-Roman or non-Orthodox churches. It seems appropriate because of the unique history of Anglicanism to begin this essay with a brief resume of theology and polity.

There are approximately 64 million Anglicans today in churches on the continents of Europe, Africa, North and South America, and Asia. The Lambeth Conference of 1930 described these churches as "a fellowship, within the one Holy, Catholic and Apostolic Church, of those duly constituted Dioceses, Provinces or Regional Churches in communion with the See of Canterbury. . . . " They "uphold and propagate the Catholic and Apostolic faith and order as they are generally set forth in the Book of Common Prayer as authorized in the several Churches. . . . "

They are therefore particular or national, expressing their faith within the nations of which they are a part. There is no central organization or legislative body; they are "bound together ... by mutual loyalty sustained through the common counsel of the Bishops in conference."[1] The most visible expressions of "common counsel" are the Lambeth Conferences which have convened about every ten years since 1867. The conferences have adopted resolutions on the pertinent issues and worldwide situations of the times. They have made theological statements which represent the positions of the bishops and through them the churches. In 1888 the bishops set forth four tenets of their theology as a basis upon which ecumenical dialogue might proceed. The Lambeth Quadrilateral, as this statement has come to be known, affirmed their belief: in the Old and New Testaments as containing " 'all things necessary to salvation,' and as being the rule and ultimate standard of faith;" in the Apostles' and Nicene Creeds as the "sufficient statement of the Christian faith;" in the sacraments of baptism and the Eucharist "ministered with unfailing use of Christ's words of Institution, and of the elements ordained by Him;" and in the "Historic Episcopate, locally adapted in the methods of its administration to the varying needs of the nations and peoples called of God into the Unity of His Church."[2] This fourth article places Anglicanism in the Catholic tradition and declares a different doctrine of the ordained ministry than is found among the Protestant churches of the Reformation. In 1948 the Lambeth bishops agreed that the following commentary on the doctrine of the historic episcopate is in harmony with the Quadrilateral. The historic episcopate according to the commentary involved "acceptance, in the form of a fact, of the three-fold ministry of bishops, priests and deacons, and the acceptance of it also as accompanied by the claim that it is a ministerial succession tracing back to the 'Apostles' time'."[3]

In the Roman and Orthodox churches this historic episcopate with its threefold order of ordained ministers has been expressed through a male priesthood. This has been the case in Anglicanism also. It can be argued, therefore, or so it seems, that this Catholic heritage in Anglicanism with the centrality of a male priesthood poses special issues both for professional lay women and for those seeking ordination. It has affected the participation of women in the counsels of the churches. To make this claim is not to discount the influence of other theological issues or the social and cultural pressures of the times in the movement of women into leadership positions in the churches; it is to suggest, however, that this Catholic heritage provides theological and traditional issues that women in the Presbyterian or Lutheran churches, for example, need not encounter.

The Catholic heritage exists within a democratic polity in the churches of the Anglican Communion, and it is this polity which has permitted in recent years the emergence of female leadership in varying degrees in some of the churches. Nevertheless, the way has not been an easy one for the women involved nor for many of the communicants in the parishes. The leadership is more visible in some churches than others. It is almost non-existent in the African churches, for example, but much more prevalent in the Episcopal Church, U.S.A. This essay proposes to examine the leadership positions of women in two of the churches of the Anglican Communion, the Church of England and the Episcopal Church, U.S.A. To discern the history of women's ministries in the Anglican Communion and the position of the bishops one must examine the Lambeth Resolutions from 1867 to 1978.[4] Although these resolutions have no canonical or legislative authority unless adopted by the appropriate body in each church, they reflect the thinking of the bishops and through them of the churches. After examining the large number of resolutions on the participation of women in the public life of the churches, this essay will present a profile of the activities of women in leadership roles on a national level in the Church of England and the Episcopal Church, U.S.A. The narrowing of the discussion to the national scene in the churches is necessary for the purposes of a short essay. The contributions of faithful parish lay women are a matter of historical record, and there is no intent to minimize them.

THE LAMBETH RESOLUTIONS

The eleven Lambeth Conferences issued resolutions on the important events of the times, as the bishops discerned them; among them are a large number pertaining to women in the

churches. The bishops composed committee reports, deliber-
ated, and adopted resolutions pertaining to the laity, members
of religious communities, deaconesses, women workers, deacons, priests, and bishops. A careful reading of this material
reveals the movement of the churches from a conservative, re-
strictive stance to the more recent emerging affirmation of wom-
en's vocations in the churches. The Lambeth fathers, the episcopal
representatives of their churches, do not appear to have acted
in any creative or prophetic ways; rather they seem to have
moved with or a bit behind the culture. They noted the stirrings
in the secular world as women found new areas of endeavor.
They saw that women were not treated equally with men in the
churches and set about to remedy the situation in so far as they
could theologically bring themselves to do so. By 1968 and 1978
the bishops had embraced a far wider vision of the contributions
of women than had existed fifty years earlier.

Laity

Anglicanism has been and is largely today hierarchical and
clerical, that is dominated by the clergy in its leadership. At the
beginning of the century the place of the laity in the churches
was, therefore, an important issue. Thus in 1908 a resolution
spoke to the relationship of clergy to laity in the churches; it
recognized the ministry of the laity as "side by side with the
ministry of the clergy, in the work, the administration and the
discipline of the Church."[5] In 1920 the Lambeth discussions
moved to the place of women among the laity. A comprehensive
pre-conference report on the "Position of Women in the Councils
and Ministrations of the Church" reflected the awareness among
the bishops that women were becoming better educated, entering universities, and holding prominent positions in society. As
the committee commented on the competence of these women,
it obviously sought to move with the times; it declared that
"difference of function between man and woman in the Church,
as in the world, and the relative subordination of woman in no
way imply an inferiority of woman in regard to man." Yet the
Lambeth fathers could move only so far. Their uneasiness is
seen as they cautioned that the "elementary facts of human

nature" must not be forgotten and that "women have the power of moving men." They were unable to resist noting that there is "deep wisdom in the words of the New Testament which say of a faithful Christian woman 'she shall be saved through her child bearing.' "[6] The two resolutions from the Conference of 1920 which addressed women's issues did not contain any of the committee's language on the chemistry between the sexes. They urged that laywomen be admitted on an equal basis in the councils where laymen were active. They further permitted men and women "to speak in consecrated or unconsecrated buildings, and to lead in prayer, at other than the regular and appointed services of the Church."[7]

Stronger theological statements on the laity in the ministry of the churches came in 1958 when the bishops recognized that the laity shared in the priestly ministry of the church through baptism. The bishops called on all Anglican men and women to realize this by taking part in the life of the church.[8] In 1968 there were four resolutions recommending lay involvement with opportunities for training and education. Resolution 24 cautioned that all major issues in the life of the church be decided with the full participation of the laity.[9]

Members of the Religious Communities

The religious life is one of the traditional vocations for women in the Christian church; it originated in the third century in the East and has continued through nearly 1600 years. Even in the twentieth century when there is a wider scope of vocations for women, this way of life remains a viable one for many devout women. The term "the religious life" is a technical one in monastic literature and refers to those Christians living in communities who have taken the traditional vows of poverty, chastity, and obedience.

In sixteenth-century England the religious life was dissolved by Henry VIII, the great old monastic houses were closed, and the members of the communities were scattered about. By the end of the nineteenth century the religious life had been revived in England, and communities again existed. This came to the attention of the bishops at the 1897 conference. They noted "with thankfulness" the existence again of brotherhoods, sisterhoods, and deaconesses.[10] In 1930 the conference again recognized "with thankfulness" the growth of religious communities in the Anglican Communion and advised a closer cooperation between the episcopate and the communities along the lines recommended in a pre-conference committee report, "The Ministry of the Church." This report sought for a kind of supervision of the communities by the diocesan bishops.[11] A resolution in 1948 referred to the value of this "special vocation" but pointed out that Christians were "generally called by God to take their part in the life of the world, and through the power of God's grace to transform it."[12] The Lambeth bishops in 1958 commended this "special form of vocation" to the Anglican Communion.[13] Finally in 1968 came the strongest resolution from the bishops. It recognized the contributions of the religious life to the church and expressed its appreciation for the "witness to the absolute character of the claims of God on the life of man, to the fruitfulness of a life given to prayer and service, and to the unity of the Church across the divisions which at present exist." It called upon the communities to take a part in the renewal of the church.[14]

On Deaconesses

The ministry of deaconesses flourished in the early church. Janet Grierson's carefully documented and useful book, *The Deaconess*,[15] traces the history of this vocation for women from those early years to the present. The deaconesses were quite active in the fourth and fifth centuries in what Grierson calls the "golden age of deaconesses" in the East. One recalls Olympias who served at the cathedral in Constantinople when John Chrysostom was patriarch. By the twelfth century the ministry had declined in the East. In the West it is less easy to trace, and in the Middle Ages it came into competition with the religious communities. In the early years, it appears that deaconesses visited the sick, the poor, and those in need. Generally they ministered to women; they assisted in their baptism, anointing them and providing instruction.

In the nineteenth century, leaders in the Church of England "restored" the ancient Order of Deaconesses. Elizabeth Catherine Ferard was set apart by the Right Reverend A.C. Tait of the Diocese of London in 1862 and became the first episcopally ordained deaconess in England since the Reformation. Deaconess Grierson traces the expansion of this ministry to women by women as the deaconesses became social workers, nurses, teachers, and parish workers, and their numbers increased. By 1900 there were at least 180 in England and Wales, and in 1918 at least 340.[16] The Lambeth Conference of 1897 convened in the midst of this growth and took note "with thankfulness" of the revival of the office of deaconess.[17]

At the Lambeth Conferences in 1920, 1930, and 1948 there were extended resolutions that sought to describe the order of deaconess in relationship to the historic threefold order of ministry and further to detail appropriate responsibilities for this ministry of women.

"The Report of the Committee Appointed to Consider and Report upon the Position of Women in the Councils and Ministrations of the Church" prepared by thirty-two bishops for the Lambeth Conference of 1920 closely examined the position of the deaconesses and their participation in the church. It referred to the "large measure of uncertainty" that prevailed on the status of a deaconess. It asked, "Is a Deaconess set apart for a religious office? Or is she in the full sense of the word Ordained so that she possesses Holy Orders?" The committee stated clearly: "In our judgment the ordination of a Deaconess confers on her Holy Orders. In ordination she receives the 'character' of a Deaconess in the Church of God; and, therefore, the status of a woman ordained to the Diaconate has the permanence which belongs to Holy Orders." It also declared that "for Women the Order of Deaconesses is the one and only Order of the Ministry which has the stamp of Apostolic approval (Rom. 16:1; 1 Tim. 3:2); and for Women it is the one and only Order which we can recommend that our Branch of the Catholic church should recognize and use."[18] The resolutions of the conference did not fully incorporate the committee's judgment that the ordination of a deaconess conferred holy orders, although in Resolution 47 it used the term "the Diaconate of Women" and recommended that it "should be restored formally and canonically."[19] Resolution 48 followed word for word the statement in the committee report that this is the "only Order of the Ministry which we can recommend. . . . "[20] In Resolution 49 the office was described as following "the lines of the primitive rather than of the modern Diaconate of men."[21] Many clergy and deaconesses in the Church of England interpreted the committee report and the conference resolutions to mean that deaconesses were removed from a lay status and were therefore a part of the ordained ministry. This understanding seems to be the basis of the present confusion on the status of deaconesses,[22] wherein some deaconesses consider themselves within the ordained ministry while others see themselves as lay people. Resolutions 49 to 52 described the office of a deaconess, prescribed the ingredients in a "Form and Manner of Making of Deaconesses," and listed appropriate functions. The form provided for prayer by the bishop with the laying on of hands, a formula to give "the authority to execute the Office of a Deaconess in the Church of God," and the delivery by the bishop of the New Testament to each candidate. The functions entrusted to deaconesses were to prepare people for baptism and confirmation, to assist at the administration of baptism with the authority to administer it in "cases of necessity," to pray with and counsel women, to read morning and evening prayer and the litany in church except those parts assigned to the priest, to "lead the prayer" in church, and to "instruct and exhort the Congregation."[23]

In the ten years between Lambeth Conferences the status of the deaconess was not fully clarified, and resolutions on the subject were drawn up again. The 1930 Committee Report, "The Ministry of the Church," prepared by fifty-one bishops, did not accept a deaconess as "the female equivalent of the existing Deacon." It affirmed the order of deaconess as an "Order *sui generis*" and "the only Order of Ministry open to women." It further recognized that "this may be thought to be a departure from primitive practice, but the times have changed. . . ."[24] Thus any emphasis on the woman deacon as the counterpart of a male deacon believed by some to be a part of the New Testament church seems to have been lost. The Resolutions of the 1930 Lambeth Conference reaffirmed that the "Order of Deaconess is for women the one and only Order of the Ministry which we can recommend our branch of the Catholic Church to recognize and use." Reference was made to the "Ordination of a Deacon-ess," but it was not to be "combined with an ordination of Priests or Deacons. . . . " In Resolution 70 the functions of the deaconess were listed: they were those of the 1920 Conference with certain additions; the deaconess could "officiate at the Churching of Women," instruct, and preach—but not during the service of holy communion.[25]

At the 1948 Lambeth Conference the bishops reaffirmed Res-olution 67 of the 1930 Conference that the order of deaconess was for women "the one and only Order of the Ministry" which they could recommend. It further urged that the work of dea-conesses should be encouraged throughout the Anglican Communion.[26]

In 1968 the theological climate was changing in the churches as the bishops gathered at Lambeth. Resolution 32 recom-mended that "those made deaconesses by laying on of hands with appropriate prayers be declared to be within the diacon-ate."[27] The vote was a close one with 221 voting for and 183 against. It was reconsidered at the conference in 1978 when Resolution 32 (c) of 1968 was recalled and there was a recom-mendation that the churches admit women to the diaconate and not ordain them to a "separate order of deaconesses."[28]

Women Workers

Women have had a long history of dedicated service to the people in their parishes and to the poor in their communities. Out of these voluntary services the more professional positions of "women workers" emerged. The first resolution pertaining to women workers came in 1920. In the pre-Lambeth committee report on the "Position of Women," the bishops expressed ap-preciation for the work of women in the churches and set about to consider the subject. The committee thought that laywomen could speak in "consecrated and unconsecrated buildings" and that they could lead in prayer in a service other than the "regular and appointed" ones of the churches. Recognizing that women workers should have some kind of oversight, the committee recommended the establishment of a Board of Women's Work in every diocese to provide for a kind of certification and to consider training, employment, and stipends for women workers. Resolution 54 sought to do some consciousness raising among the bishops and their churches on the care of women workers, their employment, and their salaries.[29]

In 1930 the committee report, "The Ministry of the Church," welcomed the progress "in training and organization, both central and diocesan, for lay women workers." It emphasized that "all paid workers should receive an adequate stipend together with a place in a recognized pension scheme, and work under a formal agreement which specifies terms of employment, including time for study and devotion and provision for holidays." Thus the bishops were moving toward a professional vocation with appropriate benefits. In keeping with the presence of women in professional jobs in the secular work force, the bishops realized the importance of "proper scope and real opportunity" for the talents of women.[30] Resolution 72 admonished that diocesan bishops should determine that an "adequate stipend" and pension be paid women workers and that the women have formal work agreements.[31]

In 1948 the conference welcomed the contributions of women "in many walks of life" but prefaced the statement by "recognizing that marriage and motherhood remain the normal vocation of women."[32] Resolution 93 in 1958 again acknowledged the contributions of women and urged fuller use of talents of "trained and qualified women."[33] After 1958 there are no specific resolutions pertaining to women workers. The interest of many women in ordination to the priesthood seems to have overshadowed the earlier emphasis on lay vocations for women in the churches.

Ordained Ministry

The Lambeth Conferences have not recommended the ordination of women to the priesthood. The committee report in 1920, which considered rather fully the position of women in the church and argued for more equality and opportunity in the "Councils and Ministrations of the Church," stopped short of recommending the ordination of women to the priesthood. In 1930 the pre-Lambeth report, "The Ministry of the Church," referred to an "urgent plea for admission of women to the Priest-hood" that had come to their attention, but they did not rec-ommend any action for three reasons: the times were not right, a majority of the members of the sub-committee thought that there were theological reasons against such ordination, and oth-ers foresaw practical problems.[34]

A concrete situation in the Diocese of Hong Kong brought the subject of the ordination of women to the attention of the 1948 Lambeth Conference. In 1944 Bishop R.0.Hall of Hong Kong and South China ordained Deaconess Florence Lee Tim Oi to the priesthood in order that the sacraments might be available in Macao and the surrounding area. The Holy Catholic Church of China (Chung Hua Sheng Kung Hui, C.H.S.K.H.) felt that it could not approve of this "ordination," and Florence Lee Tim Oi resigned but continued to work as a deaconess. Then the General Synod of C.H.S.K.H. received a proposal from the Di-ocese of South China for a new canon permitting an experimental period of twenty years wherein a deaconess might be ordained to the priesthood. The General Synod sought the advice of the Lambeth Conference of 1948 as to "whether or not such liberty to experiment within the framework of the Anglican Commun-ion would be in accordance with Anglican tradition and order." The reply was negative; the bishops feared that this would "gravely affect the internal and external relations of the Anglican Communion."[35]

In 1968 a report, "The Renewal of the Church in Ministry," considered the ordination of women and began its theological section with the statement: "We find no conclusive theological reasons for withholding ordination to the priesthood from women as such."[36] The resolution from the conference did not follow the report; it stated "that the theological arguments as at present presented for and against the ordination of women to the priest-hood are inconclusive."[37] Resolution 35 requested all churches "to give careful study to the question of the ordination of women to the priesthood and report its findings" either to the Anglican Consultative Council (or the Lambeth Consultative Body)."[38] Resolution 37 recommended that the advice of one of these two bodies be sought and considered before a church made the de-cision to ordain women.[39]

By the time the 1978 conference was convened ten years later, four churches had admitted women to the priesthood: the Diocese of Hong Kong, the Anglican Church of Canada, the Episcopal Church, U.S.A., and the Church of the Province of New Zealand. Eight other churches had "either agreed or approved in principle or stated that there are either no fundamental or no theological objections to the ordination of women to the historic threefold ministry of the Church." The bishops remained divided on the subject, with some objecting to the ordination of women to the priesthood and others not having made a decision and, of course, others approving. Resolution 21 was an obvious attempt to retain the fellowship among the bishops; it referred to "distress and pain to many on both sides" but also recognized the autonomy of the member churches. It declared its "acceptance of those member Churches which now ordain women," its "acceptance of those member Churches which do not ordain women," and its awareness of the variety of doctrine in its midst. The bishops also attempted to regulate the passage of ordained women from one church to another by recommending that their priesthood should be exercised only "where such a ministry is agreeable to the bishop, clergy, and people where the ministry is to be exercised and where it is approved by the legally responsible body of the parish, area, or institution where such a ministry is to be exercised." Out of 370 bishops 316 voted that further conversations be pursued, 37 voted against such conversations, and there were 17 abstentions.[40]

The 1968 and 1978 Conferences moved more rapidly in the area of the diaconate. The bishops in 1968 recommended, as was noted in the sections on deaconesses, that "those made deaconesses by laying on of hands with appropriate prayers be declared to be within the diaconate." They sought to deal with the basic theological issues pertaining to the office of deacon and suggested the removal of references to "an inferior office."[41] In 1978 the Conference urged that churches not ordaining women deacons do so.[42]

The first resolution on consecrating a woman to the episcopate came in 1978. It urged that "consultation with the episcopate through the primates" be made previous to such consecration and that a church have "overwhelming support" within "lest the bishop's office should become a cause of disunity instead of a focus of unity."[43]

THE PRESENT SCENE

The resolutions document the thinking of Anglican bishops and their churches for more than 100 years. They trace a measure of acceptance of women's vocations. What, then, is the situation in the churches of the early 1980s? Are women in the leadership of the churches? More specifically, what leadership positions do women hold in two of the churches of the Anglican Communion, the Church of England and the Episcopal Church, U.S.A.? The Lambeth resolutions on women's ministries have been discussed under the categories of laity, members of religious communities, deaconesses, women workers, and the ordained ministry. These same categories will be followed in examining the present scene.

Laity

Women have been members of the legislative body of the Church of England since 1919 when they were a part of the Church Assembly. The General Synod, the modern successor of the Church Assembly, is composed of the House of Bishops, the House of Clergy, and the House of Laity. Of the 250 members of the House of Laity in 1983 there are eighty-six women; that is, 34.4% of the members are women.[44] Eleven of these are deaconesses, two are members of religious communities, and seventy-three are laywomen. A survey of the persons serving on General Synod committees and other boards, councils, and commissions indicates only a small number of women participants. Among the eighteen elected members of the Standing Committee of the General Synod there are four women. The appointed member is a woman. The large Central Board of Finance with a possible membership of nearly seventy has no elected women, but there are three appointed by the Standing Committee of the General Synod. The Advisory Council for the Church's Ministry which coordinates the concerns of accredited lay and ordained ministries has recently employed a full-time staff person, a woman, to work with women's ministries. Three other women are listed on the staff, and there are five among the twenty-six Council members. The twenty-member Board for Mission and Unity includes three women plus a newly appointed study secretary, who is a woman. For the most part there are women representatives on the various boards and commissions with the notable exception of the Commission on Doctrine. The Church Commissioners who administer the stipends for clergy, deaconesses, and licensed lay workers include four women among a membership of nearly one hundred. A woman holds the prestigious appointment of Third Estates Church Commissioner; she is the second one to do so. There has been a woman in that position since 1972.

Laywomen serve on the staffs of theological schools in the Church of England. In fact, all of the theological schools except one have women staff persons. One theological college, St. John's, Durham, has a woman principal.

In the Episcopal Church, U.S.A. the national legislative body is the General Convention with a House of Bishops and a House of Deputies. Clergy and laypersons compose the House of Deputies. Women were not admitted as deputies until fairly recently; the first ones were seated in the House in 1970. At the 1982 General Convention, less than 20% of the 816 deputies were women. There were about 150 laywomen and less than ten women clergy. The Interim Bodies of the Convention initiate legislation for the Convention. There are women on each of the fifteen committees and commissions listed in the Convention Journal. The average membership of each is around twelve and includes at least two women. The present director for the Board of Theological Education is a woman and a layperson. The chair for the Standing Commission of Program, Budget, and Finance was a women during the past triennium. The Executive Council elected by the General Convention to implement the actions of the Convention has eight women among the forty members.[45] A woman is chair for one of the six standing committees of the Council. At the Church Center in New York City there was a woman executive for a major division, the National Mission in Church and Society. She resigned at the end of 1983, and there was no woman executive at the beginning of 1985. A woman has recently been appointed in another division to coordinate women's ministries.

The church's ten accredited seminaries have women staff in all schools. These women are both lay and ordained; they are professors and instructors.

Members of the Religious Communities

The unique witness of the religious life in the Anglican churches was restored in the nineteenth century in the Church of England. From there it spread to the new churches. Recently the Reverend George B. Braund, associate secretary of the Anglican Consultative Council, compiled a list of religious communities in the Anglican Communion. The predominance of women's communities is seen in his statistics of ninety-nine for women and thirty-nine for men. Of these ninety-nine communities, forty-two are in the Church of England, eighteen in the Episcopal Church, U.S.A., and thirty-nine in other provinces of the Anglican Communion.[46]

The religious communities have been an integral part of the lives of communicants in the Church of England. Today they continue as Houses of Prayer and also provide places for spiritual counsel and retreat to those living in the world; yet the religious life, generally speaking, does not seem to be thriving in the Church of England. Many of the communities are not receiving vocations and numbers are dwindling. Some of the large old convents have only a few sisters living in them. Statistics for 1961 list 1,501 women religious, and those for 1980 give 1,347.[47] A new book, *Bound for Life* by the Reverend Alan Harrison, secretary to the Advisory Council on the Relations of Bishops and Religious Communities, reviews the status of the communities and discusses this traditional life in the modern world.[48]

Although there is a decline in numbers this should not necessarily be viewed with undue pessimism. Account must be taken of the careers that are opening up in the secular "helping professions"; today a woman is less apt than she was in the past to enter a religious community in order to teach, nurse, or work

with the poor. In 1968 the report, "Women in Ministry: A Study,"
describes this situation:

The emphasis on "good works" of the early days of religious communities has changed to a stress on the essence of the religious life
itself as being of greatest value. Therefore ministry is seen . . . in terms
of *worship*, in intercession and reparation for the needs of the world
through the eucharist, daily offices and private prayer. In *witness*, ex-
ternally by distinctive dress and pattern of life expressed in the evangelical counsels of poverty, chastity and obedience, and the sharing of
the common family life. . . . In *work*, as centres of spirituality on which
the world can draw, and "out-going" service such as evangelistic, pastoral, educational and institutional work.[49]

It is the call to this "essence of the religious life" that appears
to draw women today. And it is this life that is shared in retreats,
centers for prayer, and spiritual counselling. It may be that the
number of religious will be less in the future, but it may also be
the case that God calls only a few to this way. In any event
might not this be an opportunity to examine once again the basic
ingredients in the vocation? The "essence of the religious life"
is quite visible in the contemplative or enclosed communities in
the Church of England where the sisters do not go out into the
world. These are vital, healthy communities that continue to
receive postulants. They are sources of spiritual direction to the
many who visit them. Finally, one should note the revival of
the eremitical or hermit life in the Church of England with at
least three women offering this ancient way to God and the
church.

Religious communities have never had the influence in the
Episcopal Church which is seen in the English Church. In fact,
there are Episcopalians in the United States who are unaware
that this vocation is an option for women. And yet, whereas
there is not a canon on the religious life in the Church of England,
there is a canon in the Episcopal Church which was amended
at the 1982 General Convention.[50]

The communities in the Episcopal Church appear to be less
traditional than those in England. Modern habits have been
adopted in many cases and there has been experimentation with
the rules. There are at least four ordained women in religious

communities. As in England there seems to be less emphasis on "works," that is institutions, and more concern with living the "essence of the religious life." Most of the communities have closed the convent schools which were a vital part of their service to the church. Today they contribute to the well being of the church by sharing their way of life and providing centers for prayer and the spiritual life. Contemplative, enclosed communities have never been strong; most women drawn to this way of life have joined communities in the Church of England. There has been one very small enclosed community in the Episcopal Church, but it has never flourished. It is difficult to compile figures on the numbers of women religious today in the Episcopal Church. Some communities are expanding; two of them have built new Mother Houses recently and have a reasonable number of postulants and novices. Some of the older communities have fewer members.

Members of religious communities have held or hold responsible positions in both the Church of England and the Episcopal Church. There are two women religious in the House of Laity of the General Synod and recently the superior of an American community was elected to the Executive Council by the General Convention.

On Deaconesses

"At no time in their long history have deaconesses in the Church of England had an assured place in the ministry of the Church and today when the whole question of ministry is under discussion the future is far from clear." Thus Deaconess Grierson describes the position of deaconesses in the Church of England in the early 1980s.[51] She points out that in spite of this there are more candidates for the order of deaconesses today than ever in the order's history. She is raising questions concerning status in this ministry. Are deaconesses ordained? To what? To the third order of the historic threefold ministry? To a distinct order as deaconesses? In 1968 the report "Women in Ministry: A Study" described the "confusion" in the church at that time and the lack of clarification surrounding the status of deaconesses:

The preparatory commission on the ministry of women for the Lambeth Conference 1920 was of the opinion that the ordination of a deaconess confers on her Holy Orders, but this is not stated in the Conference Resolutions. The special committee of the 1930 Lambeth Conference did not regard the deaconess and deacon as equivalent in Order and affirmed that the Deaconess Order was *sui generis*. Some deaconesses ordained between 1920 and 1930 undoubtedly *thought* that they had been admitted to the third order of ministry, and in these circumstances the Lambeth Conference resolution of 1930 appeared to them a backward step.

Within the Church of England, the Archbishops' Commission on the Ministry of Women (1935) referred to the Order of Deaconesses as "a Holy Order", but the 1939–41 Convocation Resolutions on Deaconesses made no mention of "Holy Order" at all.[52]

Deaconess Grierson points out that about a dozen years later the status of deaconess remains "unclear" and that the historical problems continue. Who is the deaconess? What is her status in the ministry of the church? What functions pertain to her ministry?

The Church of England today has a significant number of deaconesses, though an exact count is difficult to obtain. Deaconesses are licensed; there are those with episcopal permission to work, and there are non-stipendiary ones. Others are retired. Church of England statistics for 1980 list 198 full-time and ninety-one part-time deaconesses.[53] Deaconess training is normally obtained in one of the theological colleges along with men who are preparing for the ordained ministry. Women applying for deaconess training must be sponsored by their bishops and attend a selection conference. If a woman is accepted, she may with the bishop's approval apply to a theological college; this is the same procedure followed by male candidates for the priesthood. Thus deaconesses and lay workers are selected by the same national process and attend the same theological colleges. In September 1983 a new part-time post was created on the staff of the Archbishop of Canterbury to assist in the placing of deaconesses and accredited lay workers in their first positions. The incumbent in this new post is a deaconess. The lay assistant on the archbishop's staff has this responsibility for men ordained to the diaconate.

The function of the deaconess is governed by canons of the church. She may preside at morning and evening prayer, distribute the "holy sacrament" of the Eucharist, and read the epistle and gospel. She may preach, church women, baptize, bury the dead, and publish banns of marriage. She cannot pronounce absolution or preside at the Eucharist.[54]

The most recent action taken by the General Synod on the status of deaconesses occurred at its meetings in York in July 1983. The synod passed legislation which can begin the process of opening the diaconate to women. The "Draft Ordination of Women as Deacons Measure" passed with a combined vote in the three houses of 257 for and 66 against. Synod debate centered around the position of deaconesses who wanted to become deacons. Would this involve a "conditional ordination" or a "supplemental ordination"? In either case the church did not vote to declare deaconesses to be deacons.[55]

Today there are no deaconesses in the Episcopal Church. In 1970 the General Convention adopted the resolution "that those made Deaconesses by the laying on of hands, with appropriate prayers, be declared to be within the Diaconate."[56] Deputies may recall the joy of one deaconess as she stood and clapped her hands after the vote. A new canon, "On Women in the Diaconate," was enacted which directed that the women deacons must fulfill all of the requirements for candidates for holy orders except those relating to the priesthood. Pension plans were also a part of the canon.[57] The Central House for Deaconesses in Evanston, Illinois, was closed in the late 1970s.

The earliest action concerning deaconesses in the Episcopal Church's General Convention was in 1871 when a joint committee was appointed to report in 1873 "on the expediency of reviving in this Church the primitive order of Deaconesses."[58] Canon 10, passed in 1889, gave official status to the office of a deaconess. It did not contain the term "ordain"; the bishop appointed a deaconess and she was "set apart" for the office. She assisted "the Minister in the care of the poor and sick, the religious training of the young and others, and the work of moral reformation." Other sections of the canon prescribed certain requirements, and among these was that she should be unmarried.[59]

The deaconesses were never a large group in the Episcopal Church, and there seems to have been, as there was in England, a lack of clarity about function. The report of the Advisory Commission on the Work of Deaconesses in 1949 explicitly declared that the "setting apart of a Deaconess" was not an ordination but the acceptance of a vocation.[60] In 1961 the report of the Joint Commission on the Work of Deaconesses referred to eighty-one deaconesses of whom fifty-one were over sixty-five years of age.[61] Finally in 1970 the Joint Commission on Women Church Workers referred to the decline in the number of active deaconesses with fewer than thirty that year. Again there were questions about "the nature and function" of the ministry of deaconesses.[62] At the General Convention in 1970 action was taken to make deaconesses deacons (see footnote 56).

Women Workers

These women include deaconesses, lay workers, Church Army members, and social workers. Statistics for the Church of England in 1980 list 198 full-time and ninety-one part-time deaconesses for a total of 289; 145 full-time and fifty-nine part-time lay workers for a total of 204; eighty-two Church Army sisters; seventy-six full-time and sixty-five part-time social workers for a total of 141.[63] Statistics for 1961 had listed 469 moral welfare workers (social workers), 446 licensed lay workers, 261 Church Army sisters, and sixty-five deaconesses.[64] This data for a period of twenty years shows a sharp decrease in the number of lay workers, who are for the most part women, except in the order of deaconesses where the numbers have more than quadrupled. Yet the visitor to the Church of England today is immediately aware of a history of dedicated laywomen, who have been licensed or commissioned by the appropriate authorities, and are carrying out liturgical, instructional, and social responsibilities.

The duties of a lay worker are outlined in Canon E7 of the Church of England. Such a worker, whether man or woman, must be licensed by the bishop or obtain his permission in the diocese in which he or she serves. He or she may "lead the people in public worship, exercise pastoral care, evangelize, instruct the people in the Christian faith, and prepare them for the reception of the sacraments." A lay worker may "say or sing Morning or Evening Prayer (save for the Absolution)," "distribute the holy sacrament of the Lord's Supper to the people and . . . read the Epistle and the Gospel," "preach at divine service," "church women," "bury the dead or read the burial service," and "publish banns of marriage at Morning and Evening Prayer." These duties are similar to those in Canon D for deaconesses.[65] At the present time lay workers attend the same theological schools as deaconesses and candidates for the priesthood.

A small number of women in the Church of England are sisters in the Church Army. This is a semi-independent organization although its members may work with church authorities. It was founded in 1882 for laymen and by laywomen involved in evangelistic and social welfare services. In 1980 there were eighty-two sisters and 167 captains (men).[66] The newly appointed coordinator of women's ministries at Church House is a member of the Church Army.

Through the years there have been dedicated women involved in social services and licensed by the bishops in their dioceses. They cared for the needy and the poor and were also licensed for liturgical functions. Today these women are under the Board for Social Responsibility, one of the advisory committees of the General Synod.

To this point, discussion has centered on stipendiary workers who receive salaries for their labors, but there are those who do not receive stipends. Among these are women who are licensed lay readers. In 1980 there were 662 licensed women lay readers out of a total of 6,791 lay readers.[67] Canon E4 directs that "it shall be lawful" for a reader "to visit the sick, to read and pray with them, to teach in Sunday School and elsewhere, and generally to undertake such pastoral and educational work and to give such assistance to any minister as the bishop may direct." The readers may "read Morning and Evening Prayer (save for the absolution)," "publish banns of marriage at Morning and Evening Prayer," "read the Word of God," preach, catechize the children, "receive and present the offerings of the people," and "bury the dead or read the burial service before or after a cremation."[68] One immediately observes the similarity of these duties to those of deaconesses and women workers.

This phenomenon of women lay workers with liturgical, social, and pastoral duties is not found in the Episcopal Church; neither has it been an integral part of its history. Title III, Canon 28, "Of Professional Church Workers," pertains to women who are employed "as Christian Education, College, or Social Worker, in the service of this Church in any Diocese"[69] and outlines qualifications; but there is no active group of "Professional Church Workers" in the church at this time. In the last Church Year Book listing of "Women Church Workers" in 1978, about 250 were described as "Women Church Workers in Christian Education and National Executive Offices."[70]

In the 1960s there was an active "Association of Professional Women Church Workers" which listed its purposes: to develop the profession in the "general field of Christian Education and College Work;" to aid members in developing professional competence and to deepen the spiritual life; to be aware of possibilities for growth and expansion of the role of women workers; to encourage attainment of professional standards; and to recruit women workers.[71] In 1965 there were about 300 names listed in the Church Annual.[72] At that time there were two training schools for women workers which were closed in the late 1960s when women were permitted to enter seminaries of the Episcopal Church.

The Church Army was organized in the Episcopal Church in 1927. Twenty-two sisters are listed in 1983.[73]

There are large numbers of women lay readers in the Episcopal Church, whose activities are governed by Title III, Canon 26. They are licensed by the diocesan bishops and are under the supervision of the clergy of the parish, congregation, or mission where they serve. Lay readers must be "specially licensed" by the diocesan bishop to prepare sermons and preach. They may also "deliver the Cup at the Holy Communion" if so licensed by the bishop. They may read those portions of morning and evening prayer that are appropriate for a layperson.[74]

Ordained Ministry

The ordination of women to the priesthood has not come easily for the Anglican Communion; today there are no ordained women priests in the mother church of the Anglican Communion, the Church of England. There is a strong movement in some areas for such ordination, but there is also enough opposition to prevent the passage of any favorable legislation in the General Synod. At the General Synod in July 1975 there was a vote of 225 ayes and 180 noes on the motion, "That this Synod considers that there are no fundamental objections to the ordination of women to the priesthood." At that time the largest number of noes were in the House of Clergy. This same General Synod rejected a motion to remove "the legal and other barriers."[75] In November 1978 the General Synod voted 272 to 246 against removing legal barriers to the ordination of women. The large negative vote was again in the House of Clergy.[76] The following year at the General Synod in July a motion to prepare temporary legislation allowing legally ordained women from other Anglican provinces to officiate when visiting in England was defeated in the House of Clergy. The overall vote was 223 ayes and 188 noes, but the vote in the House of Clergy was 87 ayes and 113 noes.[77]

The subject of women's ordination is not a recent one in the Church of England. The *Report* of the Archbishops' Commission on the Ministry of Women in 1935 referred to a "strongly represented" demand for admission of women to the priesthood but also saw more opposition to such action than approval. The lack of evidence of women priests in the New Testament, tradition, the ecumenical concerns, and practical considerations were cited against the ordination of women.[78] *Women's Work in the Church* in 1942 noted that the ordination of women to the priesthood was outside its terms of reference.[79] In *Gender and Ministry* in 1962 the writers thought that the reasons for withholding ordained priesthood from women (theological, traditional, instinctive, anthropological, social, and emotional) should be more thoroughly examined.[80] The Working Party's *Women in Ministry* in 1968 noted that although ordination was not its assignment, the question came to the attention of the group. It was however unable to "provide a unanimous" answer.[81] A carefully balanced survey of the "present state of opinion" is found in Christian Howard's *Ordination of Women to the Priesthood*, published in 1972.[82]

There are genteel rumblings today as women become impatient with the slow pace of the Church of England. These seem to stem for the most part from women who are against any kind of illegal action and seek to approach the matter within the theological and legal bounds of their church. In July 1983 fourteen women walked out of an ordination service at Southwark Cathedral in London and participated in what they called a "wilderness liturgy." Thirteen deacons and eighteen priests were ordained at that time, but the fourteen women could only be licensed for lay ministries. 21 and 28 January 1984 were designated by the Movement for the Ordination of Women as an occasion for the celebration of the fortieth anniversary of the ordination of Lee Tim Oi in Hong Kong in 1944. She was the first woman ordained in the Anglican Communion. Services were scheduled at Westminster Abbey and Sheffield Cathedral. The organization that is the focal point for this ordination of women in the Church of England is the Movement for the Ordination of Women, known as M.O.W. It has a subscribing membership, publishes pamphlets and other literature, and provides a forum for discussion.

The Episcopal Church has a fair number of woman priests, but even in North America the opposition continues. An article in the *New York Times* (10 April 1983) by Charles Austin, describing the ordination of women in the United States, reports that the "strongest resistance to ordained women in a major denomination" is found in the Episcopal Church.[83]

There are 411 women priests in the Episcopal Church according to statistics compiled by the Reverend Sandra Boyd and the Reverend Suzanne Hiatt for *Rauch* (Fall 1983), the publication for the Episcopal Women's Caucus, Inc. The data is interesting; there are thirty-two rectors, forty-one vicars, 142 assistants or associates in parishes, and six co-pastors. Seventeen women are chaplains in hospitals or prisons, and twenty-three are chaplains in colleges or schools. Some ordained women are non-stipendiary. Only nine are listed as unemployed.[84]

In the early part of the 1970s the subject of women's ordination came to the attention of the House of Bishops and the House of Deputies of the General Convention. In October 1972 at the meeting of the House of Bishops, the bishops voted for the ordination of women to the priesthood and the episcopate;[85] the following year at the General Convention the House of Deputies voted against the ordination of women.[86] In 1974 eleven women were irregularly ordained to the priesthood by three retired bishops in the Episcopal Church and the active Bishop of Costa Rica, the Rt. Rev. José A. Ramos. The retired bishops were the Rt. Rev. Edward R. Wells, the Rt. Rev. Robert L. Dewitt, and the Rt. Rev. Daniel Corrigan. At the following General Convention of 1976, the House of Bishops approved by a vote of 95 to 61 the legislation that would make the ordination canons applicable to men and women. The House of Deputies concurred with 124 votes for, 75 against, and 28 divided (a divided vote according to voting procedures counted as a no).[87] The first ordinations in the Episcopal Church were in January 1977. The corpus of literature on the subject of women's ordination is extensive, and the reader will find the Reverend Sandra Boyd's bibliography useful.[88]

Other churches in the Anglican Communion are ordaining women to the priesthood. Mr. John Martin, communications officer for the Anglican Consultative Council, has compiled statistics which reflect this.[89] The Anglican Church of Canada, the Diocese of Hong Kong and Macao, the Church of the Province of New Zealand, the Church of the Province of Uganda, and the Episcopal Church, U.S.A. have active women priests. The Bishop of Mesano South in the Church of the Province of Kenya ordained a woman, but there are apparently questions about her status. The Church in Wales has ordained women deacons, but there appears to be no movement toward priesthood for these women. Legislative action making possible the ordination of women priests is in motion in the Anglican Church of Australia, but it looks as if it will be defeated.

The Episcopal Women's Caucus is the most visible organization in the Episcopal Church that is "affirming the role of women in the changing church," as it states in its publications. It has subscribing members, publishes *Rauch*, and functions as a forum for issues pertaining to women's ministries. It is a seasoned organization that has not only worked for the ordination of women but also addressed itself to other issues of women's ministry.

The Episcopal Church's concentrated movement in recent years toward the ordination of women has been so all-absorbing that other ministries for women have been less visible. Today this seems to be changing somewhat, and there appears to be an effort to recognize the roles of laywomen by their ordained sisters. Evidence of this is the newly formed Council of Women's Ministries which seeks to include representatives from all of the women's organizations, both traditional and more recent.

CONCLUSIONS

Discussions on the participation of women in leadership positions in the Church of England and the Episcopal Church, U.S.A. seem to be overshadowed today by the move for ordination of women to the priesthood. Vocations for women seem to be understood as vocations to the priesthood in the minds of many. The great numbers of lay ministers among women in the Church of England are diminishing with the exception of those who are deaconesses. Yet the ordination of women priests in the Church of England does not appear to be a possibility in the near future; as the conflicting parties in the General Synod seem no nearer agreement, the women seeking ordination continue to present their arguments, with ever more determination. There have been women priests in the Episcopal Church since January 1977, but they have not been accepted in all parts of the church. Opposition continues from a number of bishops, other clergy, and lay people who present discouraging situations to many seeking ordination.

Lay vocations for women seem not to have a high priority, although more women hold leadership roles than at any time in the history of the Christian Church. There are women leaders in the Church of England, the Episcopal Church, U.S.A., the Anglican Church in Canada, and the Episcopal Church in Wales, for example, but in the Asian and African churches women have less visibility in the secular as well as ecclesiastical society.

A fitting way to conclude this essay may be to return to the Lambeth Conference of 1920 with its committee report and resolutions on the ministry of women and their position in the councils of the church. The committee report notes:

It is now, we believe, generally, if not universally, recognized that the future must be different from the past. The education of women has advanced in a way which would have seemed incredible to our fathers. Witness the place which women take in the new and even in the ancient universities. Again, in most parts of our Communion the Church is in a new environment of social life which it is impossible for us to neglect. Women sit in legislative and in municipal assemblies. They speak at public meetings on all manner of questions social, economic, political; and that with a grasp of their subject of which the women of a former generation would have been incapable. We may see dangers in this revolution, but we cannot ignore it or refuse to allow it a practical influence on our judgment.

To be sure, in the following paragraph of the report the committee cautioned that the bishops are not to forget "the elementary facts of human nature" and the chemistry between the sexes; but the church fathers are obviously moving into the main stream of a changing society. The encyclical letter recognized that different cultures were represented among the bishops, but it specifically states that there must be room for the work of the Spirit "so that the fellowship of the Ministry may be strengthened by the co-operation of women and the fellowship of the Church be enriched by their spiritual gifts."[90]

These bishops of 1920 might be surprised at the wider range of leadership exercised by women in parts of the Anglican Communion in the 1980s. Obviously the scope of women's ministries is greatly extended. One might expect them nevertheless as they surveyed the churches scattered over the world to remark that much remains to be accomplished in this area. They might well note how slowly the churches have moved during these years in recognizing women's issues. Surely they would plead again, as they did in the past and as the church today must, that room be made for the work of the Spirit in the continuing movement toward a fuller recognition of women's gifts in the ministry of the church.

NOTES

1. The reports, resolutions, and encyclical letters have been published after the Conferences: The Most Reverend Lord Davidson of Lambeth, comp., *The Six Lambeth Conferences, 1867–1920* (London: S.P.C.K., 1929); *The Lambeth Conference, 1930, Encyclical Letter from the*

Bishops with Resolutions and Reports (London: S.P.C.K., n.d.); *The Lambeth Conference, 1948, The Encyclical Letter from the Bishops; Together with Resolutions and Reports* (London: S.P.C.K., 1948); *The Lambeth Conference, 1958, The Encyclical Letter from the Bishops Together with the Resolutions and Reports* (Greenwich, Conn.: Seabury, 1958); *The Lambeth Conference, 1968, Resolutions and Reports* (New York: Seabury, 1968); *The Report of the Lambeth Conference, 1978* (London: Church Information Office, 1978). Footnotes will have the following form with an abbreviation for Lambeth Conference, the date, either the resolution number, the report number, or a reference to the encyclical and the page. This footnote for the material in the text is L.C., 1930, Res. 49, p. 55.

2. L.C., 1888, Res. 11, p. 122.

3. L.C., 1948, Res. 59 (Part 1), p. 41. This commentary is found in the Statement of Faith and Order prepared by the Joint Commission on Approaches to Unity of the Protestant Episcopal Church, U.S.A. See *Journal of the General Convention of the Protestant Episcopal Church in the United States of America, 1949* (Hammond, Ind.: W.B. Conkey Company, 1949), pp. 354, 662–70. Hereafter all Journals will be cited as follows: *Journal*, date, page.

4. For an arrangement of these resolutions according to categories, see V. Nelle Bellamy, "Participation of Women in the Public Life of the Church from Lambeth Conference, 1867–1978," *Historical Magazine of the Protestant Episcopal Church* 51 (1982): 81–98.

5. L.C., 1908, Res. 46, p. 327.

6. L.C., 1920, Rep. V, pp. 95–106.

7. L.C., 1920, Res. 46, p. 39; Res. 53, p. 41.

8. L.C., 1958, Res. 94, p. 1.52.

9. L.C., 1968, Res. 24, 25, 26, 27, pp. 37–38.

10. L.C., 1897, Res. 11, p. 201.

11. L.C., 1930, Res. 74, p. 62; Rep. V, pp. 183–87.

12. L.C., 1948, Res. 40 (Part 1), p. 36.

13. L.C., 1958, Res. 92, p. 1.51.

14. L.C., 1968, Res. 5, p. 30.

15. Janet Grierson, *The Deaconess* (London: Church Information Office, 1981).

16. Ibid., p. 36.

17. L.C., 1897, Res. 11, p. 201.

18. L.C., 1920, Rep. V, pp. 95–106.

19. L.C., 1920, Res. 47, pp. 39–40.

20. L.C., 1920, Res. 48, p. 40.

21. L.C., 1920, Res. 49, p. 40.

22. Grierson, *The Deaconess*, pp. 47–56.

23. L.C., 1920, Res. 49–52, pp. 40–41.
24. L.C., 1930, Rep. V, pp. 177–80.
25. L.C., 1930, Res. 67–70, pp. 60–61.
26. L.C., 1948, Res. 114, 116 (Part I), pp. 52–53.
27. L.C., 1968, Res. 32 (c), p. 39.
28. L.C., 1978, Res. 20, pp. 44–45.
29. L.C., 1920, Rep. V, pp. 95–106; Res. 54, p. 41.
30. L.C., 1930, Rep. V, pp. 180–82.
31. L.C., 1930, Res. 72, p. 61.
32. L.C., 1948, Res. 48 (Part I), p. 37.
33. L.C., 1958, Res. 93, pp. 1.51–52.
34. L.C., 1930, Rep. V, pp. 179–80.
35. L.C., 1948, Rep. V (c), (Part II), pp. 119–20; Res. 113 (Part I), p. 52.
36. L.C., 1968, Rep. "Renewal in Ministry," p. 106.
37. L.C., 1968, Res. 34, p. 39.
38. L.C., 1968, Res. 35, p. 39.
39. L.C., 1968, Res. 37, p. 40.
40. L.C., 1978, Res. 21, pp. 45–47.
41. L.C., 1968, Res. 32, pp. 38–39.
42. L.C., 1978, Res. 20, pp. 44–45.
43. L.C., 1978, Res. 22, p. 47.
44. These statistics are taken from *The Church of England Year Book, 1983, The Official Year Book of the General Synod of the Church of England* (London: Church Information Office, 1983).
45. These statistics are taken from *Journal*, 1982, pp. A7–A61.
46. This list has not been published, but the data is available through the Office of the Anglican Consultative Council, 14 Great Peter Street, London SWIP 3NQ.
47. *Gender and Ministry, A Report Prepared for the Church Assembly by the Central Advisory Council for the Ministry* (London: Church Information Office, 1962), p. 27; *Statistical Supplement to the Church of England Yearbook 1982* (London: Church Information Office, 1982), pp. 20–21.
48. Alan Harrison, *Bound for Life* (London: Mowbray, 1983).
49. *Women in Ministry: A Study, Report of the Working Party Set Up Jointly by the Ministry Committee of the Advisory Council for the Church's Ministry and the Council for Women's Ministry in the Church* (London: Church Information Office, 1968), pp. 20–21. Hereafter this study will be referred to as *Women in Ministry*.
50. *Constitution and Canons for the Government of the Protestant Episcopal Church in the United States of America Otherwise Known as the Episcopal Church, Adopted in General Convention 1789–1982 Together with the Rules of Order* (New York: Seabury, 1982), Title III, Canon 27, pp. 106–7.

51. Grierson, *The Deaconess*, p. 116.

52. *Women in Ministry*, p. 15; "Convocation Resolutions on Deaconesses Passed by Both Houses of Both Convocations, 1939–41," pp. 64–66; Archbishops' Commission on the Ministry of Women, *Report* (London: Press and Publications Board of the Church Assembly, 1935), pp. 36–53.

53. *Statistical Supplement*, pp. 20–21.

54. *Canons of the Church of England* (London: Church Information Office, 1975), Canons Dl, D2, D3, C15, pp. 67–69, 87–91.

55. The proceedings of the July 1983 meetings of the General Synod have not been published at this time. This data is taken from *The Church Times* (22 July 1983), p. 5.

56. *Journal*, 1970, p. 270.

57. Ibid., p. 249.

58. *Journal*, 1871, pp. 172–73, 208. See Edwin Augustine White, *Annotated Constitution and Canons for the Government of the Protestant Episcopal Church in the United States of America*, rev. Jackson A. Dykman, 2nd ed. (Greenwich, Conn.: Seabury, 1954), 2: 257–67 for a history of the canon pertaining to deaconesses. The revision of White and Dykman is under way.

59. *Journal*, 1889, pp. 134–35.

60. "Report of the Advisory Commission on the Work of Deaconesses," *Journal*, 1949, pp. 389–92.

61. "Report of the Joint Commission on the Work of Deaconesses," *Journal*, 1961, pp. 491–96.

62. "Joint Commission on Women Church Workers," *Journal*, 1970, pp. 769–70.

63. *Statistical Supplement*, pp. 20–21.

64. *Gender and Ministry*, p. 27.

65. *Canons of the Church of England*, Canons E7 and E8, pp. 99–100a.

66. *Statistical Supplement*, pp. 20–21.

67. Ibid.

68. *Canons of the Church of England*, Canon E4, p. 96.

69. *Constitution and Canons*, Title III, Canon 28, pp. 107–8.

70. *The Episcopal Church Annual, 1978*, ed. Margaret L. Sheriff (Wilton, Conn.: Morehouse-Barlow, 1978), pp. 86–89.

71. Ibid., 1960, pp. 135–41.

72. Ibid., 1965, pp. 132–35.

73. Ibid., 1983, pp. 80–81.

74. *Constitutions and Canons*, Title III, Canon 26, pp. 104–5.

75. General Synod, *Report of Proceedings, 1975* (London: Church In-

formation Office, 1975), VI, no. 2, pp. 542, 573, 602. The debates are found on pp. 542–616.

76. General Synod, *Report of Proceedings, 1978* (London: Church Information Office, 1978), IX, no. 3, p. 1070. The debates are found on pp. 996–1070.

77. General Synod, *Report of Proceedings, 1979* (London: Church Information Office, 1979), X, no. 2, p. 879. The debates are found on pp. 842–79. See the Report of a Working Group Appointed by the Standing Committee, *Woman Lawfully Ordained Abroad*, GS415, Option 7 (London: Church Information Office, 1979).

78. Archbishops' Commission on the Ministry of Women, *Report* (London: The Press and Publication Board of the Church Assembly, 1935), pp. 8–10.

79. *Women's Work in the Church: Being the Report of a Committee Appointed by the Archbishops of Canterbury and York in 1942* (London: The Press and Publications Board of the Church Assembly, 1943), p. 6 n.

80. *Gender and Ministry*, p. 20.

81. *Women in Ministry*, p. 39.

82. General Synod, *The Ordination of Women to the Priesthood: A Consultative Document Presented by the Advisory Council for the Church's Ministry* (Oxford: Church Army Press, 1972).

83. Charles Austin, "Women Ministers Feel Responsibility of Dual Role," *New York Times* (10 April 1983), p. 12.

84. Sandra Hughes Boyd and Suzanne Hiatt, "Tabulations of Clergy Women Statistics—July 7, 1983," *Rauch* 5 (1983).

85. "It is the mind of this House that it endorses the principle of the Ordination of Women to the Priesthood and to the Ordination and Consecration of women to the Episcopate." Special Meeting of the House of Bishops, 1971, *Journal*, 1973, pp. 1114–32.

86. Ibid., pp. 216–25. Convention action must pass both houses.

87. *Journal*, 1976, pp. C–51–-C–52, B–195–-B–201. The bishops voted 128 to 9 with 9 abstentions that the Philadelphia ordinations did not include "the necessary conditions for valid ordination to the priesthood. . . ." After the convention changed the canon to permit the ordination of women, the House of Bishops approved for what it called "pastoral reasons" legislation for a "completion of the ritual acts performed in Philadelphia." Pp. B–120–-B–126.

88. Sandra Hughes Boyd, "The History of Women in the Episcopal Church; A Select Annotated Bibliography," *Historical Magazine of the Protestant Episcopal Church* 50 (1981): 423–33.

89. This data has not been published. It was obtained from John K.

Martin, Communications Officer, Anglican Consultative Council, 14 Great Peter Street, London, SWlP 3NQ. The Movement for the Ordination of Women also compiles data on the ordination of women. The office is in Napier Hall, Hide Place, Vincent Street, London SWlP 4NJ.

90. L.C., 1920, Rep. 5, pp. 99–101; Encyclical Letter, p. 15.

Suggestions for Further Reading

The books and articles listed here represent only a selection of the better works relevant to the study of women in Protestant history.

GENERAL

Bailey, D.S. *Sexual Relation in Christian Thought*. New York: Harper, 1959.

Baker, Derek, ed. *Medieval Women: Studies in Church History*. Oxford: Basil Blackwell for the Ecclesiastical History Society, 1978.

Bliss, Kathleen.*The Service and Status of Women in the Churches*. London: SCM Press, 1952.

Bridenthal, Renate, and Koonz, Claudia, eds. *Becoming Visible: Women in European History*. Boston: Houghton Mifflin Company, 1977.

Bullough, Vern L. *The Subordinate Sex*. Baltimore: Penguin Books, 1974.

Clark, Elizabeth, and Richardson, Herbert, eds. *Women and Religion*. New York: Harper and Row, 1977.

Crook, Margaret Brackenbury. *Women and Religion*. Boston: Beacon Press, 1964.

Culver, Elsie Thomas. *Women in the World of Religion*. Garden City, N.Y.: Doubleday, 1967.

Daly, Mary. *The Church and the Second Sex*. New York: Harper and Row, 1968.

Danielou, Jean. *The Ministry of Women in the Early Church*. London: Faith Press, 1961.

Doely, Sarah, ed. *Women's Liberation and the Church*. New York: Association Press, 1970.

Ermarth, Margaret Sitter. *Adam's Fractured Rib*. Philadelphia: Fortress Press, 1970.

Gage, Matilda. *Woman, Church, and State: A Historical Account of Woman Through the Christian Ages*. Chicago: C.H. Kerr, 1893.

Gibson, Elsie. *When the Minister Is a Woman*. New York: Holt, Rinehart and Winston, 1970.

Harkness, Georgia. *Women in Church and Society*. New York and Nashville: Abingdon Press, 1972.

James, Janet Wilson, ed. *Women in American Religion*. Philadelphia: University of Pennsylvania Press, 1980.

Johnson, Dale A., ed. *Women in English Religion 1700–1925*. Studies in Women and Religion, vol. 10. New York and Toronto: Edward Mellen Press, 1983.

O'Faolain, Julia, and Martines, Lauro, eds., *Not in God's Image*. London: Temple Smith, 1973.

Power, Eileen. *Medieval English Nunneries, 1275–1535*. Cambridge: Cambridge University Press, 1922.

Ruether, Rosemary Radford, ed. *Religion and Sexism: Images of Woman in the Jewish and Christian Traditions*. New York: Simon and Schuster, 1974.

Ruether, Rosemary, and McLaughlin, Eleanor, eds. *Women of Spirit*. New York: Simon and Schuster, 1979.

Stock, Phyllis. *Better Than Rubies: A History of Women's Education*. New York: G.P. Putnam and Sons, 1978.

Tavard, George H. *Woman in Christian Tradition*. Notre Dame: University of Notre Dame Press, 1973.

LUTHERAN AND REFORMED WOMEN

Bainton, Roland. *Women of the Reformation, from Spain to Scandinavia*. Minneapolis: Augsburg Publishing House, 1977.

———. *Women of the Reformation in France and England*. Minneapolis: Augsburg Publishing House, 1973.

———. *Women of the Reformation in Germany and Italy*. Minneapolis: Augsburg Publishing House, 1971.

Biéler, Andre. *L'homme et la femme dans le morale calviniste*. Geneva: Labor et Fides, 1963.

Blaisdell, Charmarie J. "Calvin's Letters to Women." *Sixteenth Century Journal* 12 (1982): 77–84.

————. "Renée de France Between Reform and Counter Reform." *Archiv für Reformationsgeschichte* 63 (1972): 196–226.

Bratt, John H. "The Role and Status of Women in the Writings of John Calvin." In *Proceedings of a Colloquium on Calvin and Calvin Studies*, edited by Peter der Klerk. Grand Rapids: Calvin College and Seminary, 1976.

Buck, Lawrence, and Zophy, Jonathan. *The Social History of the Reformation*. Columbus: Ohio State University Press, 1972.

Chrisman, Miriam U. "Women and the Reformation in Strasbourg, 1490–1530." *Archiv für Reformationsgeschichte* 63 (1972): 143–68.

Davis, Natalie Z. "City Women and Religious Change." In *Society and Culture in Early Modern France*, edited by Natalie Z. Davis. Stanford: Stanford University Press, 1975.

Davy, Yvonne. *Frau Luther*. Mountain View, Calif.: Pacific Press, 1979.

Green, Lowell. "The Education of Women in the Reformation." *History of Education Quarterly* 19 (Spring 1979): 93–116.

Karant-Nunn, Susan C. "Continuity and Change: Some Effects of the Reformation on the Women of Zuickau." *Sixteenth Century Journal* 12 (1982): 17–42.

Monter, E. William. "Women in Calvinist Geneva (1550–1800)." *Signs* 6 (Winter 1980): 189–209.

Ozment, Steven E. "Marriage and the Ministry in the Protestant Churches." In *Celibacy in the Church*, edited by William Bassett and Peter Huizing. New York: Herder and Herder, 1972.

————. *The Reformation in the Cities*. New Haven: Yale University Press, 1975.

————. *When Fathers Ruled: Family Life in Reformation Europe*. Cambridge: Harvard University Press, 1983.

Roelker, Nancy Lyman. "The Appeal of Calvinism to French Noblewomen in the Sixteenth Century." *Journal of Interdisciplinary History* 2 (Spring 1972): 391–418.

————. *Queen of Navarre: Jeanne d'Albret* Cambridge, Mass.: Belknap Press of Harvard University Press, 1968.

————. "The Role of Noblewomen in the French Reformation," *Archiv für Reformationsgeschichte* 63 (1972): 172–93.

Schreiber, Clara. *Katherine, Wife of Luther*. Philadelphia: Muhlenberg Press, 1954.

ANABAPTIST WOMEN

Clasen, Claus-Peter. *Anabaptism: A Social History, 1525–1618*. Ithaca: Cornell University Press, 1972.

Irwin, Joyce L. *Womanhood in Radical Protestantism, 1525–1675*. New York and Toronto: Edwin Mellen Press, 1979.

Keeney, William E. *The Development of Dutch Anabaptist Thought and Practice from 1539–1564*. Nieukoop: B. de Graaf, 1968.

Rupp, Gordon. *Patterns of Reformation*. Philadelphia: Fortress Press, 1969.

Schaufele, Wolfgang. "The Missionary Vision and Activity of the Anabaptist Laity." *Mennonite Quarterly Review* 36 (April 1962).

Williams, George H. *The Radical Reformation* Philadelphia: Westminster Press, 1962.

ENGLAND TO CIRCA 1640

Barstow, Anne Llewellyn "The First Generations of Anglican Clergy Wives: Heroines or Whores?" *Historical Magazine of the Protestant Episcopal Church* 52 (March 1983): 3–16.

Camden, Carroll. *The Elizabethan Woman*. Houston: Elsevier Press, 1952.

Collinson, Patrick. *The Elizabethan Puritan Movement*. Berkeley: University of California Press, 1967.

———. "The Role of Women in the English Reformation Illustrated by the Life and Friendships of Anne Locke." *Studies in Church History* 2 (1965): 258–72.

Davies, Kathleen M. "The Sacred Condition of Equality: How Original Were Puritan Doctrines of Marriage?" *Social History* 5 (1977): 563–80.

Greaves, Richard L. *Society and Religion in Elizabethan England*. Minneapolis: University of Minnesota Press, 1981.

Hill, Christopher. *Society and Puritanism in Pre-Revolutionary England*. New York: Schocken Books, 1964.

Hogrefe, Pearl. *Tudor Women: Commoners and Queens*. Ames: Iowa State University Press, 1975.

———. *Tudor Women: Queens and Commoners*. Ames: Iowa State University Press, 1979.

Johnson, James Turner. *A Society Ordained by God*. Nashville: Abingdon Press, 1970.

Leites, Edmund. "The Duty to Desire: Love, Friendship, and Sexuality in Some Puritan Theories of Marriage." *Journal of Social History* 15 (1982): 383–408.

Levin, Carol. "Women in the Book of Martyrs as Models of Behavior in Tudor England." *International Journal of Women's Studies* 4 (1981): 196–207.

McIntosh, Marjorie Keniston. "Sir Anthony Cooke: Tudor Humanist,

Educator, and Religious Reformer." *Proceedings of the American Philosophical Society* 119 (June 1975): 233–50.

Maclean, Ian. *The Renaissance Notion of Women*. Cambridge: Cambridge University Press, 1980.

Schücking, Levin L. *The Puritan Family*. Translated by Brian Battershaw. New York: Schocken Books, 1970.

Stone, Lawrence *The Family, Sex and Marriage in England, 1500–1800*. New York: Harper and Row, 1977.

Todd, Margo. "Humanists, Puritans, and the Spiritualized Household." *Church History* 49 (March 1980): 18–34.

Warnicke, Retha M. *Women of the English Renaissance and Reformation*. Westport, Conn.: Greenwood Press, 1983.

Yost, John K. "The Reformation Defense of Clerical Marriage in the Reigns of Henry VIII and Edward VI." *Church History* 50 (June 1981): 152–65.

ENGLAND, CIRCA 1640–1700

Barbour, Hugh. *The Quakers in Puritan England*. New Haven: Yale University Press, 1964.

Brailsford, Mabel. *Quaker Women 1650–1690*. London: Duckworth and Co., 1915.

Braithwaite, William C. *The Beginnings of Quakerism*. London: Macmillan and Co., 1912.

———. *The Second Period of Quakerism*. Cambridge: Cambridge University Press, 1961.

Cadbury, Henry J. "Early Quakers at Cambridge," *Proceedings of the Cambridge Historical Society* 24 (1938): 67–82.

Cohen, Alfred. "The Fifth Monarchy Mind: Mary Cary and the Origins of Totalitarianism." *Social Research* 31 (Summer 1964): 195–213.

———. "Prophecy and Madness: Women Visionaries During the Puritan Revolution," *Journal of Psychohistory* 11 (Winter 1984): 411–30.

Cross, Claire. " 'He-Goats Before the Flocks': A Note on the Part Played by Women in the Founding of Some Civil War Churches." *Studies in Church History* 8 (1972): 195–202.

Greaves, Richard L. "The Ordination Controversy and the Spirit of Reform in Puritan England." *Journal of Ecclesiastical History* 21 (1970): 225–41.

Hill, Christopher. *The World Turned Upside Down: Radical Ideas during the English Revolution*. New York: Viking Press, 1972.

Lloyd, Arnold. *Quaker Social History, 1669–1738*. London: Longmans, 1950.

McArthur, Ellen A. "Women Petitioners and the Long Parliament." *English Historical Review* 24 (October 1909): 698–709.

Mack, Phyllis. "Women as Prophets During the English Civil War." *Feminist Studies* 8 (Spring 1982): 19–38.

Ross, Isabel. *Margaret Fell: Mother of Quakerism*. London: Longmans, Green and Co., 1949.

Smith, Hilda. *Reason's Disciples: Seventeenth Century Feminists*. Urbana: University of Illinois Press, 1982.

Stenton, Doris Mary. *The English Woman in History*. London: George Allen and Unwin, 1957.

Thomas, Keith. "Women and the Civil War Sects," *Past and Present* 13 (1958): 42–62.

Thompson, Roger. *Women in Stuart England and America: A Comparative Study*. London: Routledge & Kegan Paul, 1974.

Vann, Richard T. *The Social Development of English Quakerism 1655–1755*. Cambridge: Harvard University Press, 1969.

Williams, Ethyn Morgan. "Women Preachers in the Civil War." *Journal of Modern History* 1 (1929): 561–69.

COLONIAL AMERICAN WOMEN

Axtell, James. *The School Upon a Hill: Education and Society in Colonial New England*. New Haven: Yale University Press, 1974.

Bacon, Margaret. *The Quiet Rebels: The Story of the Quakers in America*. New York: Basic Books, 1969.

Battis, Emery John. *Saints and Sectaries: Anne Hutchinson and the Antinomian Controversy in the Massachusetts Bay Colony*. Chapel Hill: University of North Carolina Press, 1962.

Bumsted, J.M. "Emotion in Colonial America: Some Relations of Conversion Experience in Freetown, Massachusetts, 1749–1770." *New England Quarterly* 49 (March 1976): 97–108.

Cohen, Ronald A. "Church and State in Seventeenth Century Massachusetts: Another Look at the Antinomian Controversy." *Journal of Church and State* 12 (1970): 475–94.

Cott, Nancy F. *The Bonds of Womanhood: "Woman's Sphere" in New England, 1780–1835*. New Haven: Yale University Press, 1977.

Demos, John. *A Little Commonwealth: Family Life in Plymouth Colony*. Oxford: Oxford University Press, 1970.

Dunn, Mary Maples. "The Role of Women in 18th Century Virginia Baptist Life." *Baptist History and Heritage* 8 (1973): 158–67.

———. "Saints and Sisters: Congregational and Quaker Women in the Early Colonial Period," *American Quarterly* 30 (1978): 582–601.

Frost, J. William. *The Quaker Family: A Portrait of the Society of Friends.* New York: St. Martin's Press, 1973.

George, Carol V.R. "Anne Hutchinson and the 'Revolution Which Never Happened,' " In *Remember the Ladies: New Perspectives on Women in American History,* edited by Carol V.R. George. Syracuse: Syracuse University Press, 1975.

Greven, Philip J., Jr. *Four Generations: Population, Land, and Family in Colonial Andover, Massachusetts.* Ithaca: Cornell University Press, 1970.

———. *The Protestant Temperament.* New York: Alfred A. Knopf, 1977.

Kerber, Linda. *Women of the Republic: Intellect and Ideology in Revolutionary America.* Chapel Hill: University of North Carolina Press, 1980.

Koehler, Lyle. "The Case of the American Jezebels: Anne Hutchinson and Female Agitation During the Years of Antinomian Turmoil, 1636–1640." *William and Mary Quarterly,* 3rd ser., 31 (1974): 55–78.

———. *A Search for Power: The "Weaker Sex" in Seventeenth-Century New England.* Urbana: University of Illinois Press, 1980.

Malmsheimer, Lonna M. "Daughters of Zion: New England Roots of American Feminism." *New England Quarterly* 50 (Septemler 1977): 484–504.

Masson, Margaret W. "The Typology of the Female as a Model for the Regenerate: Puritan Preaching, 1690–1730." *Signs* 2 (1976): 304–15.

Moran, Gerald F. "Conditions of Religious Conversion in the First Society of Norwich, Connecticut, 1718–1744." *Journal of Social History* 5 (1972): 331–43.

———. "Religious Renewal, Puritan Tribalism, and the Family in Seventeenth-Century Milford, Connecticut," *William and Mary Quarterly,* 3rd ser., 36 (1979): 236–54.

Moran, Gerald F. and Vinovskis, Maris. " 'The Great Care of Godly Parents': Early Childhood in Puritan New England." In *Child Development in the Past and Present,* edited by John Hagen and Alice Smuts. Forthcoming.

Morgan, Edmund S. *The Puritan Family: Religion and Domestic Relations in Seventeenth-Century New England.* Rev. ed. New York: Harper and Row, 1966.

Norton, Mary Beth. *Liberty's Daughters: The Revolutionary Experience of American Women.* Boston: Little, Brown, 1980.

Porterfield, Amanda. *Feminine Spirituality in America: From Sarah Edwards to Martha Graham.* Philadelphia: Temple University Press, 1980.

Ruether, Rosemary Radford, and Keller, Rosemary Skinner, eds. *Women and Religion in America: A Documentary History*. Vol. 2: *The Colonial and Revolutionary Periods*. New York: Harper and Row, 1983.

Ryan, Mary P. *Cradle of the Middle Class: The Family in Oneida County, New York, 1790–1865*. Cambridge: Cambridge University Press, 1981.

———. "A Woman's Awakening: Evangelical Religion and the Families of Utica, New York, 1800–1840," *American Quarterly* 30 (1978): 602–23.

Shiels, Richard D. "The Feminization of American Congregationalism, 1730–1835." *American Quarterly* 33 (1981): 46–62.

Ulrich, Laurel Thatcher. *Good Wives: Image and Reality in the Lives of Women in Northern New England 1650–1750*. New York: Alfred A. Knopf, 1982.

———. "Virtuous Women Found: New England Ministerial Literature." *American Quarterly* 28 (1976): 20–40.

Wilson, Joan Hoff. "The Illusion of Change: Women and the American Revolution." In *The American Revolution: Explorations in the History of American Radicalism*, edited by Alfred F. Young. DeKalb: Northern Illinois University Press, 1976.

METHODIST WOMEN

Agnew, Theodore L. "Reflections on the Women's Foreign Missionary Movement in Late 19th Century American Methodism." *Methodist History* 6 (January 1968): 3–16.

Baker, Frank. "John Wesley and Sarah Crosby." *Wesley Historical Society Proceedings* 27 (December 1949): 76–82.

Baldwin, Lewis V. "Black Women and African Union Methodism." *Methodist History* 21 (July 1983): 225–37.

Breeze, Lawrence E. "The Inskips: Union in Holiness." *Methodist History* 13 (July 1975): 25–45.

Brown, Kenneth O. " 'The World-Wide Evangelist'—The Life and Work of Martha Inskip." *Methodist History* 21 (July 1983): 179–91.

Dayton, Lucille Sider, and Dayton, Donald W. " 'Your Daughters Shall Prophesy': Feminism in the Holiness Movement." *Methodist History* 14 (January 1976): 67–92.

Hill, Patricia R. "Heathen Women's Friends: The Role of Methodist Episcopal Women in the Women's Foreign Mission Movement, 1869–1915." *Methodist History* 19 (April 1981): 146–54.

Mitchell, Norma Taylor. "From Social to Radical Feminism: A Survey

of Emerging Diversity in Methodist Women's Organizations, 1869–
1974." *Methodist History* 13 (April 1975): 21–44.

Moore, Robert. *Pit-Men, Preachers and Politics: The Effects of Methodism
in a Durham Mining Community*. Cambridge: Cambridge University Press, 1974.

Rowe, Kenneth E., ed. *Methodist Women: A Guide to the Literature*. Lake
Junaluska, N.C.: General Commission on Archives and History,
1980.

Shaw, Anna Howard. "My Ordination: Anna Howard Shaw." edited
by Nancy N. Bahmueller, *Methodist History* 14 (January 1976):
125–31.

Spencer, Ralph W. "Anna Howard Shaw." *Methodist History* 13 (January
1975): 33–51.

Thomas, Hilah F., and Keller, Rosemary Skinner, eds. *Women in New
Worlds*. 2 vols. Nashville: Abingdon Press, 1981–82.

Wall, Ernest. "I Commend unto You Phoebe." *Religion in Life* 26 (1957):
396–408.

THE ABOLITIONISTS

Calvo, Janis. "Quaker Women Ministers in Nineteenth Century America," *Quaker History* 63 (Autumn 1974): 75–93.

Cromwell, Otelia. *Lucretia Mott*. Cambridge: Harvard University Press,
1958.

DuBois, Ellen. "The Radicalism of the Woman Suffrage Movement:
Notes Toward the Reconstruction of Nineteenth-Century Feminism." *Feminist Studies* 3 (Fall 1975): 63–71.

———. "Struggling into Existence: The Feminism of Sarah and Angelina
Grimké," *Women: A Journal of Liberation* (Spring 1970); reprinted
as a pamphlet by New England Free Press, Boston.

Fellman, Michael, and Perry, Lewis, eds. *Antislavery Reconsidered*. Baton
Rouge: Louisiana State University Press, 1979.

Filler, Louis. *The Crusade Against Slavery, 1830–1860*. New York: Harper
and Row, 1960.

Fladeland, Betty. *Men and Brothers: Anglo-American Antislavery Cooperation*. Urbana: University of Illinois Press, 1972.

Frost, J. William, ed. *The Quaker Origins of Antislavery*. Norwood, Pa.:
Norwood Editions, 1980.

Hays, Elinor Rice. *Morning Star: A Biography of Lucy Stone, 1818–1893*.
New York: Harcourt, Brace and World, 1961.

Hersh, Blanche Glassman. "Am I Not a Woman and a Sister?: Abolitionist Beginnings of Nineteenth-Century Feminism." In *Anti-*

slavery Reconsidered, edited by Michael Feldman and Lewis Perry. Baton Rouge: Louisiana State University Press, 1979.

———. *The Slavery of Sex: Feminist-Abolitionists in America*. Urbana: University of Illinois Press, 1978.

———. "The 'True Woman' and the 'New Woman' in 19th Century America: Feminist Abolitionists and a New Concept of True Womanhood." In *Woman's Being, Woman's Place, Female Identity and Vocation in American History*, edited by Mary Kelley. Boston: G.K. Hall, 1979.

Kraditor, Aileen S. *Means and Ends in American Abolitionism*. New York: Pantheon Books, 1969.

Lerner, Gerda. *The Grimké Sisters from South Carolina*. Boston: Houghton Mifflin, 1967; New York: Schocken Books, 1971.

Lutz, Alma. *Crusade for Freedom: Women of the Antislavery Movement*. Boston: Beacon Press, 1968.

McPherson, James M. "Abolitionists, Woman Suffrage, and the Negro, 1865–1869." *Mid-America* 47 (January 1965): 40–47.

Melder, Keith E. *Beginnings of Sisterhood: The American Woman's Rights Movement, 1800–1850*. New York: Schocken Books, 1977.

———. "Ladies Bountiful: Organized Women's Benevolence in Early Nineteenth Century America." *New York History* 48 (July 1967): 231–54.

Perry, Lewis. *Radical Abolitionism: Anarchy and the Government of God in Antislavery Thought*. Ithaca: Cornell University Press, 1973.

Smith, Timothy L. *Revivalism and Social Reform in Mid-Nineteenth Century America*. New York: Abingdon Press, 1957.

Sterling, Dorothy. *We Are Your Sisters: Black Women in the Nineteenth Century*. New York: W.W. Norton & Co., 1984.

Walters, Ronald G. "The Erotic South: Civilization and Sexuality in American Abolitionism." *American Quarterly* 25 (May 1973): 177–201.

Welter, Barbara. "The Feminization of American Religion: 1800–1860." In *Insights and Parallels: Problems and Issues of American Social History*, edited by William O'Neill. Minneapolis: Burgess, 1973.

Wyman, Lillie Buffum Chace. "Reminiscences of Two Abolitionists." *New England Magazine* (January 1903), pp. 536–50.

Wyman, Lillie Buffum Chace and Wyman, Arthur Crawford. *Elizabeth Buffum Chace, 1806–1899: Her Life and Its Environment*. 2 vols. Boston: W.B. Clarke, 1914.

MODERN PRESBYTERIAN WOMEN

Barrus, Ben M., Baughn, Milton L., and Campbell, Thomas H. *A People Called Cumberland Presbyterians: A History of the Cumterland Church*. Memphis: Frontier Press, 1972.

Beaver, R. Pierce. *All Loves Excelling: American Protestant Women in World Mission*. Grand Rapids: Eerdmans, 1968.

Boyd, Lois A. "Presbyterian Ministers' Wives—A Nineteenth Century Portrait." *Journal of Presbyterian History* 59 (Spring 1981): 3–17.

Boyd, Lois A. and Brackenridge, R. Douglas. *Presbyterian Women in America: Two Centuries of a Quest for Status*. Westport, Conn.: Greenwood Press, 1983. Includes a full bibliography.

———. "Rachel Henderlite: Women and Church Union," *Journal of Presbyterian History* 56 (Spring 1978): 10–35.

———. "United Presbyterian Policy on Women and the Church—An Historical Overview." *Journal of Presbyterian History* 59 (Fall 1981): 383–406.

Brackenridge, R. Douglas. "Equality for Women? A Case Study in Presbyterian Polity 1926–1930," *Journal of Presbyterian History* 58 (Summer 1980): 142–65.

Carson, Mary Faith, and Price, James J.H. "The Ordination of Women and the Function of the Bible." *Journal of Presbyterian History* 59 (Summer 1981): 245–65.

Douglas, William. *Ministers' Wives*. New York: Harper & Row, 1965.

Gripe, Elizabeth Howell. "Women, Restructuring and Unrest in the 1920s." *Journal of Presbyterian History* 52 (Summer 1974): 188–99.

Hayes, Florence. *Daughters of Dorcas: The Story of the Work of Women for Home Missions Since 1802*. New York: Board of National Missions, Presbyterian Church in the U.S.A., 1952.

Hummel, Margaret. *The Amazing Heritage*. Philadelphia: Geneva Press, 1970.

Irvine, Mary D., and Eastwood, Alice L. *Pioneer Women of the Presbyterian Church, United States*. Richmond: Presbyterian Committee of Publication, 1923.

Jamison, Wallace Newlin. *The United Presbyterian Story*. Pittsburgh: Geneva Press, 1958.

Loetscher, Lefferts A. *A Brief History of the Presbyterians*. 3rd ed. Philadelphia: Westminster Press, 1978.

Miller, Page Putnam. "Women in the Vanguard of the Sunday School Movement." *Journal of Presbyterian History* 58 (Winter 1980): 311–25.

Parker, Inez Moore. *The Rise and Decline of the Program of Education for Black Presbyterians of the United Presbyterian Church, U.S.A. 1865–1970*. San Antonio: Trinity University Press, 1977.

Penfield, Janet Harbison. "Women in the Presbyterian Church—An Historical Overview." *Journal of Presbyterian History* 55 (Summer 1977): 107–24.

Smylie, James H. "Notable Presbyterian Women." *Journal of Presbyterian History* 52 (Summer 1974): 99–121.

————. "*The Woman's Bible* and the Spiritual Crisis." *Soundings* 59 (Fall 1976): 305–28.

Thompson, Ernest Trice. *Presbyterians in the South.* 3 vols. Richmond: John Knox Press, 1963, 1973.

Verdesi, Elizabeth. *In But Still Out: Women in the Church.* Philadelphia: Westminster Press, 1973, 1976.

Wheeler, Eliza DesPortes. *Women in Ministry: The Case of Anne Montgomery.* Hartford: Research Report of the Hartford Seminary Foundation, 1975.

Winsborough, Hallie Paxson. *The Women's Auxiliary, PCUS: A Brief History of Its Background, Organization and Development.* Atlanta: Presbyterian Committee of Publication, 1927.

————. *Yesteryears.* As Told to Rosa Gibbins. Atlanta: Presbyterian Committee of Publication, 1937.

MODERN ANGLICAN WOMEN

Bellamy, V. Nelle. "Participation of Women in the Public Life of the Church from Lambeth Conference, 1867–1978," *Historical Magazine of the Protestant Episcopal Church* 51 (1982): 81–98.

Boyd, Sandra Hughes. "The History of Women in the Episcopal Church: A Select Annotated Bibliography." *Historical Magazine of the Protestant Episcopal Church* 50 (1981): 423–33.

Boyd, Sandra Hughes and Hiatt, Suzanne. "Tabulations of Clergy Women Statistics—July 7, 1983," *Rauch* 5 (1983): 1.

Brown, Lawrence. "Texas Bishop Vetoes Women Council Delegates in 1921," *Historical Magazine of the Protestant Episcopal Church* 48 (March 1979): 93–102.

Gender and Ministry, A Report Prepared for the Church Assembly by the Central Advisory Council for the Ministry. London: Church Information Office, 1962.

General Synod. *The Ordination of Women to the Priesthood: A Consultative Document Presented by the Advisory Council for the Church's Ministry.* Oxford: Church Army Press, 1972.

Grierson, Janet. *The Deaconess.* London: Church Information Office, 1981.

Harrison, Alan. *Bound for Life.* London: Mowbray, 1983.

Heasman, Kathleen. *Evangelicals in Action: An Appraisal of Their Social Work in the Victorian Era.* London: Geoffrey Bles, 1962.

Heeney, Brian. "The Beginnings of Church Feminism: Women and the Councils of the Church of England 1897–1919." *Journal of Ecclesiastical History* 33 (January 1982): 89–109.

Hewitt, Emily C., and Hiatt, Suzanne K., eds. *Women Priests: Yes or No?* New York: Seabury Press, 1977.

"Joint Commission on Women Church Workers." *Journal of the General Convention of the Protestant Episcopal Church in the United States of America* (1970).

Prelinger, Catherine M. "Women and Religion, Women as Episcopalians: Some Methodological Observations," *Historical Magazine of the Protestant Episcopal Church* 52 (June 1983): 141–52.

"Report of the Advisory Commission on the Work of Deaconesses," *Journal of the General Convention of the Protestant Episcopal Church in the United States of America* (1949).

"Report of the Joint Commission on the Work of Deaconesses," *Journal of the General Convention of the Protestant Episcopal Church in the United States of America* (1961).

Women in Ministry: A Study, Report of the Working Party Set Up Jointly by the Ministry Committee of the Advisory Council for the Church's Ministry and the Council for Women's Ministry in the Church. London: Church Information Office, 1968.

Women's Work in the Church: Being the Report of a Committee Appointed by the Archbishops of Canterbury and York in 1942. London: The Press and Publications Board of the Church Assembly, 1943.

Working Group Appointed by the Standing Committee. *Women Lawfully Ordained Abroad.* London: Church Information Office, 1979.

Index

Abolitionist women: Abby Kelley's role, 185–86; attacks on racial prejudice, 195–98; feminism, 194-95; the Grimké sisters, 178–85; religious influence on leaders, 189–94; William Lloyd Garrison's appeal, 175–76; the "woman question," 186–88; work in Boston, Philadelphia, and New York, 176–78

Abolition Society, 9

Abortion, 222

Adams, Mary, 98

Adams, Widow, 86

Adman, Ursula, 110

Adultery, 18–19, 25, 60, 62, 64

Advisory Commission on the Work of Deaconesses (Episcopal), 248

Advisory Council for the Church's Ministry (Church of England), 241

Affair of the Rue St. Jacques, 31

Africa, West, 167

African Methodist Episcopal Church, 155, 160, 171 n.10

African Methodist Episcopal Zion Church, 160, 161

African Union Methodist Protestant Church, 161

Ainsworth, Henry, 83

Albert of Prussia, 25

Aldee, Joan, 83

Allen, Richard, 160

Allen, Robert, 77

American Anti-Slavery Society, 177, 180, 182, 185, 188, 194, 195, 197

American Association of Women Ministers, 11

American Methodist Ladies Centenary Association, 162

Ames, Jessie Daniel, 169

Anabaptists, 5–6, 8, 12, 25, 45–47, 95, 96; female martyrs, 66–69; revolutionary women, 63–66; role of women in churches, 51–57; theological views on women, 47, 51; views on family, sex, and marriage, 57–63

Anglican Church of Australia, 253

Anglican Church of Canada, 240, 253, 254

Anglican Communion, 11–12, 20,
229–31, 229–31, 254–55; on
deaconesses, 245–48; on the la-
ity, 241–43; on members of re-
ligious communities, 243–45;
on ordaining women, 250–54;
on women workers, 248–50.
See also Lambeth, Resolutions
Anglican Consultative Council,
243, 253
Anthony, Susan B., 195
Anticlericalism, 97
Anti-Slavery Convention of
American Women, 180, 185,
196
Anti-Slavery Movement, 9–10,
161, 167, 168, 173–99
Apostolic Church, women in, 4
Archbishops' Commission on the
Ministry of Women (1935),
246, 251
Archie, Lydia, 161
Aristotle, 50
Askew, Anne, 95
Association of Professional
Women Church Workers, 250
Association of Southern Women
for the Prevention of Lynch-
ing, 169
Astell, Mary, 117
Attaway, Mrs., 96, 97
Augsburg Confession, 16
Austin, Charles, 252
Austria, 52
Authors, female, 51, 81–83, 103–
5, 111
Auwers, Linda, 141
Avery, Elizabeth, 105
Axtell, James, 138

Backus, Isaac, 139, 143
Bacon, Anthony, 79
Bacon, Lady Ann, 79–82

Baptists, 7, 11, 76, 77, 84, 85, 96,
102, 107, 109, 111, 114, 143,
179
Barnardiston, Lady Jane, 79–80
Barrow, Henry, 81, 86
Bartlett, John, 87
Batenburgers, 66
Bath and Wells, Diocese of, 109
Bathurst, Elizabeth, 112
Bauford, Joan, 85
Baxter, Richard, 110
Beaumont, Agnes, 110–11
Beck, Balthasar, 56
Belle, Katharine, 212–16, 226
n.40
Belle, Sue, 157
Bender, Harold S., 47, 52
Bennett, Belle, 157, 159, 163, 165
Bernaerts, Jelis, 57
Berry, Mrs., 88
Bethune, Mary McLeod, 159
Bethune-Cookman Institute, 160
Beza-Tomson Bible, 84
Bigamy, 19, 61, 64
Birney, James G., 186
Blake, Eugene Carson, 219, 222
Blaurock, George, 53
Blunt, Richard, 76
Board for Mission and Unity
(Church of England), 242
Board for Social Responsibility
(Church of England), 249
Board of Christian Education
(Presbyterian), 210, 212, 216
Board of Education (Methodist),
160
Board of Foreign Missions (Pres-
byterian), 210–12, 217
Board of Home Missions (Pres-
byterian), 224 n.14
Board of Ministerial Relief and
Sustentation (Presbyterian),
210, 212

Board of Missions (Methodist), 157, 158
Board of National Missions (Presbyterian), 210, 212
Board of Theological Education (Episcopal Church, U.S.A.), 242
Board of Women's Work (Anglican), 237
Book of Common Prayer, 229
Boosers, Maeyken, 51, 60
Boston Female Anti-Slavery Society, 176, 180, 183
Boswell, James, 75
Boucher, Joan, 95
Bouwens, Leenaert, 62
Bowes, Lady, 78, 80
Bowman, Ellyn, 86
Boyd, Sandra, 252, 253
Boyle, Katherine (Lady Ranelagh), 89 n.4
Brandenburg, Elizabeth of, 24
Braund, George B., 243
Braunschweig, Duke Erich, 25
Braunschweig, Elizabeth of, 24–25
Brewster, Ann, 114
Brewster, Thomas, 114
Bridge, William, 79
Brinsley, John, 99
Broechers, Marie, 54
Brown, Richard, 139
Bucer, Martin, 21, 23, 34
Buckingham, Duke of, 101
Buckley, James M., 162–63
Bulkeley, Edward, 81
Bullinger, Heinrich, 29
Bumenin, Frena, 6, 55
Bunyan, Elizabeth, 122 n.63
Bunyan, John, 79, 108, 111
Burr, Esther, 147 n.27
Burroughs, Jeremiah, 79
Butler, Clementina, 156

Butler, Clementina Rowe, 156
Byfield, Sarah, 128

California: San Francisco, 223 n.2
Calbert, Elizabeth, 114, 116
Calvert, Giles, 114
Calvin, Idelette, 28
Calvin, John, 5, 13, 14, 32, 34–36, 41–42 n.73, 82, 84, 205; on celibacy, 27; on divorce, 29; female correspondents of, 34–35; on marriage, 27–29; on spiritual equality, 29; on women, 25–27; on women in the church, 29–30; on women rulers, 29
Calvinists, 4–5, 12–13, 25–36
Camden, Lady Elizabeth, 80
Canada, 12, 154, 240, 253, 254
Canon law, 42 n.73
Canterbury, Archbishop of, 246
Canterbury, See of, 229
Capito, Wolfgang, 23
Carleton, George, 86
Cartwright, Thomas, 81, 86
Cary, Grace, 101
Cary, Mary, 8, 83, 107
Catechisms and catechizing, 6, 20, 21, 25, 30, 77, 129, 138, 140, 249
Catherine de Medici, 31, 32
Catholics, 78
Cecil, William (Lord Burghley), 80, 81
Celibacy, 5, 14, 20, 27
Central Board of Finance (Church of England), 241
Central House for Deaconesses, Ill., 247
Channel, Elinor, 101
Channing, William Ellery, 176, 190
Chapman, John Jay, 176

Chapman, Maria Weston, 176, 180, 182, 186–88
Chappell, Winifred, 165, 169
Charles I (King of England), 101
Charles II (King of England), 108
Chauncy, Charles, 128
Chester, Diocese of, 77
Chicago Training School, 159, 169
Chidley, Katherine, 8, 79, 82, 85, 104, 121 n.45
Child, Lydia Maria, 176, 177, 182, 188, 191
Christian Methodist Episcopal Church, 160, 161
Chrysostom, John, 234
Church Army (Church of England), 248–50
Churching of women, 85, 247
Church of Wales (Anglican), 253, 254
Church of Christ of Japan, 218
Church of England, 5, 7, 9, 11–12, 78, 85, 114, 117, 151, 229–55
Church of the Nazarene, 167
Church of the Province of Kenya, 253
Church of the Province of New Zealand, 240
Church of the Province of Uganda, 253
Church widow, office of, 83–84
Claes, Weynken, 67
Claesken of Workum, 59
Clarendon Code, 108
Clarke, Samuel, 143
Clasen, Claus-Peter, 47, 52
Cleveland, John, 139
Clifford, Margaret (Countess of Cumberland), 80, 81
Cohen, Alfred, 100
Cole, Nathan, 139

Colman, Benjamin, 131
Cologne, Archbishopric of, 52
Colonies, American, 7. See also New England
Colored Methodist Episcopal Church, 161
Commissioned Church Worker (Presbyterian), 217, 227 n.51
Commission on Doctrine (Church of England), 242
Commission on Interracial Cooperation, 169
Comstock, Elizabeth, 10
Condé, Louis de, 31
Conference on Women's Status and Service in the Church (Presbyterian), 215
Congregationalists, 7, 11, 76, 78, 79, 82, 94, 107, 109, 114, 133, 134, 138, 143, 144, 179, 193, 200 n.9, 225 n.23
Congregational Union, 8
Connecticut, 136, 147 nn.25, 28; Canterbury, 147 n. 28; Milford, 147 nn.25, 28; New Haven, 133; New London, 147 n.28; Norwich, 143; Preston, 143; Stonington, 147 n.28; Suffield, 147 n.28; Windsor, 141, 147 n.28; Woodbury, 147 n.28
Connecticut River Valley, 141
Constantinople, 234
Consultation on Church Union, 221
Conventicles, 77, 108–9, 111, 142–43
Conway, Sir Edward, 81
Cooper, Thomas, Bishop of Lincoln, 81
Copinger, Edmund, 81
Corbet, Margaret, 77
Cordier, Maturin, 30
Corrigan, Daniel, 253

Corvinus, Antonius, 25
Council on Women and the
    Church (Presbyterian), 222
Council of Women's Ministries
    (Anglican), 254
Crane, Elizabeth, 78, 86
Cremin, Lawrence, 138
Cromwell, Oliver, 101
Crosby, Sarah, 153
Cumberland Presbyterian
    Church, 223 n.1
Curtis, Jane, 114–15
Cutter, Barbara, 140
Cuyler, Theodore L., 224 n.9

D'Albret, Jeanne, 32–33
Dale, Dorcas, 112
Davenport, John, 81
Davidjorists, 66
Davis, Sarah, 141
Daytona Normal and Industrial
    School for Negro Girls, 159–60
Deborah, 29
De Bure, Idelette, 28
Dedham Classis, 84
Degler, Carl, 125
De Luns, Philippe, 31
De Morel, François, 30
Demos, John, 129
Denck, Hans, 53
Dering, Edward, 80, 82
De Roore, Jacob, 60
De Swarte, Jan, 60–61
De Swarte, Klaesken, 61
Dewitt, Robert L., 253
Dexter, Gregory, 83
Diaconate and deaconesses, 4, 6,
    7, 11, 30, 51, 52, 55–56, 83,
    159, 160, 167, 203, 208–10, 217,
    232, 234–37, 239-41, 245–50,
    254
Dickey, Sarah, 164
Dircks, Lijsken, 59

Discipline of the Union Church
    of Africans, 161
District of Columbia, 199 n.8
Divorce, 18–19, 21, 25, 29, 39
    n.36, 41–42 n.73, 48, 62, 96
Dordrecht (Dort) Confession of
    Faith, 51, 55–56, 58
Douglas, Lady Eleanor, 101, 121
    n.43
Douglass, Sarah Mapps, 177,
    196, 197
Dover, Mrs. Simon, 114
Doyle, Patricia, 222
Dudley, Anne (Countess of War-
    wick), 79, 81
Dunfey, Rebecca, 140–41
Dury, John, 80
Dyke, William, 79

Eaton, H., 154
Eby, Charles, 52
Edict of Nantes, 33
Education, 10, 21, 30–32, 34, 58–
    60, 112, 137–39, 158–60
Edward VI (King of England),
    21, 29
Edwards, Jonathan, 142, 147 n.27
Edwards, Thomas, 82, 96, 97,
    119 n.18
Edwards, Timothy, 141, 142
Eighty Years War, 34
Elders, 11, 167, 203, 208–10, 213,
    216, 220, 226 n.40
Elizabeth I (Queen of England),
    6, 29, 34, 84
Elizabeth of Brandenburg, 24
Elizabeth of Braunschweig, 24–25
Elizabeth of Leeuwarden, 53
Elliott, Maggie Thompson, 164
Embury, Philip, 154, 165
England, 11, 12, 22–24, 75–89,
    197, 229–55; Abingdon, 109–10;
    Ashford, 85; Banbury, 86; Bed-

ford, 108; Birch, 80; Bristol, 79;
Bury St. Edmunds, 79; Cambridge, 34; Cheshire, 80; Cranbrook, 79; East Molesey, 86;
Ellenbrook Chapel, 80; Ely, 85;
Essex, 79; Exeter, 79; Faversham, 85; Gorhambury, 79;
Great Yarmouth, 76; Guiseley,
80; Hackness, 77; Hemel
Hempstead, 79; Lancashire,
80, 85; London, 78, 80–82, 84,
85, 87, 88, 93, 96, 97, 101, 102,
109–11, 114, 116, 187, 188, 195,
252; Manchester, 80, 85; Mid-
dlesex, 110; Newbury, 78; Nor-
folk, 96; Norwich, 76, 109;
Ormskirk, 77; Redburn, 79;
Salisbury, 85; Shrewsbury, 85;
Skipton Castle, 80; Southwark,
78; Stepney, 78; Suffolk, 79;
Surrey, 101; Westminster, 106;
Wolston, 86; York, 247
Episcopal Church, U.S.A., 231,
240–45, 247, 248, 250, 252–54
Episcopal Returns (1669), 108
Episcopal Women's Caucus, Inc.,
252, 253
Equal Rights Amendment, 222
Erasmus, Desiderius, 82
Eremetical life, 244
Evangelical Association, 158, 164
Evangelical Church, 164
Evans, Charles, 127
Evanston College for Ladies, 162

Family, role of women in, 20,
58–59, 129–30
Farret, Margaret, 88
Feicken, Hille, 66
Fellowship of the Concerned,
169
Female College of Northwestern
University, 162
Feminism and feminist move-

ment, 10, 94, 117, 167, 168,
174, 183, 184, 194, 198, 204,
221
Fenner, Dudley, 81
Feoffees for Impropriations, 79–
80
Ferard, Elizabeth Catherine, 234–
35
Ferrara, Duke of, 32
Ferris, David, 139
Field, John, 81
Fifth Monarchists, 8, 76, 83, 98,
101, 104, 105, 107, 110, 114,
121 n.38
Finney, Charles Grandison, 178
Fish, Joseph, 144
Fisher, Abigail, 112
Fletcher, Mary Bosanquet, 153
Fornication, 16, 57
Forten, Harriet, 177
Forten, James, Sr., 177
Forten, Margaretta, 177
Forten, Sarah, 177
Fosbrooke, Margaret, 79
Fox, George, 102, 113, 121 n.48
Fox, Judith, 80
Fox, Margaret Fell, 109–11
France, Renée de (Duchess of
Ferrarra), 30, 32
France, 30–34; Lyon, 33; Montar-
gis, 32; Strasbourg, 21–23, 31,
46, 49, 55, 56, 61, 63
Francis I (King of France), 32
Franck, Sebastian, 56
Frederick, Duke (the Wise), 24
Free Methodists, 167
Free Religious Association, 191
Frey, Claus, 61
Fulke, William, 81
Fundamentalism, 168

Gadbury, Mary, 8, 98
Garrettson, Catherine Livingston, 154

Garrettson, Freeborn, 154
Garrison, William Lloyd, 173, 175, 185, 188, 190
General Association of Congregationalist Ministers, 181
Geneva Bible, 77
Geneva City Council, 29, 30
Germany, 21, 23, 24, 48, 52; Augsburg, 21, 54; Emden, 62; Gottingen, 25; Hanover, 25; Ingolstadt, 24; Munster, 6, 53, 63–66, 68; Nürnberg, 61; Schleiden, 54; Ulm, 21; Windsheim, 61; Wurttemberg, 61; Zwickau, 21, 39 n.36
Gerrits, Soetken, 51, 56
Gifford, George, 81
Golding, Dame Elizabeth, 87
Goodwin, John, 84
Goodwin, Thomas, 79
Gough, John, 87
Gough, Prudence Ridgely, 154–55
Great Awakening, 8, 132, 134, 135, 140, 142–44, 147 n.26
Grebel, Barbara, 48
Grebel, Conrad, 48, 53, 55
Greenwood, John, 76, 86
Greenwood, Mrs. John, 86
Grevin, Philip, 126
Grierson, Janet, 234, 235, 245, 246
Grimké, Angelina, 178–85, 187, 192–97, 201 n.36, 202 n.46
Grimké, Sarah, 178–85, 187, 192–97, 201 n.36, 202 n.46
Grindal, Edmund, Bishop of London, 76, 87
Gynecocracy, 29

Hadewijk of Leeuwarden, 68
Hall, Bishop R.O., 239
Hargrove, Bishop R.K., 158

Harkness, Georgia, 159, 169
Harper, Frances Ellen Watkins, 197
Harris, Mary, 81
Harrison, Alan, 243
Hartzell, Jennie Culver, 156
Hastings, Selina Shirley (Countess of Huntingdon), 153
Hattinger, Margarita, 55
Hayes, Lucy Webb, 157
Hays, George P., 225 n.21
Hazzard, Dorothy, 78–79
Heathen Woman's Friend, The, 156
Heck, Barbara Ruckle, 153–54, 165
Heck, Paul, 154
Helm, Lucinda, 157
Helm, Mary, 157
Henry II (King of France), 32
Henry IV (King of France), 33
Henry VIII (King of England), 233
Herbert, Mary Sidney (Countess of Pembroke), 82
Heywood, Oliver, 110
Hiatt, Suzanne, 252
Higgins, Patricia, 106
High Commission, 75, 76, 82, 83, 88
Higher education for women, 205
Hidlersham, Arthur, 78
Hill, Christopher, 100
Hoby, Lady Margaret, 77, 78, 82
Hodge, Margaret, 212–16
Hoffman, Melchior, 23, 49, 55, 56, 63, 68
Holiness movement, 165–68
Holland. See Netherlands
Holmes, Jane, 140
Holy Catholic Church of China, 239
"Holy Maids," 100

Hong Kong, 12, 252, 253
Hong Kong and Macao, Diocese
of, 239, 240, 253
Hoover, Theressa, 161
Hospitality to clergy, 78, 154–55
Household religion in New Eng-
land, 137–39
Houses of Prayer, (Church of
England), 243
Howard, Christian, 251
Howe, Julia Ward, 10
Howgill, Mary, 112
Hubmaier, Balthasar, 48, 53
Hudson Valley, 154
Hugeline, Elsbeth, 48
Huguenots, 31–33
Humanism, 21, 31, 137
Hungary, 22
Hurt, Lilian, 219–20
Hut, Hans, 53, 61
Hutchinson, Anne, 95
Hutter, Jacob, 53
Hutterites, 46, 49, 53, 58, 60, 62

Ibbotson, Ann, 114
Iconoclasm by women, 93
Illinois, 167; Chicago, 217, 223
n.2; Evanston, 159, 247
Independents. See
Congregationalists
India, 156, 167
Indians, American, 156
Inquisition, 32
Inskip, John S., 166, 167
Inskip, Martha Foster, 166, 167
Institute for Colored Youth, 196
Intermarriage, racial, 196
International Association of
Women Ministers, 11
Ireland: Dublin, 107
Irwin, Joyce L., 55
Italy, 32

Jamaica, 110
James, St., 56
Jans, Anneken, 51, 67
Jans, Felistis, 59
Jansdochter, Adriaenken, 57
Jeremiads, 131
Jessey, Henry, 78, 88, 102
Jewel, John, 82
Johnson, Carrie Parks, 169
Johnson, Francis, 76, 78, 83
Johnson, Samuel, 75
Joint Commission on the Work
of Deaconesses, 248
Joint Commission on Women
Church Workers, 248
Jones, Sara, 82
Joris, David, 51, 65–66
Jost, Lienhard, 55
Jost, Ursula, 55, 56

Kansas, 225 n.23
Kelley, Abby, 185, 186, 188, 192,
195, 197
Kerber, Linda, 125
Kinnaird, Joan, 117
Kitchin, William, 79
Klaassen, Walter, 45, 46
Knewstub, John, 81
Knox, John, 29, 34
Knyvett, Lady, 90 n.12
Koehler, Lyle, 126

Ladies' New York City Anti-
Slavery Society, 178
Lamb, Thomas, 84, 96
Lamb, Zerviah, 143
Lambeth Conferences, 229–41,
246, 254–55
Lambeth Quadrilateral, 230
Lambeth Resolutions: on deacon-
esses, 234–37; on the laity,
232–33; on members of reli-
gious communities, 233–34; on

ordaining women, 238–41; on women workers, 237–38
Lampe, William, 218
Lathrop, John, 75, 77, 82, 88
Laud, William, Archbishop of Canterbury, 88, 101
Lee, Jarena, 155, 160
Lee, Luther, 167
Lee, Mrs. Nicholas, 87
Leeuwarden, Elizabeth of, 53
Leeuwarden, Hadewijk of, 68
Leiden, Jan van (Jan Beuckelsz), 6, 63–65
Leight, Dame Dorothy, 80
Letters on the Equality of the Sexes, and the Condition of Woman, 184, 194
Levellers, 104–7, 115
Le Vettre, Claudine, 59
Liberator, 175
Liberty Party, 186
Lilburne, Elizabeth, 122 n.63
Lilburne, John, 106
Literacy, 21, 59, 139–42
Livermore, Mary, 10, 194
Locke, Anne, 34–35, 82
Lockridge, Kenneth, 140, 141
Lollards, 7, 84, 95
London, Bishop of, 75
London, Diocese of, 235
London Common Council, 97
London Yearly Meeting (Quaker), 113
Looseveldt, Pierijntgen, 67
Louisiana: New Orleans, 156
Low Countries. *See* Netherlands
Lubbertsdochter, Judith, 56
Luther, Katherine (*née* von Bora), 17, 22
Luther, Martin, 5, 13–14, 24, 26–28, 35–36; on divorce, 18–19; on education, 21; on family relations, 20; influence of his ideas on women, 20–21; and Katherine von Bora, 17, 19, 22–23; on marriage, 16–18; on women and relations between the sexes, 14–16; on women preachers, 15, 19
Lutherans, 4–5, 12–25, 231
Lystyncx, Aeffgen, 54, 66

Macao, 12, 239, 253
McClurg, Patricia, 11
McConnell, Bishop Francis J., 169
McDowell, Fannie, 167
Mack, Phyllis, 100
Magdala, Mary of, 4
Mailly, Madelein (Comtesse de Roye), 31
Mankes-Zernike, Anna, 56
Manz, Felix, 53, 55
Margaret of Parma, 34
Marguerite de Navarre, 32
Maria, Bernhartz, 54
Maria of Monjou, 54, 68
Marprelate tracts, 78, 86
Marriage, 4–6, 14, 16–18, 25, 27–29, 57–58
Martin, John, 253
Martin, Mrs. Richard, 86
Martyr, Peter, 23, 84
Martyrs Mirror, 45, 46, 48, 51, 52, 59, 65, 66, 68, 70 n.5
Mary I (Queen of England), 6, 34
Maryland: Baltimore, 155, 198, 217
Mary of Magdala, 4
Mary Stuart (Queen of Scotland), 29
Massachusetts, 84, 181, 187, 194, 196; Boston, 128, 133, 156, 159, 175–78, 180, 186, 191, 200 n.9; Brookline, 193; Cambridge, 140; Freetown, 140–42; Lynn,

185; Nantucket, 189; North
Brookfield, 193; Salem, 133
Mather, Cotton, 127–31, 133,
135, 142, 149 n.45
Mather, Increase, 138–39
Matthijsz, Jan, 63
Maxwell, Ann, 114
May, Samuel J., 180
May, Susan, 85
Maynard, Margaret, 85, 88
Medici, Catherine de, 31, 32
Melchiorites, 46, 63
Mennonite Encyclopedia, 47, 52,
63, 66, 70 n.5
Mennonites, 46, 76
Men's Meetings (Quaker), 113
Mesano South, Bishop of, 253
Methodist Church, 165
Methodist Episcopal Church, 9,
10, 152, 154, 162, 164–66, 168,
169
Methodist Episcopal Church,
South, 157, 163, 165
Methodist Federation for Social
Service, 169
Methodist Protestant Church, 10,
158, 162, 164, 165
Methodists, 9, 179, 200 n.9; in
early America, 153–55; femin-
ism, 167; holiness movement,
165–67; impact of social gospel,
168–69; institutionalization of
women's work, 155–61; ordi-
nation of women, 164–65;
Wesleyan tradition, 151–53;
women as lay representatives,
161–64
Meyer, Lucy Rider, 159, 165
Midland Particular Baptist Association, 85
Milton, John, 83, 96, 97, 121 n.27
Missionaries, 159, 160, 207, 208,
225 n.23

Missionary Voice, 157
Missouri, 225 n.23; Kansas City,
159; St. Louis, 223 n.2
Mixed marriages among Anabap-
tists, 61–62
Monastic life, 16–17, 20, 100,
233–34, 243–45
Monjou, Maria of, 54, 68
Moody, Dwight L., 159
Moone, Susannah, 114
Moore, Robert, 80
Moravia, 52, 55
Morély, Jean, 30
Morgan, Edmund S., 137
Morse, Joshua, 143
"Mother," office of, 161
Mott, James, 187
Mott, Lucretia Coffin, 10, 177,
187–91, 194, 195, 197
Movement for the Ordination of
Women (Anglican), 252, 260
n.89
Mudge, Lewis S., 214, 218, 226
n.40
Muller, Magdalena, 6, 55
Munster, Kingdom of, 54, 63–65
Munsterites, 46, 57, 63–66
Murglen, Barbara, 55
Myller, Judith, 88

National Council of Churches,
219
National Council of Negro
Women, 160
National Mission in Church and
Society (Episcopal Church,
U.S.A.), 242
Navarre, Marguerite de, 32
Nayler, James, 121 n.48
Netherlands, 21, 33, 34, 50, 52,
54–56, 58, 63, 65, 76, 84; Am-
sterdam, 54, 56–57, 65, 66;
Antwerp, 57, 59; Bergklooster,

65; Bovenknijpe, 57; Ghent, 60; Haarlem, 56; The Hague, 56, 67; Limmen, 54; Monschau, 54; Oldeklooster, 65; Poeldijk, 65; Rotterdam, 51
Newark, Presbytery of, 206
New England, 8, 124–45, 181–82
New England Anti-Slavery Society, 176
New England Deaconess Home and Training School, 159
New England Puritans: as church members, 133–37; and education, 137–42; and Great Awakening, 143–44; and household religion, 137; lay associations, 143; as members of conventicles, 142–43; as parents, 129–30; piety of, 130–33; recent studies of, 125–26; women of virtue, 127–29
New Jersey, 169; Newark, 205; Vineland, 166
New Jersey, Synod of, 206
"New Organization," 186, 187
New Testament view of women, 3–4, 48. *See also* Paul, St.
New York, 10, 115, 154, 165, 166, 169, 197; Albany, 223 n.2; Brooklyn, 224 n.9; Champlain, 154; Geneva, 224 nn.9, 12; New York City, 178, 180, 185, 186, 200 n.9, 223 n.2, 242; Rochester, 219; Seneca Falls, 10, 167, 188, 205
New Zealand, 12, 253
Nichols, Josias, 77
Niederollesbroich, Bernhartz Maria of, 54
Niswonger, Ella, 164
Nonconformist women (English): as authors and translators, 81–83; in church government, 83–

84; as demonstrators, 85–88; as founders of churches, 78–79; hospitality to clergy, 78; as patrons, 79–81; and preaching, 84–85; as printers, 83; role in churches, 76–77; role in homes, 78; suffering of, 88; in the underground, 86
Northampton Classis, 79
Norton, Mary Beth, 125

Ochino, Bernardino, 82
Office of Church and Society (Presbyterian), 222
Ohio, 197; Cincinnati, 156
Oi, Florence Lee Tim, 12, 239, 252
Oliver, Anna, 164, 165, 167
Olympias, 234
Oosterbaan, J.A., 45
Opheral, Charity, 164
Ordination of women, 8, 9, 11–12, 57, 158, 161, 162, 164–67, 203, 204, 208–10, 213, 214, 216–21, 225 n.23, 226 n.51, 230, 235–41, 244–48, 250–54, 259 n.87
Oregon: Portland, 223 n.2
Orphanages, 56
Osborn, Sarah, 144–45
Oulton, Richard, 83
Our Homes, 157
Overton, Mary, 115

Paget, Thomas, 138
Palmer, Phoebe, 166–68
Parker, Theodore, 191
Parliament (England), 6, 78, 87, 94, 104, 105
Parma, Margaret of, 34
Parr, Susannah, 105
Patriarchy, 20

Patronage of ministers and writers, 6, 79–81
Paul, St., 3–4, 15, 25–27, 29, 56, 83, 84, 130, 151
Paul, Susan, 199 n.4
Paulet, Lady Margaret, 79
Peacham, Henry, 81
Peck, Katherine, 110
Pendarves, John, 110
Pendarves, Thomasine, 109, 122 n.59
Pennsylvania, 115; Philadelphia, 177–79, 185, 196, 200 n.9, 201 n.36, 217, 223 n.2, 259 n.87
Penry, Helen, 87
Penry, John, 78, 86, 87
Perkins, William, 78, 81
Persecution of women, 6, 7, 31, 46–48, 51, 54, 60, 65–69, 77, 88, 109–11, 114
Peterborough, Bishop of, 79
Pfersfelder, Elizabeth, 61
Philadelphia Female Anti-Slavery Society, 177, 196
Philips, Dirk, 50, 62
Philpot, John, 87
Poland, 34
Polygamy, 63–65
Ponet, John, 82
Poole, Elizabeth, 101, 110, 121 n.45, 122 n.59
Pope, Mary, 104, 105, 115
Preaching by women, 9, 10, 15, 21, 25, 52, 56, 83, 84, 93, 99, 112–14, 160, 161, 166, 167, 205, 206, 208, 214, 224 n.9, 247, 249, 250
Presbyterian Church, U.S., 273 n.1
Presbyterian Church, U.S.A., 11; boards and agencies, 209–13; female elders and deaconesses, 208–10, 213, 216–17; movement toward equality, 216–23; ordination, 213–21; the "woman question," 205–9
Presbyterians, 77, 79, 81–84, 109, 116, 178, 179, 192, 200 n.9, 203–23, 231
Presbyterian Women's Organization, 218, 220
"Priesthood of all believers," 15, 22
Prince, Thomas, 131
Printers, female, 56, 83, 114–15
Privy Council (England), 80
Prophets, female, 99–103
Prowse, Anne Locke, 82
Pruss, Margrette, 56
Prussia, Albert of, 25
Prynne, William, 83
Pugh, William Barrow, 218
Puritans, English, 5–7, 17, 34, 75–89, 94, 109, 116. See also Nonconformist women
Purvis, Robert, 177

Quakers, 6–9, 12, 52, 75, 76, 85, 93, 94, 96–98, 107, 109–12, 114–16, 119 n.23, 121 n.48, 143, 174, 177–80, 185, 187, 189–92, 195–98, 200 n.9, 201 n.36, 224 n.9

Rabstock, Barbara, 55
Radcliffe, Frances (Countess of Sussex), 34, 80
Ramos, José A., 253
Ranters, 8, 109
Rauch, 252, 253
Reeves, Hannah Pearce, 155
Religious life (Anglican), 233–34, 243–45
Remond, Charles Lenox, 197
Remond, Sarah Parker, 197

Renée de France (Duchess of Ferrara), 30, 32
Resinx, Felistis, 68
Restoration era, 108–17
Rhode Island: Newport, 144
Richardson, R.C., 77
Riedemann, Katerina, 49
Riedemann, Peter, 49, 58
Rippon, Roger, 87
Roberts, B.T., 167, 168
Robinson, John, 83
Rochester, Presbytery of, 220
Roe, Alice, 88
Rogers, Hester Ann Roe, 153
Rogers, John, 107
Rohan, Jacqueline de (Marquise de Rothelin), 32
Rosenblatt, Wibrandis, 23
Rothmann, Bernhard, 53, 64–65, 68
Russell, Lady Elizabeth, 81, 82
Russell, Lucy (Countess of Bedford), 81
Rutgers, Swaen, 62
Ryan, Mary, 125

St. John, Lady Catherine, 81
St. John's College, Durham, 242
St. Lawrence River Valley, 154
Salem Female Anti-Slavery Society, 197
Sattler, Michael, 48, 53, 62
Scandinavia, 21
Scarritt Bible and Training School, 159
Schaeff, Catharina, 56
Schleitheim Confession, 48
Schools, theoklogical: Church of England, 242, 246, 249; Episcopal Church, U.S.A., 243, 250
Scottish Confession of Faith, 34
Scotland, 29, 34, 140
Sectaries, English: female proph-
ets, 99–103; images of women, 98–99; as lay preachers, 95–98, 112–14; modern views on, 94–95; persecution of, 109–11; as printers, 114–15; relations with Levellers and Fifth Monarchists, 105–8; at the Restoration, 108-17; role models, 116–17; as writers, 103–5, 111–12
See, Isaac, 206
Senaca Falls Women's Rights Convention, 10, 167, 188, 205
Separatists, 7, 52, 76, 87–88
Settle, Mrs. Thomas, 78
Sewall, Samuel, 131
Sex ratios of church membership, New England, 133–34, 147 n.21
Sex roles and images, 35
Sexton, Lydia, 155, 164
Sexual desires and relations, 16–17, 27–28, 60, 65
Shaw, Anna Howard, 10, 164, 165, 167
Shaw, Irene, 141
Shepard, Thomas, 140
Sidney, Sir Philip, 82
Sidney Sussex College, Cambridge, 80
Simons, Geertruydt, 49
Simons, Menno, 46, 49, 50, 53, 54, 57, 58, 62, 63, 66, 68
Six Weeks' Meetings (Quaker), 113
Smiley, Sarah, 224 nn.9, 12
Smith, Amanda Berry, 160, 167
Smith, Henry, 84
Smout, T.C., 140
Smyth, John, 56, 76, 78, 83
Snape, Edmund, 79
Social Gospel, 168–69
Society of Friends. See Quakers
Southard, Madeline, 11

South Carolina, 179; Charleston, 178, 180
South China, Diocese of, 239
Southern Baptist Convention, 8
Sowle, Tace, 115
Spalatin, George, 24
Speer, Robert E., 211, 214
Spencer, Peter, 161
Spendlowe, Edward, 79
Spilsbury, John, 88
Stadler, Ulrich, 60
Stanton, Elizabeth Cady, 188, 194, 195
Stanton, Henry B., 186
Star Chamber, 81, 86
Steward, Rebecca Gould, 155
Stewardesses (Methodist), 160
Stone, Lucy, 193, 194
Strowd, John, 87
Strowd, Mrs. John, 86
Suffrage, woman's, 10, 12, 164, 193, 204, 205, 209
Sundamore, Lady, 79
Swain, Clara, 156
Swiss Brethren, 46
Switzerland, 47, 48, 50, 52; Basel, 23; Béarn, 33; Constance, 21; Geneva, 29, 30, 41 n.73; Neuchatel, 32; St. Gall, 55; Zollikon, 52; Zurich, 29, 46, 52, 55

Taffin, Jean, 82
Taft, Mary Barritt, 153
Tailour, Anna, 88
Tait, A.C., 235
Tappan, Lewis, 186
Task Force on Women (Presbyterian), 222
Taylor, William, 83
Temperance movement, 162, 168, 205
Tennessee: Nashville, 159
Texas, 199 n.8

Third Estates Commissioner (Church of England), 242
Thoburn, Isabella, 156
Thomas, Anthony, 79
Thomas, Keith, 99
Thompson, George, 179
Throckmorton, Job, 78
Tilly, Dorothy Rogers, 169
Tithes, tithing, 94, 105
Todd, Margo, 137
Towner, Margaret, 220
Townsend, Theophilia, 112
Tracy, Patricia, 126
Translators, female, 6, 81–82
Trapnel, Anna, 98, 101, 102, 104, 107, 110, 121 nn.38, 43
Traske, Mrs. John, 85
Travers, Rebecca, 112
Truth, Sojourner, 198
Tubman, Harriet, 161
Turkey, 7
Turner, Bishop Henry McNeal, 160
Tymme, Thomas, 81

Udall, John, 81
Udall, Nicholas, 82
Uemura, Tamaki, 218
Underground railroad, 172
Union American Methodist Episcopal Church, 161
Unitarians, 10, 174, 176, 180, 190, 191, 195, 198, 200 n.9
United Brethren, 155, 158, 162, 164
United Church Women (Presbyterian), 219
United Presbyterian Church, U.S.A., 223 n.1
United Presbyterian Women, 221
Universalists, 10, 191
Unwin, Katherine, 85

Van Batenburg, Jan, 65
Van Bright, Thieleman Jansz, 45, 46, 65, 66
Van Cott, Maggie (Margaret Newton), 165, 166
Van Damme, Elysabeth, 56
Van den Houte, Soetgen, 60
Vassar College, 205
Verbeeck, Joos, 59
Vere, Lady Mary, 81
Vermigli, Peter Martyr, 23, 84
Viret, Pierre, 30
Vocation, 5, 9–10, 20, 27, 28, 33–35, 232–34, 238, 241, 243, 244, 248, 254
Voetius, Gisbertus, 84
Von Bora, Katherine, 17, 22
Von Grumbach, Argula, 23–24
Voolstra, Sjouke, 51

Waitier, Jan, 58
Waldegrave, Mrs. Robert, 86
Waldegrave, Robert, 86
Wales, 79, 235, 253, 254
Walrond, Jane, 90 n.7
Walrond, John, 90 n.7
Ward, Harry F., 169
Warren, Elizabeth, 83, 104, 121 n.45
Washington, Booker T., 159
Weber, Helen, 218
Wedel, C.H., 53
Weld, Dame Mary, 80
Weld, Theodore, 183–86, 192, 193, 197
Wells, Edward, R., 253
Wentworth, Anne, 111
Wesley, Charles, 151
Wesley, John, 9, 151–52, 166, 170
Wesley, Susannah Annesley, 153
Wesleyan Methodists, 167
West, Sarah, 141
Weston, Anne Warren, 182, 183

Westwood, Mary, 115
White, Dorothy, 112
White, Elizabeth, 136
Whitehead, Anne Downer, 112, 113
Whitgift, John, Archbishop of Canterbury, 12, 81, 84, 86
Wife beating, 58
Wight, Sara, 102
Wigston, Mrs. Roger, 86
Wildbloud, Humphrey, 79
Willard, Emma Hart, 10
Willard, Frances, 162, 163, 165, 168
Williams, George H., 65, 67
Willoughby, Catherine (Duchess of Suffolk), 34
Wilson, John, 79
Winkler, Conrad, 52
Winton, Diocese of, 109
Wives, subordination of, 18, 25–27, 58
Wollstonecraft, Mary, 10
"Woman question": in the Abolitionist movement, 186–88; in the Presbyterian Church, U.S.A., 205–9
Woman's Board of Foreign Missions (Presbyterian), 209, 223 n.2
Woman's Board of Home Missions (Presbyterian), 209, 224–25 n.14
Woman's Christian Temperance Union, 162, 168
Woman's Department of Church Extension (Methodist), 157
Woman's Foreign Missionary Society (Methodist), 9, 155–57, 159
Woman's Home Missionary Society (Methodist), 156, 163
Woman's Missionary Council (Methodist), 157

Woman's Parsonage and Home Mission Society (Methodist), 157

Women's Division, United Methodist Board of Global Ministries, 156

Women's Executive Committee of Home Missions (Presbyterian), 11, 223 n.2

Women's Meetings (Quaker), 112, 113

Women's Ministerial Conference, 10–11

"Women's Petitions," 106, 121 n.49

Workum, Claesken of, 59

World Council of Churches, 219

World's Anti-Slavery Convention, 187, 195

Wright, Henry C., 181

Wright, Leonard, 84

Zaller, Robert, 76

Zell, Katherine, 5, 22, 23

Zell, Matthew, 23

Zwingli, Ulrich, 46

About the Contributors

DR. V. NELLE BELLAMY, formerly professor of church history at Episcopal Theological Seminary in Kentucky, is the archivist of the Episcopal Church and adjunct professor of church history at the Episcopal Theological Seminary of the Southwest. A holder of the Ph.D. degree from Duke University, she has a special interest in the history of the Lambeth Conferences. Her most recent publication, "Participation of Women in the Public Life of the Church from Lambeth Conferences 1867–1978," appeared in the *Historical Magazine of the Protestant Episcopal Church* 51 (March 1982). She has also published several articles in archival journals as well as pieces on Jane Ayer and John Chrysostom. Dr. Bellamy served on the Corporation for the *Anglican Theological Review* and is currently a member of the Advisory Board for the Episcopal Women's History Project.

DR. CHARMARIE JENKINS BLAISDELL, associate professor of history at Northeastern University, received her Ph.D. degree from Tufts University. Before going to Northeastern, she taught at Boston College. Among her numerous professional activities, she has served as coordinator of the Committee on Women in the Historical Profession. Her publications include articles on French and Italian reformers in the *Archiv für Reformationsgeschichte* and the *Sixteenth Century Journal*. In the summer of 1982 she lectured in Dublin on Calvinist women.

LOIS A. BOYD, who holds degrees from the University of Texas and Trinity University, is editor and director of the Trinity University Press. A specialist in oral history, she co-authored *Presbyterian Women in America: Two Centuries of a Quest for Status* (Greenwood, 1983) with R. Douglas Brackenridge. She has published a number of articles in the *Journal of Presbyterian History* and *Texas Presbyterian* and has written a manual on oral history for the Presbyterian Historical Society. With George N. Boyd, she edited *Religion in Contemporary Fiction: Criticism from 1945 to the Present* (Trinity, 1972). In 1979 she was the recipient of the Conservation Society Award for her editorial work and publications dealing with historical preservation.

DR. R. DOUGLAS BRACKENRIDGE, professor of religion at Trinity University, received his Ph.D. degree from the University of Glasgow. A Danforth Associate, he has served as president of the Presbyterian Historical Society (1977–80) and is a member of its board of trustees. With Lois A. Boyd he wrote *Presbyterian Women in America: Two Centuries of a Quest for Status* (Greenwood, 1983). He is also author of *Eugene Carson Blake: Prophet with Portfolio* (Seabury, 1978); *Beckoning Frontiers: A Biography of James W. Laurie* (Trinity, 1976); *Voice in the Wilderness: A History of the Cumlerland Presbyterian Church in Texas* (Trinity, 1969); and, with Francisco Garcia, *Iglesia Presbiteriana: Presbyterians and Mexican Americans in the Southwest* (Trinity, 1974). In 1981 he received the Distinguished Service Award from the Presbyterian Historical Society.

DR. RICHARD L. GREAVES, professor of history at Florida State University, received the Ph.D. degree from the University of London. Before joining the history faculty at Florida State, he taught at Michigan State University. His publications include *Deliver Us from Evil: The Radical Underground in Britain, 1660–1663* (Oxford, forthcoming); *Society and Religion in Elizabethan England*

(Minnesota, 1981); *Saints and Rebels: Seven Nonconformists in Stuart England* (Mercer, 1985); *Theology and Revolution in the Scottish Reformation: Studies in the Thought of John Knox* (Christian University Press, Eerdmans, 1980); *The Puritan Revolution and Educational Thought: Background for Reform* (Rutgers, 1969); and *John Bunyan* (Eerdmans, Sutton Courtney, 1969). He has edited *Elizabeth I, Queen of England* (D.C. Heath, 1974); four volumes of *The Miscellaneous Works of John Bunyan* (Oxford, 1976 ff.); and, with Robert Zaller, the three-volume *Biographical Dictionary of British Radicals in the Seventeenth Century* (Harvester, 1982–84). With James Forrest he has also written *John Bunyan: A Reference Guide* (G.K. Hall, 1982). He has published some three dozen journal articles and has received fellowships from the American Council of Learned Societies, the National Endowment for the Humanities, the Huntington Library, the William Andrews Clark Memorial Library, and the Andrew Mellon Foundation.

DR. BLANCHE GLASSMAN HERSH, who received her Ph.D. degree in American history from the University of Illinois at Chicago Circle, recently retired from her position as coordinator of the Women's Studies Program at Northeastern Illinois University. She also taught at Roosevelt University in Chicago. A specialist in abolitionist women, she is the author of *The Slavery of Sex: Feminist-Abolitionists in America* (Illinois, 1978) as well as *Re-Entry Women and Women's Studies: A Planning Study* (National Institute of Education, 1980). Her articles include "Am I Not a Woman and a Sister? Abolitionist Beginnings of Nineteenth-Century Feminism," in *Antislavery Reconsidered*, edited by M. Fellman and L. Perry (Louisiana State, 1979). Dr. Hersh has served on the Coordinating Council of the National Women's Studies Association and the Coordinating Committee for the Chicago Area Women's Studies Association.

DR. DOROTHY P. LUDLOW, who received her Ph.D. degree at Indiana University, is assistant professor of history at California State University, Fresno, where she is active in the Women's Studies Program. Dr. Ludlow is the author of *"Arise and Be Doing": English "Preaching Women," 1640–1660* (University Microfilms, 1978). She wrote seven articles on women for the *Bi-*

ographical Dictionary of British Radicals in the Seventeenth Century, edited by R. Greaves and R. Zaller (Harvester, 1982–84). A specialist in the history of Stuart England, she has been the recipient of a Woodrow Wilson Doctoral Dissertation Fellowship and a Fulbright-Hays Fellowship. Among the professional societies to which she has read papers are the American Historical Association, the Conference on British Studies, and the Economic and Business Historical Society.

DR. GERALD F. MORAN is associate professor of history and chairman of the Department of Social Sciences at the University of Michigan, Dearborn. The recipient of a Ph.D. degree from Rutgers University, he has also taught at Douglass College, Rutgers, and at the University of California, Irvine. An authority on Colonial American history, he contributed an essay to *Women in American Religion* (Pennsylvania, 1980), edited by Janet Wilson James. His other publications include "Religious Renewal, Puritan Tribalism, and the Family in Seventeenth-Century Milford, Connecticut," *William and Mary Quarterly* 36 (April 1979); and other articles in the *Journal of Social History*; the *Michigan Law Review*; and the *Eerdman's Handbook of the History of Christianity in America*. His book, *The Puritan Saint: Church Membership and Piety in Colonial Connecticut*, is forthcoming.

DR. FREDERICK A. NORWOOD, a recipient of the Ph.D. degree from Yale University, taught at Baldwin-Wallace College before beginning a distinguished career as professor of the history of Christianity at Garrett Theological Seminary. A Guggenheim Fellow, he has served as a member of the Editorial Board of both the History of American Methodism and Evangelical World Methodism. His many publications include *The Reformation Refugees as an Economic Force* (American Society of Church History, 1942); *The Development of Modern Christianity* (Abingdon, 1956); *Church Membership in the Methodist Tradition* (Methodist Publishing House, 1958); *Great Moments of Church History* (Abingdon, 1962); *Strangers and Exiles: A History of Religious Refugees*, 2 vols. (Abingdon, 1969); *The Story of American Methodism* (Abingdon, 1974); and numerous journal articles. His *Sourcebook of American Methodism* (Abingdon, 1982), a collection of readings, includes a chapter on Methodist women. Dr. Norwood is a recipient of the Brewer Prize of the American Society of Church History.

DR. KEITH L. SPRUNGER is the Oswald H. Wedel Professor of History at Bethel College in Kansas. The holder of a Ph.D. degree from the University of Illinois, he is the recipient of awards and grants from the Danforth Foundation, the American Council of Learned Societies, the American Philosophical Society, and the Social Science Research Council. His publications include *The Learned Doctor William Ames* (Illinois, 1972); *Dutch Puritanism* (Brill, 1982); and fifteen journal articles in such publications as *Church History*; the *Journal of the History of Ideas*; the *Harvard Theological Review*; the *New England Quarterly*; and the *Mennonite Quarterly Review*.